The Kitchen Gardener's Handbook

The Kitchen Gardener's Handbook

JENNIFER R. BARTLEY

TIMBER PRESS
Portland * London

Frontispiece: A bounty of squash, potatoes, onions, peppers, corn, melon, tomatoes, beans, and flowers from the summer garden.

Photographs are by the author unless otherwise indicated.

Published in 2010 by Timber Press, Inc.

The Haseltine Building
133 S.W. Second Avenue, Suite 450
Portland, Oregon 97204-3527
www.timberpress.com

2 The Quadrant
135 Salusbury Road
London NW6 6RJ
www.timberpress.co.uk

ISBN-13: 978-0-88192-956-0

Printed in China

Library of Congress Cataloging-in-Publication Data

Bartley, Jennifer R.
  The kitchen garden companion / Jennifer R. Bartley.
    p. cm.
  Includes bibliographical references and index.
  ISBN 978-0-88192-956-0
1. Kitchen gardens. 2. Plants, Ornamental—Seasonal variations. 3. Seasonal cookery. 4. Floral decorations. I. Title.
  SB321.B384 2010
  635—dc22   2010005070

A catalog record for this book is also available from the British Library.

To my parents, James E. Matson and Ruth R. Matson

Happy is it, indeed, for me that my heart
is capable of feeling the same simple and
innocent pleasure as the peasant whose
table is covered with food of his own rearing,
and who not only enjoys his meal, but
remembers with delight the happy days and
sunny mornings when he planted it, the soft
evenings when he watered it, and the pleasure
he experienced in watching its daily growth.

—J. W. VON GOETHE, *The Sorrows of Werther*

A variety of red and green lettuces surrounded by a small boxwood hedge in the potager of the Bourton House Garden in Gloucestershire, England. The intensively planted garden provides food without sacrificing artistry.

Contents

Spring

Summer

Acknowledgments

I really am a lucky girl to spend much of my days designing, photographing, writing about, and walking in gardens. There are many people who make that possible and I am indebted to them.

Thank you to all of my clients who allow me to design their special garden spaces. I am humbled and honored. A special thanks to one who would rather remain anonymous. Thank you for your trust and the opportunity to create your elegant and edible paradise. It has been and continues to be an amazing process of garden building and friendship.

Thank you to Dean and Sally Schmitt for your support and help. You allowed me to take over your kitchen, house, and schedule for many days. I do appreciate the shared hours of cooking, setting the table, eating, and cleaning up just so I could take a few snapshots.

Thank you to my husband, Terry Bartley, who is a true comrade in this ongoing process of growing, cooking, and eating from the garden. You truly keep all things together so that I can create. Thank you to my kids who make cooking and eating together so much fun. You had great patience while I set up photo shoots in the middle of family dinners.

Thank you to Timber Press and everyone there, especially Tom Fischer for your enthusiasm for the project and Linda Willms for your attention to detail.

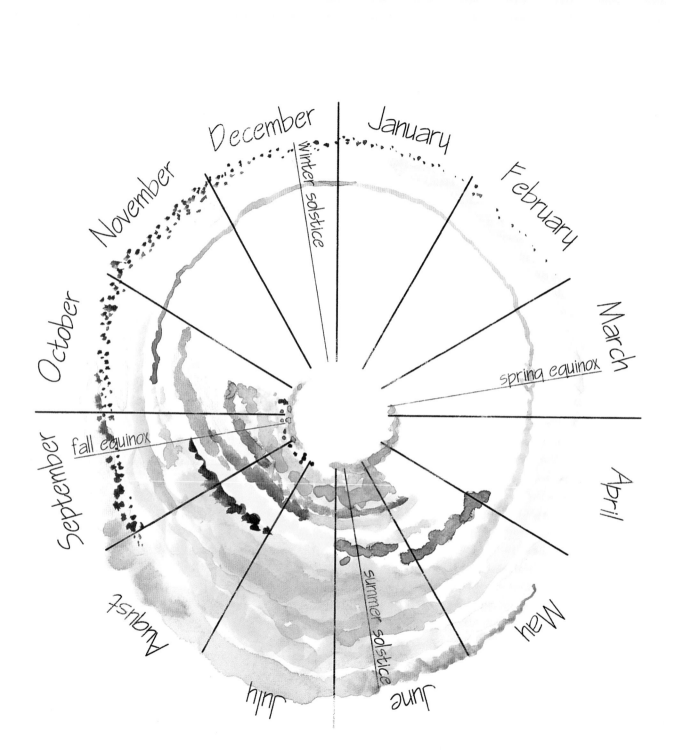

A seasonal map of the author's garden hints at the changing landscape, with flowers, fruits, and vegetables each in season in its time. The frost-free days are evident: the growing season for tender crops is 15 May to 15 October. If you look carefully at your landscape throughout the year, you will always find something remarkable in every season.

Introduction

This is a book that will help you live with the seasons, embracing what each has to offer. Many cookbooks are organized in this way; this one is special because it is also a home book with ideas for cutting the complementary perennial flowers, greens, blossoms, and twigs that bloom when you are ready to harvest the edibles and prepare a meal.

It's a book of recipes from the kitchen garden and ideas of when to use the flowers, trees, and shrubs growing around your home. Cooking is like gardening; it takes experimentation and an adventurous spirit. This is the way I cook. I try to keep it as simple and uncomplicated as possible. Sometimes the recipes are everyday (what I call peasant food) simple one-dish meals: al dente pasta with extra-virgin olive oil, garlic, something from the garden, preferably 'Genovese' basil, a few toasted walnuts, and a little grated hard cheese.

This is also a design book. It will show you how to create a more sustainable landscape around your home. Plans and sketches from my own garden (outside the formal kitchen garden) and those I've designed for clients demonstrate how to reduce the lawn and create a seasonal, edible, and useful garden. These designs are not complicated but they have layers of plants. Sometimes edibles are selected; sometimes a shrub or flower for cutting. All of the plants work together to create a garden.

Here's how the book is laid out: Each of the four main sections focuses on a season and begins with an in-depth look at the vegetables, fruits, greens, and herbs that are at their peak at that particular point in the year. Growing information is included for each plant, and many of the profiles are accompanied by recipes. Seasonal menus round out this section. Then we turn to shrubs and flowers that can be used to decorate the table, garden designs, and the particular tasks that need doing in that season.

Each season has its special gifts. Strawberries last a few weeks in late spring. Cherries last a few weeks in the summer. Fresh basil is just for warm weather. Kale is sweetest in the fall after a frost. The more we live seasonally the more thankful we become for the little things. It's about savoring and receiving with thankfulness. Good food doesn't have to be fancy or complicated. Simple is best, right off the vine. Getting to that simplicity is the problem.

This is our modern challenge, our frontier: to create our properties so that trees, shrubs, grasses, perennials, annuals, fruits, herbs, and vegetables are planted in a way that makes sense. My goal is to use plants to create shade, enclosure, volume, structure, fragrance, bloom, bouquets, shelter, beauty, texture, or something to eat for the birds or me. Each plant, whether it's edible or not has its place in the garden. Groundcovers on the ground plane protect the soil. Shrubs and perennials form the next layer of planting and provide cover for birds and wildlife. These plants also create space. Medium and large shrubs create enclosure and define the space of the garden. The final and top layer is the canopy. Here trees provide shade and a boundary to the garden.

Edible gardening is not like a canoe that floats by and, if missed, cannot be recaptured. There is no single perfect planting, growing, or harvesting moment. Instead, edible gardening is a continuous process; you can participate at any stage in the time continuum. Each season offers an opportunity to plant something or harvest something. In early spring try peas, in late spring try quick-growing radishes, in early summer plant squash, in late summer try broccoli, in early fall plant spinach, in late fall plant mâche, and so on. Growing your own food and harvesting your own flowers is a satisfying venture. Join the growing journey at any scale from a pot to your entire landscape. The best gardening lessons are the ones you learn by doing. Plant a seed and watch it grow.

The Edible Front Yard

This drawing shows how to mix up some edibles with multiseason shrubs and flowers for a useful and practical garden in a front yard. It is the actual plan of my front yard, and I am using this design to illustrate the process of selecting plants for multiseason use. My goal is to have something either to eat or to cut for an arrangement through the year. That means ideally something is blooming or has spectacular color throughout the year. We will see this garden again in each of the seasons: spring (p. 60), summer (p. 128), fall (p. 174), and winter (p. 210). For readers interested in re-creating all or part of this garden, a planting plan and master plant list can be found on pages 18-19.

Isometric drawing of an edible, colorful seasonal front yard.

MASTER PLANTING PLAN AND PLANT LIST FOR THE EDIBLE FRONT YARD

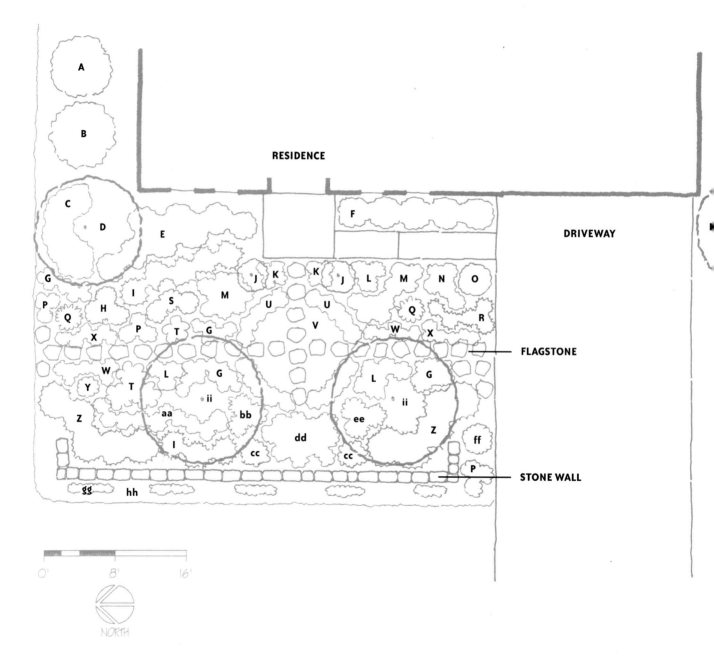

LABEL	NO. OF PLANTS	COMMON NAME	SCIENTIFIC NAME	ZONE	NOTES
A	1	'Winter Red' winterberry holly	Ilex verticillata 'Winter Red'	3–9	red berries in winter
B	1	'Southern Gentlemen' winterberry holly	Ilex verticillata 'Southern Gentlemen'	3–9	pollinator for 'Winter Red'
C	33	sweet woodruff	Galium odoratum	4–8	spring blooms
D	2	crabapple tree	Malus spp.	—	existing tree; spring blossoms
E	8	dwarf fothergilla	Fothergilla gardenii	5–8	white flowers in spring; fall–winter color
F	5	bird's nest spruce	Picea abies 'Nidiformis'	—	existing evergreen shrub
G	28	'Moerheim Beauty' sneezeweed	Helenium autumnale 'Moerheim Beauty'	4–9	orange-red flowers in fall
H	3	'Ruffled Clouds' peony	Paeonia 'Ruffled Clouds'	2–7	light pink blooms in spring
I	8	'Shenandoah' switch grass	Panicum virgatum 'Shenandoah'	4–9	burgundy-red fall color; 4 ft. high; summer–winter interest
J	2	'Britzensis' coral bark willow	Salix alba 'Britzensis'	2–8	pollard at 5 ft. high; year-round interest
K	8	bloody sorrel	Rumex sanguineus	6–8	edible leaves in spring; spring–fall interest
L	12	'Becky' shasta daisy	Leucanthemum 'Becky'	5–8	white flowers in early summer
M	18	'Tiki Torch' orange coneflower	Echinacea 'Tiki Torch'	4–9	bright orange flowers in summer and fall; winter interest
N	5	'Purple Haze' anise hyssop	Agastache 'Purple Haze'	6–9	leaves and flowers for tea; summer–fall interest
O	1	'Cayuga' fragrant viburnum	Viburnum carlesii 'Cayuga'	5–8	fragrant blooms in spring; year-round interest
P	9	'Autumn Joy' stonecrop	Sedum 'Autumn Joy'	3–11	summer and fall flowers; winter interest
Q	2	'Fireworks' goldenrod	Solidago rugosa 'Fireworks'	5–9	yellow flowers in fall
R	5	'Sapphire' blue oat grass	Helictotrichon sempervirens 'Sapphire'	4–8	evergreen grass
S	3	globe thistle	Echinops ritro	3–10	blue cut flowers in summer and fall
T	4	rhubarb	Rheum spp.	4–8	edible stalks in spring
U	20	'Walkers Low' catmint	Nepeta faassenii 'Walkers Low'	3–8	spring–fall bloom
V	—	seasonal edible annuals	—	—	spring–winter
W	12	'October Skies' aster	Aster oblongifolius 'October Skies'	4–8	purple flowers in fall
X	12	Rozanne geranium	Geranium 'Gerwat'	4–8	blue-purple flowers in summer; spring–fall
Y	1	Hubricht's blue star	Amsonia hubrichtii	5–9	spring blooms; vivid fall color
Z	10	currant	Ribes sativum	3–8	5 ft. high; edible fall fruit; good hedge spring–fall
aa	10	'White Swan' coneflower	Echinacea purpurea 'White Swan'	3–9	white flowers in summer and fall into winter
bb	3	'Peach Strudel' daylily	Hemerocallis 'Peach Strudel'	2–8	orange flowers in summer
cc	2	Autumn Sun black-eyed Susan	Rudbeckia nitida 'Herbstsonne'	4–9	yellow flowers in fall
dd	11	'Henry Eilers' sweet coneflower	Rudbeckia subtomentosa 'Henry Eilers'	4–8	yellow flowers in fall
ee	3	'Nectarine Tango' daylily	Hemerocallis 'Nectarine Tango'	3–8	orange flowers in summer
ff	1	'O Yashima' flowering quince	Chaenomeles 'O Yashima'	5–9	fragrant blooms late winter; spring & fall interest
gg	5	apple trees	Malus spp.	—	espaliered; fruit in fall; spring bloom
hh		strawberries	Fragaria spp.	—	fruit in spring; edible groundcover
ii	2	ash trees	Fraxinus spp.	—	existing tree; fall color; winter bark; spring and summer foliage

Spring

ONE OF THE FIRST SIGNS of spring is the slight color change in the willows. The slender weeping branches faintly shift to yellow before any deciduous trees leaf out. I first notice the subtle change in the seasons as I drive the country roads near my home and gaze at the woods along the road. Even forsythia with its glaring yellow is welcome at this time. In the woodland, wildflowers, wild onions, and wild leeks appear; ramps grow beside May apples, spring beauties, and trilliums.

Alliums in all of their forms are either blooming or their spiky leaves are ready for harvest. Whether you eat them or just enjoy seeing them in the garden, ramps, chives, garlic chives, green garlic, leeks, shallots, sweet onions, nodding onions, or the purely ornamental onion *Allium* 'Globemaster', with its giant 10-inch (25-cm) spherical purple blooms, are the joys of spring.

Perennials that have been dormant all winter begin to emerge from the soil. Many of the perennial herbs are leafing out and can be harvested in the early spring. Some biennial vegetables and herbs have remained in the garden all winter (sometimes with needed protection) and can be harvested in the early spring. Annuals that have self-seeded, like

Chives burst with bright magenta edible blossoms in the spring and can be grown in the perennial border if you don't have a separate herb garden.

Ramps have an oniony, garlicky flavor. Use them like you would use green onions. The entire plant is edible except for the root tip.

Spring Vegetables

borage, calendula, and dill, pop up around the garden. As you weed, pick these edible wanderers when they are young and use them. Dill can go into salad dressings, borage flowers into chilled drinks.

Spring is the time to add compost and prepare the beds if you can steal a warm dry day when the soil is not soggy. This is the time to plant cool-season varieties of vegetables, those that tolerate frost. There is always a chance of freezing temperatures until the frost-free date for your area, so until then, plant only vegetables that like it cool. Spring is the time to plant seeds of warm-season vegetables indoors under lights.

ARTICHOKE (*Cynara scolymus*)
Perennial in zone 8, grown as an annual in cooler climates
Seed to table: 85 to 100 days

Artichokes are perennial plants in warm climates. They originated from the cardoon (*Cynara cardunculus*), a wide, attractive plant with spiny leaves. Artichokes are quite majestic with their serrated leaves. Perennial artichokes can be harvested in late spring and early summer. Each stem produces one artichoke bud at the tip and several smaller ones below. Harvest the central bud when scales are still tightly closed, then harvest the smaller ones before they open.

Freshly picked asparagus, pink dogwood blossoms, and found morel mushrooms are part of the fleeting joys of spring.

'Iride' beets are very sweet and can be eaten raw without cooking. The leaves can be used in salads or cooked as greens.

In colder climates artichokes can be grown as annuals but the seeds must be started indoors in midwinter (January) to be large enough to set out by spring. Try 'Green Globe', 'Imperial Star', or 'Violetto di Romagna'. See more on artichoke in the Fall chapter (page 134).

ASPARAGUS (*Asparagus officinalis*)
Perennial in zones 4 to 8
Planting to table: 2 years for first harvest, then annually

Fresh, succulent asparagus is one of the joys of the spring garden. Asparagus is a long-lasting perennial so find a place to plant it that will be permanent. A thriving asparagus bed can produce purple or green pointy spears for twenty-five years or more.

Choose male hybrids like 'Jersey Giant', 'Jersey Prince', and 'Jersey Knight' for the best production. 'Purple Passion' produces purple spears. Order one-year-old crowns from a catalog and plant them 18 inches (45 cm) apart in rows 5 feet (1.5 m) apart.

It's fine to harvest spears the second and third years after planting, but do not harvest spears the first year. Using a small knife, cut the spears at the base almost at soil level. When the harvest is finished for spring, new spears will fern out creating a feathery screen 4 to 5 feet (1.2–1.5 m) high. Let these billowy fronds stay in the garden.

BEETS (*Beta vulgaris*)
Biennial grown as an annual
Seed to table: 45 to 58 days

Sow beets outdoors in early spring when ground can be worked in rows 6 to 8 inches (15–20 cm) apart. Sow at 2-week intervals for a continuous supply of baby beets and greens. Thin seedlings to 4 to 6 inches (10–15 cm) apart and use the thinnings, including the roots, in salads.

For an earlier harvest, sow beets indoors under lights and set out in the garden in early spring as transplants. Transplants are usually available at nurseries as well.

Roasted beet salad is best when you use early spring beets picked when they are small and tender. Beets are naturally sweet and go well with sweet onions and walnuts.

Roasted Beet Salad

Serves 6

12 early spring beets, such as Bull's blood or golden
    beets or a mix
1 large sweet onion, sliced, then halved
½ cup walnuts, coarsely chopped
1 teaspoon white vinegar
1 tablespoon olive oil, plus more for drizzle
Salt to taste

Preheat oven to 400°F. Wash the entire beet—root, stems, and leaves. Cut off stems and leaves and store those in the refrigerator for another use. Cut off root tip and peel beets. Cut into large chunks. Place beets, onions, and walnuts in a roasting pan, drizzle with a little olive oil. Mix well and roast for 45 minutes. Place in serving bowl and cool. When beets are cool, add the vinegar and 1 tablespoon olive oil. Chill to blend flavors.

To roast beets, wash thoroughly and then cut off the tops and roots. Place the beets in a single layer in a roasting pan. Drizzle with a good olive oil and roast at 400°F until tender, about 45 minutes for 8 to 10 medium beets.

To boil beets, wash and trim them before placing them in a saucepan with water to cover. Boil until tender. Cool and remove outer skin before using beets in a recipe. To reduce bleeding of red varieties, leave beets whole with the roots and some of the stems attached, then trim after cooking. Serve warm or cool to use in salads.

Harvest beets when they are small, before they become tough and woody. Use the tops raw for salads or cooked as greens.

There are many varieties of beets, some grown for their leaves and some for their roots. Among the best varieties are 'Bull's Blood', 'Chioggia', 'Golden', and 'Iride'. 'Bull's Blood is an heirloom with deep red leaves and roots. It was the first beet I grew and the sweet taste converted me to a beet lover. See more on beets in the Fall chapter (page 134).

BROCCOLI (*Brassica oleracea* Italica Group)
Annual
Seed to table: 45 to 95 days

For a spring harvest, it's easiest to set out broccoli as transplants but you can sow indoors under lights eight weeks before you plant. Set out the plants a month before the frost-free date. Because broccoli is frost tolerant, it is one of the first vegetables to be planted as soon as you can get out to the garden. In the spring use varieties that mature quickly like 'De Ciccio', an Italian heirloom with multiple heads that matures in 48 days.

It's true; the broccoli we love to eat is a cluster of immature unopened flower buds. Harvest the broccoli heads when they are 4 to 6 inches (10–15 cm) wide by cutting the stem close to the base of the plant with a sharp knife. Headless broccoli looks rather strange in the garden but let the stalks remain in the

24

garden for a few weeks. After you harvest the central head, side shoots of broccoli florets will appear, extending the harvest. Some varieties are better for producing a single central head, while others are good for producing side shoots. 'Coronado Crown' is very heat tolerant. 'Waltham 29' produces a main head and also many side shoots.

If you miss the ideal harvest time, which can occur from one day to the next, do not worry about it; the closed dark green florets will open into bright yellow flowers. These are edible and lovely to add to salads or anywhere you would use broccoli. Unseasonably warm days in spring will hurry this process along and cause the broccoli to bolt when the heads are still small. Every part of home grown broccoli is sweet; the head, stem, leaf, and flower are tasty when harvested young. See more on broccoli in the Fall chapter (page 134).

CARROTS (*Daucus carota*)
Biennial grown as an annual
Seed to table: 52 to 70 days

Carrots like a loamy sandy soil that is free of small rocks so they can grow straight. Raised beds work well as you can prepare a deep, loose, well-drained soil. Carrots need a consistent supply of water through the growing season. They are not tolerant of drought.

Plant seeds directly in the garden in early spring. They will germinate in cool soil. Because the seeds can take up to two weeks to germinate, some gardeners like to mark rows of slower-growing carrots with fast-growing radishes.

Try white, orange, yellow, or purple carrots for fun. 'Atomic Red' produces brilliant red carrots. 'Cosmic Purple' is purple on the outside and yellow to orange on the inside. 'Lunar White' is a mild white carrot. See more on carrots in the Summer and Fall chapters (pages 66 and 136, respectively).

Broccoli planted in the spring should be set out early and harvested when young before the buds open to yellow flowers.

CAULIFLOWER (*Brassica oleracea* Botrytis Group)
Biennial grown as an annual
Seed to table: 54 to 80 days

Cauliflower is a cool-season crop that can be grown in the spring or fall garden. It often does best as a fall crop. If planted in the spring set out transplants in cool weather a few weeks before the last frost. See more on cauliflower in the Fall chapter (page 136).

FIDDLEHEADS

Fiddleheads that emerge in the spring are one of the few edibles that thrive in shady conditions so if you lack sunlight consider Ostrich fern (*Matteuccia struthiopteris*) for an edible woodland. The green fern fronds emerge out of the ground in the spring as tightly wound coils. These coils are the fiddleheads of the young fronds waiting to unfurl.

Ostrich fern grows in moist shady woodlands. It is a perennial in zones 4 to 8 and naturalizes freely

Green garlic can be used like green onions and is harvested from the early spring potager before the bulbs are mature, along with flat-leaf parsley and 'Monstruoso' Swiss chard.

in the right conditions. The plants are widely available from nurseries; your local nursery will likely carry them. One caveat: make sure the fronds you eat come from *Matteuccia struthiopteris* because many ferns send up fronds in the spring, and every baby frond you find is not edible.

GREEN GARLIC (*Allium sativum*)
Annual bulb
Planting to table: 120 to 150 days

Spring is the time to harvest green, or immature, garlic, not the time to plant it. The bulbs are planted

in the fall when you plant your daffodils and tulips. To harvest green garlic, dig up immature bulbs and use them like you would green onions. They look like large green onions or leeks at this point. The bulb is swelling but has not formed yet, so it and the entire stem of the young garlic can be used in recipes that call for garlic or green onions. Green garlic has a milder flavor than mature garlic cloves. This transient taste can only be savored in the spring, before the garlic matures. See more on garlic in the Summer and Fall chapters (pages 71 and 138, respectively).

LEEKS (*Allium ampeloprasum* Porrum Group)
Annual
Seed to table: 120 to 150 days

Harvest mature leeks that were planted last fall and allowed to overwinter in the garden or cold frame.

Stuffed trout with green garlic and herbs is served with quinoa with spring vegetables.

Stuffed Trout with Green Garlic and Herbs

Herbs from the garden can be used to flavor any meat, chicken, or fish. My niece and nephew, Kelly and Jesse Tetirick, caught some trout while fishing a tributary of the Mad River in Ohio. I was blessed with their good luck. Trout is easy to prepare because it has no scales, but use your favorite fish in place of the trout if you like, preferably fresh. The tarragon and dill infuse the fish with a wonderful flavor. The foil keeps the fish moist and seals in all the flavor; it makes clean up simple too. This goes well with Quinoa Pilaf with Spring Vegetables (see page 42).

Serves 2
2 whole trout, gutted and cleaned
Salt and freshly ground pepper
2 stalks green garlic, sliced lengthwise in strips
1 small sweet onion, sliced, then halved
1 bunch fresh tarragon leaves, stems and all
1 bunch fresh dill leaves and stems
3 tablespoons butter, cut into pieces, divided
Juice of ½ lemon
Lemon slices (optional)

Preheat the broiler to 450°. Wash the fresh trout under cold running water and gently scrape the skin with a knife to clean; pat dry. Place each fish on its own piece of aluminum foil, making sure the foil is large enough to wrap the fish. Salt and pepper the inside of the fish.

(continued)

Prepare the stuffing. Mix together the green garlic, onion, and sprigs of dill and tarragon. Add in some of the butter. Divide the mixture in half, stuffing each fish with its half of the mixture.

Divide the remaining butter between the two fish and lay it on the outside of each fish. Squeeze some lemon on the fish. Wrap each fish tightly with the aluminum foil and seal the edges.

Place the foil packets of fish on a shallow roasting pan, in case the packets leak. Broil on the top rack of a hot oven for 7 minutes. Turn the packets over and cook them on the other side for 7–8 minutes.

Carefully unseal the foil and serve immediately with lemon slices.

You can also cook the fish this way on a hot grill outside if you prefer.

Use a trowel to dig near the base, while twisting and pulling the stalk.

Set out additional leeks as transplants in early spring or start from seed indoors. Leeks are frost tolerant and can be set out in cool soil as soon as you can work it. Dig a trench and lay the small leeks upright in the soil, about 2 or 3 inches (5–7.5 cm) apart. Fill in the soil around the leeks. As the leeks grow, continue to mound up soil around the leeks to ensure a long white shaft. Harvest every other leek as they grow for pencil-thin, baby leeks.

The blue-green tops look like onions but will not die back when ready for harvest. Water the leek bed thoroughly each week, as leeks do not like dry periods. See more on leeks in the Fall chapter (page 138).

MORELS (*Morchella*)

Morels are a fleeting delicacy of spring and foraging for the treats is a tradition for those who live near woods. Talk to avid mushroom hunters about their favorite hunting grounds and you are likely to get evasive answers on the precise location of the secret spot. Near an old apple orchard? At the base of some

Cold leek and potato soup can be made one day and served the next. Have guests snip chives into their own soup bowls at the table. I put flowering pink chives in a vase and passed some scissors and everyone added their own. The pink chive flowers look pretty too.

Spring Leek and Potato Soup

This is the classic vichyssoise traditionally served cold, here without the cream. I have no objection to cream; this soup just doesn't need it. You could serve it with a dollop of crème fraîche or sour cream.

Serves 8
5 large (3–4 cups) leeks, chopped
8–10 small (4–5 cups) potatoes
2 tablespoons butter
5–6 cups chicken stock, plus more as needed
Salt and pepper to taste
Fresh chives (optional)

Thoroughly wash the leeks and peel the potatoes before coarsely chopping them. Melt the butter in a large soup pot. Add the chopped vegetables and sauté until the leeks are cooked through. Add the chicken stock and cover the pot with a lid slightly ajar to allow the steam to escape. Simmer over medium-low heat until the potatoes and leeks are soft, about 1 to 1½ hours. Add more broth if necessary to keep the soup from getting too thick.

Cool slightly and puree in food processor until the soup is smooth. Return the pureed mixture to the pot and add more broth to the right consistency. Chill for a few hours or overnight. Serve chilled with freshly chopped chives.

dead elm trees? On the south side of a hill? Possibly. Your chances of finding these treats do increase after a fire. When you do find morels, save the precious water you rinse them in to throw out in the garden in a shady place with the hope that the spores will magically produce next year. If you don't happen to find any morels on your walks through the woods in spring, the markets are filled with lovely local mushrooms of many kinds.

ONIONS (*Allium cepa*)
Biennial grown as an annual
Seed to table: 40 to 50 days for green onions, 90 to 120 days for bulb onions

Onions can be grown from seeds or sets, thrive in cool weather and cool soil, and can be set out weeks before the frost-free date. Start onions from seed in late winter and grow indoors under lights until ready to be put out in the spring. Seed catalogs sell sets of onions to make it easy—just order and set out when they arrive.

When the sets arrive, they are bound together like a bunch of small green onions. Separate them and place in the soil an inch (2.5 cm) deep about 6 inches (15 cm) apart. Plant so the bulb is completely covered. Onions grow for a long time in the garden. They need full sun. Try a few in the perennial border—the dark green upright vertical leaves are attractive.

Any onion can be harvested at the green onion stage and enjoyed for the tiny bulblet and stalk, but some onions are bred for the white linear stalks with green edible tops and not for the fat layered bulb.

Egyptian onions, sometimes called walking onions because they move around the garden, are perennial onions that produce small bulblets on top of long stems. These bulbs have a mild onion taste and are ready to use in the spring. See more on onions in the Summer and Fall chapters (pages 74 and 138, respectively).

PEAS (*Pisum sativum*)
Annual
Seed to table: 54 to 72 days

Peas have the remarkable ability to form a beneficial relationship with certain bacteria that naturally occur in soil. The bacteria form nodules on the roots of peas and beans that extract nitrogen directly from the air to feed the plant. All legumes share this quality. Farmers have known about this symbiotic relationship for eons. That bacteria are probably already living in your soil if you've grown peas before.

To insure the pea roots have easy access to the bacteria you can inoculate the seeds yourself. Pea inoculants is available from online seed sources. When you are ready to plant, moisten the seeds and dust with the dormant *rhizobia*.

Choose peas you like to eat and plant them when the daffodils bloom, or so goes the old saying. They tolerate cool soil and cool weather, in fact prefer it. Pea vines will languish with the hot weather. Plant seeds directly in spring soil about 6 inches apart. Not all peas require staking but the tendrils will appreciate some support; a few branches pruned from the yard and stuck in the soil will do. Some varieties are more avid climbers and will need tall trellises or poles.

POTATOES (*Solanum tuberosum*)
Annual grown from a tuber
Planting to table: 50 to 120 days

Use certified potato seed to ensure the tubers are disease free and have not been treated with a sprout inhibitor. Chances are the potatoes from the grocery store have been treated, so order from a seed catalog. Keep seed tubers in a cool dark place until ready to plant. Potatoes are a cool-season crop and can be planted outside a month before the last frost in your area. Plant them even earlier if the ground is not wet.

Cut seed potatoes so that there are two eyes per potato. Lay them on newspapers for a couple of

Spring peas with mint cream are a meal in themselves, or serve them for a special occasion. Make this dish with homegrown English peas that you shell yourself.

Spring Peas with Mint Cream

Serves 4
1 tablespoon butter
2–3 small shallots, chopped
½ cup cream
3–5 fresh mint leaves, plus more for garnish
2 cups fresh English peas, shelled just before cooking

Melt the butter in a saucepan. Add the shallots and sauté until they are soft. Add the cream and mint leaves. Heat the mixture to the boiling stage, but don't boil the cream. Crush the mint leaves with a wooden spoon as you heat the mixture. Add the peas and heat through. Remove the mint leaves before serving. Serve immediately, or chill and serve cold. Garnish with fresh mint leaves.

days to dry. Plant individual tubers with the sprouts pointed up, about 3 inches (7.5 cm) deep. Space about 9 to 12 inches (22.5–30 cm) apart. Early varieties will be ready for harvest in early summer, possibly sooner.

When plants are 12 inches (30 cm) tall, add some compost and hill up the soil around each plant. The goal is to keep light from the underground potatoes. Exposure to light prompts the potato to produce chlorophyll and accumulate a toxin called solanine. This will be concentrated at the surface of the potato, so peeling should remove it.

Small spring potatoes are ready to harvest 50 days from planting. To harvest the earliest potatoes, move the loamy soil away from the edges of the plant's roots and gather the small tubers growing on the edge. Mound the soil back and cover the roots.

'Red Gold' is excellent for new (early) potatoes. 'Adirondack Blue' produces deep blue potatoes. 'Russian Banana' is a fingerling with good flavor. See more on potatoes in the Summer and Fall chapters (pages 80 and 140, respectively).

Dilly Heirloom Potato Salad

This is a simple potato salad with just a few ingredients and is always a favorite at family events. I use celery seed in potato salad because that's how my mom made it; it is out of fondness for the memory of watching her make it as a young girl that I include it. That and it tastes good.

Serves 8–10
3 dozen (5–6 cups) small early potatoes with skins
Salt to taste
½ cup sour cream
½ cup real mayonnaise
2 tablespoons white wine vinegar
3 tablespoons fresh dill weed, chopped
2 tablespoons fresh flat-leaf parsley, chopped
½ teaspoon celery seed
3–4 green onions, finely chopped
Freshly ground pepper to taste

Wash the potatoes but don't peel them. If they are small enough, leave whole; otherwise cut them in half or quarters. Place the cut potatoes in a pot and just cover with water. Boil until the potatoes are soft (but not mushy) when poked with a fork. Drain the water and set the potatoes aside to cool down.

In a separate small bowl, combine the remaining ingredients to make the dressing. While the potatoes are still warm, cut them into bite-size cubes, place them in a serving bowl, and sprinkle with salt. Pour the dressing on the potatoes and stir well before storing the potato salad in the refrigerator. Serve cold.

Make this salad the day before you serve it; it always tastes better for some reason.

RADISHES (*Raphanus sativus*)
Annual
Seed to table: 22 to 40 days

Plant a tiny radish seed in cool spring soil, and in 22 to 40 days you will have a crunchy radish to garnish your salad or eat straight from the garden, after rinsing it off first. Sow seeds in rows or broadcast them, then cover lightly with soil. As you thin the tiny plants, put the greens in salads. 'Purple Plum' is a favorite sweet purple variety almost too stunning to eat.

Daikon radishes are used in Japanese cooking. These long, white radishes look like fat, white carrots, only bigger. The roots can be boiled, roasted, grated in salads, or pickled. The leaves are large, serrated, and attractive. They also can be eaten when young whether cooked like turnip greens, stir-fried like Swiss chard, or raw in salads. They have a spicy mustard flavor. See more on radishes in the Fall chapter (page 141).

RAMPS (*Allium tricoccum*)

Wild leeks can be found in early spring as you walk through any woods in eastern North America and this is the time to harvest the young flavorful bulbs. Their flat, elongated leaves can be found near the first spring wildflowers. Trillium, spring beauty (*Claytonia*), Dutchman's breeches (*Dicentra cucullaria*) , and trout lily (*Erythronium*) share the same need for moist, rich woodland soil.

The Cherokee enjoyed ramps as the first green of the spring and used it as a spring tonic and for colds. The new green leaves that poke through the decaying leaves of fall in the woodland are still a most welcome sign of spring. The leaves of this ephemeral appear for only a few weeks in the spring; look for the lilylike green leaves in mid to late April in the Midwest, before the deciduous trees have leafed out.

Ramp season lasts just a few weeks because the leaves disappear as it gets warm. Later, in late sum-

mer, ramps will shoot up a stalk of seed producing flowers. Ramps can be propagated from seed which appears in the fall, or by transplanting clumps in the spring. Ramps will spread and naturalize and can be planted in the home shade garden along with other wildflowers or shade loving plants, if you can duplicate the woodland conditions.

Harvest ramps sustainably by taking only a few roots and leaves in each clump and leave many to return the following years. Dig down deep enough to ensure you harvest the entire bulb. Gather only the amount you plan to use immediately; ramps do not store well. Use in any recipe that calls for green onions, leeks, or shallots. The white bulb and the

(top right) *'Purple Plum' radishes are bright purple and so pretty on their own.*

(top left) *Daikon radishes and 'Osaka Purple' mustard in the spring garden.*

(bottom) *Ramps appear in early spring at the same time the first wildflowers appear in the woodland garden.*

Ramp and morel quiche is served with freshly picked asparagus and roasted beet salad. Lilacs for the table were picked at the same time as the asparagus.

Ramp and Morel Quiche

If you don't live near woods where you can forage for morels or if you do but aren't lucky enough to find them, you can always substitute locally grown oyster or shitake mushrooms in this recipe.

Makes 1 (10-inch) quiche
1 unbaked whole wheat pie crust (recipe follows)
12–14 ramps
5–6 morels (about 1 cup, sliced)
2 tablespoons butter
4 eggs
1 cup milk
6 ounces Gruyere cheese, grated
1 ounce parmesan cheese, coarsely grated
Salt and freshly ground pepper

Preheat oven to 350°F. Wash the ramps and cut off the roots. Chop the white bulb, white stem, and green leaves. Heat the butter in a saucepan. Sauté the morels and ramps until the mushrooms are soft. Set aside to cool slightly.

In a mixing bowl, whisk the eggs with the milk. Add the cheeses and a dash each of salt and freshly ground pepper. Mix in sautéed ramps and morels. Pour into unbaked pie shell. Bake for 45 minutes.

Whole Wheat Pie Crust

Makes 1 (9- or 10-inch) bottom pie shell
½ cup plus 2 tablespoons cold butter, cut into pieces
½ cup whole wheat flour
1 cup unbleached flour
½ teaspoon salt
2–3 tablespoons cold water

Process butter, flours, and salt in a food processor until crumbly. With processor running, slowly add cold water a tablespoon at a time; sometimes the amount of water needed depends on the humidity of the day. Process in pulses just until dough clings together. Roll out the dough on a floured board to the size of your quiche pan. Place dough in the bottom and sides of pan. Straighten out the crust and crimp the edges as desired.

green leaf are edible. Ramps have a mild onion garlic flavor and the aroma is evident when you are harvesting the roots.

SHALLOTS (*Allium cepa* Aggreatum Group)
Annual bulb
Planting to table: 80 to 90 days

Shallots, like garlic, are planted in the fall. They are ready to harvest in spring when the green tops fall over. Shallots can be harvested at any stage and used like green onions. When you dig shallots in the late spring or early summer, you will find that the single bulb you planted in the fall will have multiplied into a cluster of six to eight bulbs. See more on shallots in the Fall chapter (page 142).

Caramelized shallots in red wine served with pasta is a simple and elegant dish. Crunchy garden peas go well on the side. Peonies for the vase.

Caramelized Shallots in Red Wine with Pasta

Serves 6
1 pound Italian pasta, uncooked
3–4 tablespoons extra-virgin olive oil
12–14 shallots, sliced lengthwise
½ cup red wine
Salt and freshly ground pepper

Bring a large pot of water to a boil, add the pasta and cook to the al dente stage. Drain and keep warm while making the sauce.

Heat the oil in a skillet. Sauté the shallots in the oil over medium low heat until they are caramelized (about an hour). Stir every so often to prevent sticking and burning. Add red wine and deglaze the pan, stirring and cooking for another 10 minutes.

Pour sauce over pasta and serve immediately with chopped fresh sorrel and parmesan cheese.

Stewed Rhubarb Topping

Makes 2 cups
6–8 stalks rhubarb, sliced in ½-inch pieces
¾–1 cup sugar
½ cup water

Put rhubarb, sugar, and water in a saucepan. Bring the mixture to a boil and simmer uncovered until the rhubarb is soft. Serve warm or cold over pancakes or ice cream.

Spring Sweets

RHUBARB (*Rheum rhabarbarum*)
Perennial in zones 2 to 9
Planting to table: 2 years for first harvest, then annually

Rhubarb is an easy, long-lasting perennial. Find a permanent place for it in the garden; it will last for many years. Make sure it has plenty of room to grow; a mature rhubarb plant will spread 4 to 5 feet (1.2–1.5 m). Order bareroot plants or buy containers from a nursery in the spring. Harvest stalks the second year after planting. Cut stalks with a sharp knife and use in recipes. The leaves are toxic, so forego those. Your grandmother or great-grandmother probably made stewed rhubarb which is easy to make. Rhubarb is sweet when stewed, but do not limit yourself by thinking rhubarb has to always partner with sugar. I find the raw, tart, crunchy pieces are good in salads. I like the twang.

Rhubarb Custard Pie

This is a comforting dessert and it's even better served the next day for breakfast.

Makes 1 (9-inch) pie
1 unbaked whole wheat pie crust (page 32)
5–6 stalks rhubarb, sliced in ½-inch pieces
3 eggs
¼ cup brown sugar
¾ cup sugar
1 cup milk
1 teaspoon vanilla
Dash of cinnamon
Dash of nutmeg

Preheat oven to 400°F. Place rhubarb pieces on top of an unbaked pie crust. In a small bowl, whisk the eggs. Add the sugars, milk, vanilla, and spices to the eggs and mix together. Pour the mixture over the rhubarb. Bake for 35 minutes or until just set on top.

STRAWBERRIES (*Fragaria*)

Perennial in zones 3 to 9

Planting to table: 2 years for first harvest, then annually

Nothing is as wonderful as fresh local strawberries in season.

Strawberries make an excellent edible groundcover and can be tucked under shrubs and trees. I have mine planted under the peonies inside the fence of my potager. The plants look good throughout the season with white flowers in early spring, bright berries in early summer, and reddish-bronze leaf color in the fall. Used in this way my small patch produces a few handfuls of berries every year, if the chipmunks don't eat them first.

Strawberries are perennial and will fruit for many years, but they have their best production the first year. Most commercial growers treat them as annuals for this reason. June-bearing berries send out prolific runners. These runners are the baby plants and will be the most productive next season. One strategy is to have berries in two planting swaths. One year let the berries send out runners into the unplanted bed that has been amended with organic matter. Dig up the patch that has already produced berries and amend that soil leaving a new bed for the strawberries to send runners to.

Existing beds can be renovated to allow the younger plants to thrive by removing the older plants adding compost and giving room for the new runners. Strawberries need at least six hours of sunlight a day and because of their shallow root system a regular supply of water. They also need a rich soil with room to spread.

Strawberry-rhubarb crumble is a sweet way to eat whole grains. Strawberries and rhubarb are always a great combination.

Strawberry-Rhubarb Granola Crumble

Serves 6–8
⅓ cup walnuts, coarsely chopped
⅓ cup sliced almonds
⅓ cup pecans, coarsely chopped
2 cups whole oats
3 tablespoons butter
⅓ cup pure maple syrup
2 tablespoons molasses
6–7 stalks rhubarb
1 pound (about 4 cups) fresh strawberries
½ cup sugar
2 tablespoons all-purpose flour

Preheat oven to 350°F. Combine the nuts with the oats, then spread in a 9- by 13-inch pan. Melt the butter and combine with the maple syrup and molasses. Pour the mixture over the oats and nuts. Toast the granola in the oven for about 10 minutes, check for browning and stir. Roast for another 5 minutes until the granola is slightly brown and crispy. Remove the granola topping to another dish.

Meanwhile, prepare the rhubarb and strawberries. Wash and chop the rhubarb into bite-size pieces. Wash and hull the berries. Butter the bottom of the 9- by 13-inch pan and add the berries and rhubarb pieces. Sprinkle the sugar and flour on top. Sprinkle the granola over all. Bake for 45–60 minutes until filling is hot and bubbly. Cover with foil if the top becomes to brown. Serve warm or cold. This is also great for breakfast the next morning.

Another classic combination: melted chocolate, fresh strawberries, and real whipped cream layered in a glass.

Strawberry-Chocolate Parfait

Serves 6
6 clear glass parfait glasses
3 cups fresh strawberries
6 Heath bars, broken into small pieces
¼ cup evaporated milk
1 cup heavy whipping cream
2 tablespoons sugar
Fresh mint or chocolate mint leaves (optional)

Wash and hull the strawberries. Put ½ cup prepared strawberries in each parfait glass. Put the Heath bars pieces in a small saucepan and add the evaporated milk. Cook and stir, breaking up the pieces of candy until it all melts into a delicious caramel chocolate mixture. This process takes a while, so keep stirring. Remove the mixture from heat and cool slightly.

In a separate bowl, whip the cream on high speed until soft peaks form. With the mixer running, slowly add the sugar. Continue mixing until the whipped cream is stiff.

Divide the strawberries among the parfait glasses. Pour some of the chocolate mixture on the strawberries, add a generous dollop of whipped cream, and end with a drizzle of chocolate. Garnish with mint or chocolate mint. Serve immediately.

If you are in a hurry, skip melting the chocolate, just crush the Heath bars over the strawberries.

Spring is the season of greens. So many lettuces, kales, and Asian greens prefer the cool weather.

Spring Greens

There was a time when salad meant torn up leaves of pale iceberg lettuce. Americans got accustomed to such bland fare because that lettuce could travel long distances in a truck and then stay on a grocery store shelf even longer. Fresh, tasty salad greens are easy to grow in the potager or in a large container on the deck for an instant meal. Grow your own for a salad that explodes with texture and flavor; include pale green only if you want to. Pink, red, burgundy, viridian, and chartreuse are also options. The colors and textures available are so elegant you may not even want to make a salad; in that case, just leave the ornamental greens in the garden. The frilly, speck-led, lacy, swirled leaves are so pretty they rival any fussy flower in the border. There are many greens besides lettuce to put in salads.

ARUGULA (Rocket) (*Eruca sativa*)
Annual
Seed to table: 50 days

Sow seeds in early spring by broadcast seeding or plant in rows 6 to 8 inches (15–20 cm) apart. Harvest the tangy leaves while young; the greens are flavorful but slightly bitter. Arugula is best raw in salads. The plants will bolt in hot weather.

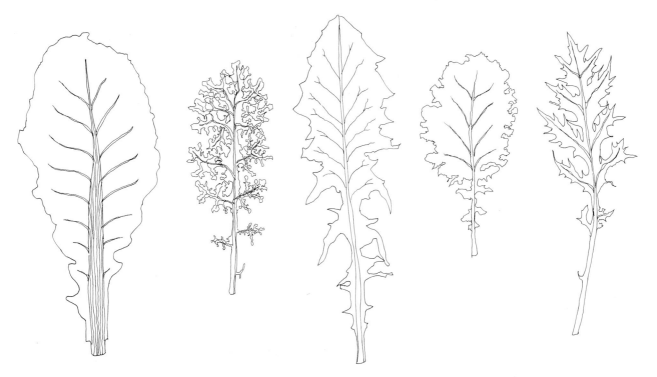

Greens for salads and stir fries come in an abundant array of flavors and textures: (left to right) red mustard, golden frill mustard, dandelion, red Russian kale, and mizuna.

BOK CHOY (*Brassica rapa* Chinensis Group)
Biennial grown as an annual
Seed to table: 25 to 45 days

Bok choy, also called pac choi, is a Chinese cabbage grown for its crunchy white stems and flavorful deep green leaves. It is excellent in stir-fries and soups, and is also great raw in salads. The leaves can be used instead of bread for a sandwich.

Bok choy is easy to grow by direct seeding in the garden in early spring. Nurseries sell plants to transplant outdoors, or you can grow your own seedlings from seed indoors beginning a few weeks before setting out. The leaves can be harvested in a cut-and-come-again fashion or the whole plant can be harvested.

'Tatsoi' is a flat-to-the-ground rosette variety. The dark leaves are very tasty. 'Golden Yellow' has bright yellow leaves on a fan-shaped plant. 'Toy Choy' is a miniature variety. All parts of the plants can be used at any stage from baby leaf to full maturity.

BROCCOLI RAAB (*Brassica rapa* Ruvo Group)
Biennial grown as an annual
Seed to table: 28 to 60 days

This sprouting broccoli (also known as rapini) is grown for the greens and small unopened buds on loose multiple shoots unlike its cousin which is grown for its one main large head. Broccoli raab is fast growing and can be harvested in a cut-and-come-again fashion, that is, cut the leaves at the base and they will regrow. The mild, sweet broccoli taste is great raw in salads, slightly cooked in stir-fries, or steamed.

Broccoli raab is easy to grow. Broadcast seed in the garden and cover lightly with soil then water in. When the plants are 2 inches (5 cm) high, thin the seedlings (use in a salad) to 4 to 5 inches (10–12.5 cm) apart.

'Spring' raab has large leaves and will tolerate some heat, so it may transition into the warmer days of summer. 'Cima di Rape Spigarello' is an Italian variety with serrated leaves. *Brassica oleracea* Italica Group 'Early Purple Sprouting' is an English heirloom variety that is very frost tolerant and produces purple sprouts. See more on broccoli raab in the Fall chapter (page 155).

CABBAGE (*Brassica oleracea* Capitata Group)
Biennial grown as an annual
Seed to table: 60 to 95 days

Cabbage, like the other brassicas, is a heavy feeder, preferring fertile soil with adequate moisture throughout the season. Choose early varieties for spring planting so they mature before it gets too hot. Sow seeds indoors under lights 8 weeks before the frost-free date, then plant outside about a month before the last frost date or buy transplants from a nursery and set them out. Cabbage prefers a cool growing season and tolerates frost. See more on cabbage in the Summer and Fall chapters (pages 102 and 156, respectively).

DANDELION (*Taraxacum officinale*)
Perennial grown as an annual
Seed to table: 45 to 55 days

The dandelion of salads is not the common dandelion that is growing in your front yard, although the leaves and flowers of that ubiquitous weed are edible if they haven't been sprayed with pesticides. The seeds I plant are cultivated to produce large leaves for salads. 'Amélioré', meaning improved, is a French variety with large mild leaves. Sow seeds directly outside 2 to 4 weeks before the frost-free date. The spiky leaves are larger than the weed and can be used in salads or cooked. The leaves are bitter and best paired with other greens in a salad.

'Ruby Perfection' red cabbage is set out in the garden when there is still a chance of frost. Cabbage prefers cool weather.

KALE (*Brassica oleracea* Acephala Group)
Biennial grown as an annual
Seed to table: 45 to 65 days

If you only plant one type of spring green, plant kale. It's really underrated as a vegetable. You can eat it raw in salads or chop it up and add it to stir-fries, soups, and dips. If you get distracted from your kitchen garden, don't worry; some varieties of kale look stunning all season, even if you never eat them. Kale is a biennial so will go to seed the second season. That's when you can take it out and plant some more. Here are two favorites that can be planted now and will look vibrant in the garden through the heat of summer and on into the cool of fall, an entire year in the garden.

'Nero di Toscano' (also called black palm kale) has large palmlike blue-green leaves that are upright and very bumpy. This kale is tolerant of heat and cold so will transition into the summer garden. You can harvest tender leaves at the baby stage in only 30 days. 'Redbor' cabbage grows 2 to 3 feet (60–90 cm) tall and has a central stalk and frilly dark red leaves. I often plant it in containers where it thrives all season. It's very ornamental and I've seen it in perennial borders. See more on kale in the Fall chapter (page 158).

LETTUCE (*Lactuca sativa*)
Annual
Seed to table: 40 to 70 days

Lettuce varieties come in a tapestry of colors and textures. With heirloom names like 'Amish Deer Tongue', 'Cimmaron', 'Dark Lollo Rossa', 'Devil's Ears', 'Mascara', and 'Speckled Trout Back', it's not hard to imagine that lettuce can be deep red, bright green, chartreuse, speckled, spotted, and everything in between. The leaf can be shaped like a deeply lobed oakleaf and be frilly, curly, serrated, and swirly or small, smooth, and round.

Lettuce can be harvested in a cut-and-come-again fashion when the leaves are young. Just snip with scissors when leaves are at least an inch (2.5 cm) tall. The leaves will keep growing for another harvest. Lettuce can also be left in the garden to grow to its full size.

To grow lettuce, sprinkle seeds evenly over prepared soil. Cover with ¼ inch (6 mm) of soil and water thoroughly. Keep consistently watered. With sun and cool weather, lettuce will do fine.

MESCLUN MIX

The word *mesclun* comes from the French and means a mix of salad greens. Seed companies offer combinations in packets to make planting convenient. The blends contain a variety of lettuces, kales, mustards, and other greens—not unlike the mixes of baby leaves at the grocery store, but these are seeds. Sometimes they vary the combinations. Last spring I planted an Asian mesclun mix with mustards, Asian greens, and mizuna. These pre-mixed seed packets are great for small gardens because they allow many colors, flavors, and textures in a tight space.

Sow every few weeks only what your family can eat. An area that is 2 feet by 2 feet (60 cm by 60 cm) may be all you need. The greens can be thinned and harvested in a cut-and-come-again fashion, until it gets too hot. Many lettuces, mustards, and kales bolt when the late spring days get too warm.

MUSTARD GREENS (*Brassica juncea*)
Annual
Seed to table: 40 to 60 days

Mustard greens look pretty in the spring garden and add spiciness to salads or sandwiches. Some of my favorites are 'Osaka Purple', which has giant red leaves, and 'Golden Frill', which has frilly, delicate lime green serrated leaves.

Dig a small trench with your finger in pliable spring soil, sprinkle in some seeds, and gently cover. Water the seeds when you have planted them. Thin when the seedlings get 2 or 3 inches (5–7.5 cm) high by removing the entire baby plant. Toss into a salad—roots, stems, leaves, and all.

Mizuna (*Brassica rapa* Nipposinica Group) is Japanese mustard with deeply serrated leaves. The leaves and stems are used in stir-fries, soups, and stews. This mustard is really flavorful, sweet and mustardy at the same time.

All of the mustards are easy to grow. Your questions should be how much will you really eat? It's easy to plant too much. A better time to plant mustards to stay in the garden for a long period of time is in the fall. (See photo of 'Osaka Purple' mustard on page 31.)

Basic Vinaigrette

Never buy salad dressing again! I stopped buying salad dressings a long time ago. Have you tried reading the labels? With good olive oil and vinegar and some lemons or limes you can easily make a simple dressing for fresh picked lettuces and greens. Sometimes it's as simple as a drizzle of olive oil and a squeeze from a slice of lemon.

Makes about a cup
½ cup extra virgin olive oil
⅓ cup mild vinegar, such as white wine or rice vinegar
Juice of 1 lemon
1 garlic clove, quartered
Salt and freshly ground pepper

Mix all ingredients and serve immediately or store in refrigerator for a week. The garlic clove imparts a mild flavor—not too much.

Creamy Green Goddess Dressing

Makes about a cup
3 tablespoons fresh flat-leaf parsley
1 garlic clove
1 green onion
½ avocado
1 cup Greek yogurt
1 tablespoon fresh tarragon leaves, chopped (optional)
1 tablespoon fresh cilantro, chopped (optional)

Chop the parsley, garlic, and green onion in a food processor. Add the avocado and process until it is finely chopped. Add the sour cream and yogurt and process briefly until smooth. Serve immediately over greens or chill and serve within a week. Try variations of this by adding a tablespoon of fresh tarragon or fresh cilantro.

Bloody sorrel emerges in the spring. The leaves are attractive all season.

SORREL (*Rumex*)
Perennial in zones 5 to 9
Seed to table: 60 days

Bloody sorrel (*Rumex sanguineus*) emerges in the spring with green leaves that are spiked with deep red veins, hence the name. The long, oval leaves are attractive and the edible plant will shine in any perennial border through fall, even if you don't eat it. Sorrel prefers full sun with ample water to part shade. It may languish in heat and drought, but thorough watering usually revives it.

French sorrel (*Rumex scutatus*) has been grown as an edible green for hundreds of years. When introduced into England in 1596 it was used as a substitute for spinach but it was popular before that and used by the Egyptians, Greeks, and Romans. Shred the fresh leaves and add to soups or use the young leaves in salads.

Rumex acetosa 'Sterile' is a flower-free variety that doesn't produce seeds.

SPINACH (*Spinacia oleracea*)
Annual
Seed to table: 35 to 40 days

I used to think there was only one kind of spinach, namely, the kind that came in a bag from the grocery store. In reality, spinach leaves can be heavily savoyed and crinkly or smooth and flat. The heavily crinkled leaf types tend to fare better through the winter. Harvest the fresh greens in the early spring from the garden or cold frame if you live in mild climate. Plant seeds early in the garden as soon as the soil can be worked. See more on spinach in the Fall and Winter chapters (pages 159 and 180, respectively).

SWISS CHARD (*Beta vulgaris* Cicla Group)
Biennial grown as an annual
Seed to table: 50 days

Swiss chard is easy to grow, tastes great, and is ornamental in the garden. It should be planted in every border even if you do not plan to eat it. Plant seeds of Swiss chard directly in the garden when the soil is about 50°F, or plant indoors under lights earlier and set the plants out in the garden when they are a few inches tall.

In mild climates Swiss chard will overwinter in the garden or in cold frames and the leaves can be harvested all season. In my garden (zone 5) I cover Swiss chard with glass cloches through the winter. This offers enough protection to harvest the newly emerging green leaves in early spring. Swiss chard, like beets and parsley, is a biennial. It will go to seed the next season. The Swiss chard left in the garden over the winter allows me to harvest the new leaves in early spring, but later the plant thins out as the plant transitions to making seed instead of leaves. Take it out at this point. By this time the newly planted chard is growing well. Treat it like an annual that lasts for a full year with protection in cold climates.

A container of 'Bright Lights' Swiss chard and pansies brightens the author's front porch.

'Bright Lights' Swiss chard is a mix of yellow, red, orange, and white. 'Fordhook Giant' has large leaves and white stems. 'Oriole' has bright orange stems. 'Monstruoso' is one of my favorites for the kitchen. It has huge green leaves and large white stems. The crunchy stems are good in stir-fries or raw for dips or as a substitute for celery. This Italian heirloom also looks striking in the garden or in a container with annual or perennial flowers.

An easy spring container is Swiss chard with pansies. If you place the container in part shade, it may last all summer. See more on Swiss chard in the Fall chapter (page 159).

Quinoa Pilaf with Spring Vegetables

Quinoa is a whole grain with all kinds of health benefits. Native to Peru, where the Incas considered it a sacred crop, it is actually the seed from a plant related to beets and Swiss chard. You can find two varieties of quinoa—red or white—at a grocery that sells bulk whole foods. Use half of each for a pleasant mix. I have used quinoa in this pilaf; you could easily substitute brown rice or barley but the cooking times would change. Quinoa cooks relatively quickly.

Serves 6
1 cup red quinoa
1 cup white quinoa
4 cups chicken or vegetable stock
3–4 stalks Swiss chard with leaves
2–3 stalks green garlic
broccoli florets as desired
1 tablespoon extra virgin olive oil
1 tablespoon butter
½ cup fresh English peas, shelled
½ cup fresh flat-leaf parsley, chopped
Salt and freshly ground pepper

Rinse quinoa seeds in a strainer with a tight mesh or swirl in a pot of water, then gingerly pour out the water while holding back the seeds with a lid. Place the chicken stock in a saucepan and add the quinoa. Bring to a boil and simmer uncovered, stirring every once in a while for about 15–20 minutes. The grains will begin to open. Turn off the heat and cover with a lid until all of the liquid is absorbed.

Coarsely chop the Swiss chard stalks and leaves. Chop the green garlic, using the entire stalk, like you would a green onion. Coarsely chop the broccoli.

In a large skillet over medium-high heat add the olive oil and butter. Add the peas and cook for a few minutes. Add the rest of the vegetables and the parsley and cook until the Swiss chard begins to wilt, about 5–7 minutes. Add the cooked quinoa to the skillet and serve in one dish.

When cooking Swiss chard with other ingredients, I like to use the white-ribbed varieties, like 'Monstruoso', as they do not bleed, but any Swiss chard will be fine in most recipes.

Spring Herbs

BORAGE (*Borago officinalis*)
Annual
Seed to table: 80 days

Borage flowers are one of the first edible flowers to bloom in the spring. The blue or purple drooping blossoms can be used in salads or drinks. Borage is a reseeding annual and it will reseed all around your garden. I enjoy the edible flowers so much that I always keep some. The plant is coarse and sprawling and not for gardeners who like neat and well-behaved plants. The stems and leaves are hairy and prickly; I tend to get a rash if I handle the plants. Have I discouraged you? I have a fondness for borage and allow it to reseed in certain places. Growing borage requires vigilance as it will spread.

CHIVES (*Allium schoenoprasum*)
Perennial in zones 3 to 11
Seed to table: 40 to 50 days

Chives are a member of the onion family and, like many alliums, bloom in the spring. Their flowers are bright magenta pink and one of the first perennials to bloom in the border. The round fluffy oniony balls are cheery as the weather transitions to warmer days. The flowers respond well to deadheading and will continue to bloom sporadically through the summer. Clip all parts of the plant to brighten the look, flavor, and taste of practically anything.

Chives can be harvested anytime spring through fall, but the flowers look best in spring and can even be used in flower arrangements. Spring is a good time to plant additional chives. They prefer full sun

(next page top) *Sweet marjoram is not hardy in zone 5 and must be planted annually. It's a type of oregano and very fragrant. Excellent for cooking.*

(bottom) *Edible borage flowers are great for salads or drinks.*

Grilled Lamb Kabobs

Serves 4–6
¼ cup extra virgin olive oil
Juice of 1 lemon
3 garlic cloves, chopped
½ cup fresh marjoram, chopped
2 tablespoons fresh tarragon leaves, chopped
Salt and freshly ground pepper
2 pounds lamb, cut into cubes

Combine the marinade ingredients and pour over the meat chunks that have been placed in a non-reactive container. Cover and marinate overnight or for 2 to 3 hours.

Place the meat on skewers and roast over hot coals until done. Serve with mint chutney and cool yogurt sauce (page 111).

Mint Chutney

Makes 2 cups
½ cup (1 bunch) fresh mint leaves
½ cup (1 bunch) fresh flat-leaf parsley
½ cup (1 bunch) fresh cilantro
2 garlic cloves
1 cayenne pepper, stemmed and seeded
⅓ cup white golden raisins
1 tablespoon brown sugar
1 tablespoon extra virgin olive oil
Juice of ½ orange

Pulse all ingredients briefly in a food processor until coarsely chopped. Serve immediately with lamb kabobs.

and well-drained soil. Chives have a place in the herb garden or even the mixed perennial border, and can even be used to line a raised bed in the potager. See more on chives in the Summer chapter (page 106).

CULINARY HERBS

Many of the culinary perennial and self-seeding annual herbs emerge early in the spring in cool weather and will continue until frost. The young leaves of mint, thyme, tarragon, dill, and cilantro are at their peak at the beginning of the season. During this growth stage the flavor of the oils is at the peak. Later in the summer when herbs flower the herb oils are not as pungent. When starting a new bed of dill and cilantro, continue to sow seeds every few weeks until the plants are established and reseed themselves. Dill will often come up where you don't want it so harvest those seedlings for fish or a dip. Pluck wayward seedlings while young.

LEMON BALM (*Melissa officinalis*)
Perennial in zones 5 to 11
Seed to table: 120 days

This ancient medicinal mint was originally grown in monastery gardens. The leaves have a delicious lemon scent and flavor, but the plant itself is a mint and behaves like all mints: unless it is contained it will take over your garden. I innocently bought mine from my niece who was selling plants to support her school. That was a decade ago and I am still trying to eradicate it from certain beds. Lemon balm is perfect for a spot in the garden that has an edge to it, perhaps between a sidewalk and a driveway, or keep it in pots. It is a nice mint for drinks and teas.

SWEET WOODRUFF (*Galium odoratum*)
Perennial in zones 4 to 8
Seed to table: 60 days

Sweet woodruff prefers part shade to full shade where the soil is moist. This fragrant herb will naturalize in an area if it is kept out of full sun and the soil is not allowed to dry out. It is an excellent ground cover when given the right conditions. The palm-tree-like whorled leaves are attractive all season but in late spring (May in my garden) the plant produces tiny white flowers. These flowers and the bits of new green leaves are used to flavor May Wine, the drink that celebrates spring.

Fresh Lemon Balm Tea

The new young leaves of lemon balm emerge in early spring so a hot tea is welcome when the days are still cool in spring. This recipe came from Bunnie Geroux, an octogenarian who is the director of the Ohio Herb Education Center in Gahanna, Ohio. This is a lemony tea made with fresh mint leaves.

1 cup fresh young lemon balm leaves
1 cup boiling water

Wash the leaves and pack them in a mug. Pour boiling water over the leaves and let steep for a few minutes. Strain and serve immediately.

May wine is served with fresh strawberries and edible herbs and flowers from the spring garden.

May Wine

1 bottle of German white wine, such as a Riesling
4–5 sprigs young sweet woodruff leaves
Sweet woodruff leaves and flowers for garnish
Fresh strawberries for garnish
Borage flowers for garnish

Dry the sweet woodruff in the microwave on high for 30 seconds. Turn the plate and continue at 30-second intervals until the leaves are dried. Pour the wine into a pitcher and add the dried leaves to steep. Cover and keep in the refrigerator overnight. Strain out the leaves. Pour the flavored wine into serving glasses and garnish each glass with strawberries, borage flowers, and sprigs of sweet woodruff flowers and leaves.

Shrubs and Flowers for the Table

Spring seems to come slowly then pass quickly in the American Midwest. In early and mid spring (March and April) there is a cold, dreary, bare-twigged anticipation of warmth. Then blink; the magnolia, cherry, and dogwood trees are blooming. Soon I'm swooning with all of the color and fragrance. One moment the red shoots of peonies emerge from the ground signaling spring and the next moment I am cutting back the spent stems that have bowed to the ground and are now barren. Blink again and the crabapples have leafed out and their blossoms have disappeared.

Relish the short-lived beauty of this season with its blossoms and fragrance. Enjoy the tastes of the season along with the flowers of the season. Picking flowers and twigs from your own garden doesn't have to be fancy or formal. I sometimes send my guests, or my children when they are home, to the garden to pick whatever they can find that's blooming. My son Jim, for his May birthday, was sent with a vase full of water and a pair of clippers to gather peonies, irises, salvias, and alliums for the centerpiece. The arrangement was his choice, his creation; however the flowers landed in the vase was perfect. There is no way to mess it up.

BULBS FOR SPRING

Bulbs are often overlooked as a layer of early spring color in the perennial border. They can be mixed in with perennials to extend the bloom season. Daffodils, chives (or alliums), and tulips bloom as the perennials are just emerging from the soil. When the bulbs are done blooming the perennials are large enough to cover the dying foliage.

Daffodils (*Narcissus*) are one of the easiest plants to grow for spring color, indoors and out. Varieties

Peonies are one of the classic flowers of spring. In the beginning of the season the red shoots pierce the soil; by late spring they are in full fragrant bloom. Lizzie and Ethan Zink help me pick a bouquet of flowers including peonies and Siberian iris for the dinner table.

The easiest cut flowers to grow are daffodils and tulips. These bright pink tulips grow in a children's garden at the entrance to Hanby Arts Magnet School in Westerville, Ohio.

can be chosen so that you have a staggered succession of bloom from early spring to late spring. Daffodils will naturalize over the years expanding the area they cover. Every few years divide the bulbs for more bloom. Tulips (*Tulipa*) are treated as annuals. Plant them in the fall for one season of bloom in the spring. Ornamental onions (*Allium*) produce pink to purple spheres ranging in size from a ping-pong ball to a soccer ball.

Cut flower stems any time of day; trim at the base and put them in water. Daffodils and tulips make wonderful spring arrangements. Alliums are bet-

ter left to enjoy in the garden. When the blooms are spent, let the foliage die back naturally, then tie back if it looks unsightly. When the foliage is completely brown, remove it and put in the compost.

Plant bulbs in the fall for cut flowers in the spring. For an easy bulb design, see page 172 in the Fall chapter.

CRABAPPLE (*Malus*)
Deciduous ornamental tree in zones 4 to 8
Site conditions: Full sun; moist, well-drained soil

Crabapples are an excellent ornamental tree for spring blossoms. Flowers can be white, pale pink, coral, mauve, dark pink, red, and shades in between. The trees are fast growing and short-lived (about fifteen to twenty years). Older, mature trees are best for pruning so you don't damage the tree by removing branches. Just save the pruning chores for spring so that you can bring the colorful, fragrant twigs full of blossoms indoors.

Crabapples usually grow no larger than 20 feet (6 m) tall but range in size and form from wide and horizontal to upright and narrow; some look like lollipops. 'Prairie Fire' has coral red blossoms. 'Strawberry Parfait' has pink-red blossoms. 'Holiday Gold' has white blossoms and gold fruit. Just make sure to choose varieties that are disease resistant so the leaves do not turn brown and mottled with scab. The fruit is edible, although not so tasty. We'll find them useful in the fall when making jelly. See more on crabapple in the Fall chapter (page 163).

DOGWOOD (*Cornus*)
Deciduous ornamental tree in zones 5 to 8
Site conditions: Part to full sun

Flowering dogwood (*Cornus florida*) is a native North American tree loved for the showy cross-shaped bracts that bloom white or pink in spring. The tree is revered for its branching form and spring bloom. It is an understory tree in the wild, so it makes sense

to imitate those conditions and give it part sun in the landscape, especially in the afternoon. That is the natural place to plant the tree, but some experts now recommend planting in sun to decrease susceptibility to dogwood anthracnose. Trees grown in moist, shady areas are more prone to fungal diseases, especially during cool weather.

Anthracnose is a fungus that has spread to many trees and kills them usually with in three years. Check with experts in your region before planting. 'Appalachian Spring' is a cultivar derived from a lone tree that survived a blight in a Maryland woods where every other dogwood was wiped out by dogwood anthracnose. It is believed to carry resistant genes to the fungus. Kousa dogwood (*Cornus kousa*) is an alternative too, but won't have spring bloom or the sacredness to American gardeners. Some research indicates that there is variation in resistance among cultivars of kousa dogwood.

FORSYTHIA (*Forsythia*)
Deciduous flowering shrub in zones 4 to 8
Site conditions: Prefers full sun; well-drained soil

Love it or hate it, forsythia does make a bright yellow show in the spring. It's often the first thing to bloom and after a dreary, gray winter is a welcome sight. Some will plant it because their grandmothers grew it; some won't grow it because it's everywhere. *Forsythia viridissima* var. *koreana* 'Kumson' has foliage that looks nothing like the typical forsythia; the leaves are wider, variegated, and very attractive.

Cornelian cherry dogwood (*Cornus mas*), also hardy in zones 4 to 8, is an alternative to forsythia for yellow color if you find forsythia too garish or ubiquitous. It is a small ornamental tree that grows 15 to 20 feet (4.5–6 m) tall with tiny pale yellow flowers in early spring. In midsummer it produces edible, tart, oblong red fruits for preserves or jelly. 'Elegant', 'Pioneer', and 'Redstone' have the best fruit set.

'Crandall' clove currant (*Ribes odoratum*) is another alternative with yellow spring bloom. Native to the eastern and central United States, it produces black edible currants in late summer (July). See more on currants in the Summer chapter (page 94).

IRIS (*Iris*)
Perennial in zones 3 to 9
Site conditions: Full sun to light shade; well-drained soil

Bearded irises (*Iris germanica*) bloom when the early daffodils and tulips have finished blooming. There are hundreds of cultivars and the color range is wide. Pale lavender to bright purple, pale peach to russet orange, pale cream to vivid yellow you could search specialty catalogs for your favorite. They are an old fashioned plant often passed down through generations; I received mine from my mother-in-law and hers came from her mother. Periodically the plants are susceptible to iris borer. The larvae thrive in the rhizomes. I have dug up rhizomes, cut the slimy larvae out of roots, thrown rotten rhizomes away and replanted the good ones. I am much more diligent to clean up in fall and remove foliage that has died back. I have never had a problem since.

Siberian iris (*Iris sibirica*) has a smaller bloom and prefers moist sites. The colors are white, blue, purple and violet. One of my favorite cut flowers for spring is 'Caesar's Brother' The Siberian irises are not as prone to the root borer, another reason to like them. They grow well in northern climates.

Tall forsythia branches fill the space in a kitchen with an immense ceiling. Dr. Elsie Freeman found an old shrub and cut these long branches while she and I were out walking in the fields near her Maine home one April.

LILAC (*Syringa vulgaris*)
Deciduous flowering shrub in zones 3 to 7
Site conditions: Full sun; rich, alkaline soil

Lilacs are another iconic blossom of spring. The soft pinkish lavender to deep purple fragrant blooms are unsurpassed if you are lucky enough to have one or more. The blooms do not last long in the vase; nevertheless, they are still remarkable when brought indoors. Pounding the base of the woody stem to flatten it so it absorbs more water doesn't seem to work for me. Lilacs are not for the small yard, they can grow 12 feet (3.6 m) tall and wide , depending on the cultivar. 'President Lincoln' produces clusters of single blue flowers. 'Président Grévy' is an old variety with lilac double flowers. There are over a thousand varieties of French hybrid lilacs.

PANSIES (*Viola*)
Annual
Site conditions: Prefers full sun; cool temperatures

There is a reason you see pansies everywhere in the spring. They are one of the few annuals that tolerate and prefer cool weather. In contrast, the summer annuals cannot be planted outside until the frost-free date has passed. I am not a pansy snob. I like to plant them as a border in the raised beds of the potager. They grow next to the spring greens and peas. Pansies take full sun and tolerate many types of soil, even clay soil.

PEONY (*Paeonia*)
Perennial in zones 2 to 8
Site conditions: Full sun or part shade; rich, well-
  drained soil

Ask your mother what her favorite flower is and the answer is apt to be peony. At least it's my favorite flower. No perennial matches it for showy, reliable, and spectacular blooms in the garden or in the vase.

The glorious color lasts only for a few weeks in the spring but peonies deserve a place in the border. They attract beneficial insects as well. Drive around older communities in the spring and you are apt to see peonies in bloom. That is because these easy-to-grow perennials last for twenty or thirty years, often without any special care.

Peonies prefer areas with cold winters and do not do well in the heat of the American Far South. Colors range from white to yellow and pale pink to deep crimson red. The blooms range from single with a showy center to full double with a sphere of colorful petals. Shop nurseries in the spring or divide some tubers from a friend's garden. Peonies are easy to divide and transplant, and this should be done in early spring before the plants send up too many leaves.

REDBUD (*Cercis canadensis*)
Deciduous ornamental tree in zones 4 to 9
Site conditions: Prefers full sun, tolerates part shade;
  rich, moist soil

Redbud is a native ornamental tree that blooms in the spring. The bright pink blossoms appear before the branches leaf out. Save your pruning chores for the bloom season and cut a few branches to bring indoors. The magenta-purple blossoms and stark black branches look elegant as a simple arrangement for the table.

SAUCER MAGNOLIA (*Magnolia soulangiana*)
Deciduous ornamental tree in zones 5 to 9
Site conditions: Full sun; wide range of soils

Saucer magnolias blooms in shades of dark pink to pale pinkish white. The tree blooms about the same time that spring daffodils and tulips are blooming. The tulip-cup-shaped blossoms are very attractive in the landscape or cut for a vase.

Pink peonies, purple globe allium and dark blue Siberian iris are easily arranged in an informal springtime vase.

Magnolia blossoms are stunning in the spring. Clip a blossom or two to bring indoors for a vase or float them in a bowl of water.

SERVICEBERRY (*Amelanchier*)
Deciduous ornamental tree in zones 3 to 7
Site conditions: Prefers part shade, can adapt to sun

Serviceberry is another small native tree with multiseason appeal. White blossoms cover the tree in early to mid spring (late March or early April). In midsummer it produces sweet edible fruits that can be eaten right off the tree or made into jams and desserts. In the fall the leaves range in color from yellow to orange.

SWEET PEA (*Lathyrus odoratus*)
Annual
Site conditions: Prefers full sun; cool temperatures

Sweet peas are old-fashioned plants grown for their fragrant flowers and not to eat. In fact, all parts of the plants are toxic. Sweet peas add color to the kitchen garden as the vines climb and twist over fences and trellises. They also bring color and fra-

grance indoors. Cut a few blossoms to float in a bowl of water. It will stimulate the plant to produce even more.

Plant seeds outside a month to six weeks before the last spring frost. Sweet peas need support as they grow so train them up a fence or create a teepee with willow or bamboo. The bloom season will be prolonged in areas with cool summers. They do not tolerate heat.

VIBURNUM (*Viburnum*)
Deciduous or evergreen flowering shrubs in zones 5 to 8 (depending on the cultivar)
Site conditions: Full sun or part shade; rich, well-drained soil

Viburnums are excellent shrubs for the residential landscape. They add structure to the garden, help create privacy screening to divide a boundary, and provide showy blossoms in the spring. Many produce berries in the fall that range in color from bright red to pink and blue. The berries are a source of food for birds. American cranberry bush viburnum (*Viburnum trilobum*) produces edible berries for jams in the fall.

When you cut flowers for indoor arrangements you are actually pruning and shaping the shrub, and that's a good thing, so trim away. The stiff stems help to hold up other more fragile flowers in mixed bouquets in the vase. *Viburnum nudum* 'Winterthur' has attractive shiny foliage with white blooms in spring and pink and blue berries in fall. Plant with *Viburnum nudum* 'Bulk' (Brandywine) for best fruit production on both plants. The doublefile viburnums bloom heavily in spring and are very fragrant. See more on viburnum in the Fall chapter (page 165).

(right) *Sweet peas produce fragrant colorful blossoms in the late spring and early summer. A willow tee pee supports these climbers which are just starting to bloom.*

(below) *Arrowwood viburnum (*Viburnum dentatum*) adds structure to the perennial border. It is covered with flat-topped white blossoms in the spring and produces berries in the fall.*

Design for Spring

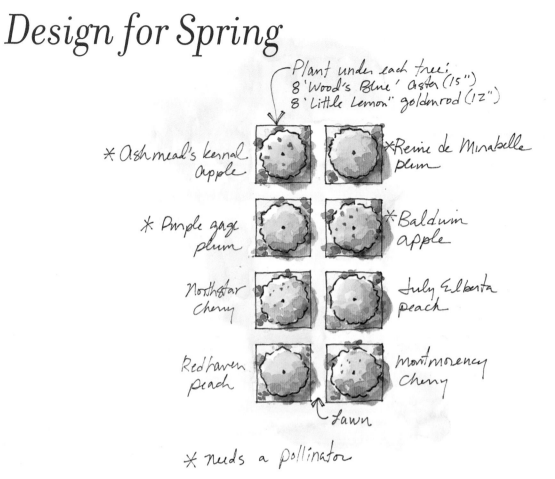

Plant under each tree:
8 'Wood's Blue' aster (15")
8 'Little Lemon" goldenrod (12")

* Ashmead's kernal apple

*Reine de Mirabelle plum

* Purple gage plum

*Baldwin apple

Northstar Cherry

July Elberta peach

Redhaven peach

Montmorency Cherry

Lawn

* needs a pollinator

PLANT AN ORCHARD

This design for a home orchard combines visions of two gardens and adapts them to my local landscape. The first garden to influence this design is Highgrove Estate, the country home and organic garden of HRH The Prince of Wales. I toured this garden one summer. Although taking photos on the 37-acre private property is forbidden, taking notes or making sketches is not. One of the many things that impressed me was the orchard where rare and endangered cooking apples are being preserved. Were they not grown here, these ancient apple varieties would otherwise vanish. The trees are laid out in a grid pattern. Each tree is planted in the center of a square of lavender (*Lavandula angustifolia* 'Royal Gem'). There were maybe eighteen plants in each

Plan view of an orchard for a large residential site. A mix of eight fruit trees, each planted in a bed of goldenrod and asters that is separated from the other beds by lawn.

square, with swaths of lawn between the squares. I saw this same pattern in an estate garden near Lexington, Kentucky, where my first thought on seeing the garden was, "Ahhh, the owner has been to the orchard of Prince Charles."

The second influence in this design comes from my visit to the vineyards of Napa valley in the winter of 2008. I was impressed with the mustard that was growing around the grape vines, which in January are dormant and look like brown pruned twigs. The yellow mustard was planted as a cover crop to cut down on weeds.

My design for a home orchard shows a mix of eight fruit trees with the centers planted 16 feet (4.8 m) apart. There is a swath of lawn that is 3 to 6 feet (90–180 cm) wide, enough for two passes of a lawn mower. The squares are 12 ½ feet (about 3.6 m) on each side and underplanted with low-growing flowers that happen to bloom in the spring. Each square has room for eight 'Wood's Blue' aster and eight Little Lemon goldenrods (*Solidago* 'Dansolitlem') planted in a grid. There are two apple trees and two plum trees, each needing a pollinator. There are two cherry trees and two peach trees although these do not require a pollinator for production.

When planting fruit trees, choose a well-drained spot on high ground, not in a valley or low spot where frost will linger in the early spring and kill blossoms. Valleys can be 10 degrees colder than hilltops.

Do not overfertilize the trees. Mitch Lynd, of Lynd Fruit Farm in Pataskala, Ohio, says, "Quality fruit is grown on trees that are on the edge of starvation." There is a parable in there somewhere about hard times being good for us, you know, producing the good fruit of character.

Fruit trees are often grafted: the fruiting section, or scion, is selected for known characteristics and it is attached to the rootstock. The scion is reproduced vegetatively so it is identical to its parent. This is important because fruit does not grow true to type; that is, if you plant the pit of a peach that you find particularly flavorful, there is no guarantee that the resulting tree will bear fruit that is exactly the same. Furthermore, you will have to wait a long time to see if you like the fruit grown from that seed. Grafting, however, ensures the variety with the characteristics that you want.

When choosing a scion, select varieties based on disease resistance, taste, and purpose. Do you want to eat the fruit fresh, make pies, store or freeze the fruit? There are thousands of cultivars; research the varieties that will meet your needs and that do well in your area.

Plant fruit trees on a ridge or hill not in a frost pocket valley where frost lingers and could kill early spring blossoms.

Each type of fruit tree has standard rootstocks that go with it. The rootstock determines the final size of the tree. A full-size apple tree can reach 20 to 30 feet (6–9 m) tall and wide and takes seven to ten years to produce fruit, not a practical size for most residential gardens. In the northern and midwestern United States, for example, consider B-9 as a rootstock for a dwarf apple tree that will be 8 to 12 feet (2.4–3.6 m) tall. The size is perfect for a small garden and you will avoid hauling out ladders and pole clippers when you crave an apple off the tree or want some fresh applesauce. B-9 is extremely cold hardy and resistant to collar rot.

Cross pollination is necessary for fruit production of most trees. This means you need to plant two different cultivars that bloom at the same time closer than 100 feet (30 m) of each other. Cross pollination is essential for apples, pears, most sweet cherries, and most Japanese plums. It is not essential for apricots, European plums, tart cherries, peaches, and nectarines, though it does improve the amount of fruit. Fruit and almond trees are pollinated by honey bees. Many nut trees are pollinated by wind and so should be planted within 50 feet (15 m) of each other.

FORMAL POTAGER: SPRING

This is a formal potager design for a client in the southeastern United States, in zone 8, where the climate allows her to grow many greens and vegetables through the winter. The potager is where the owner grows annual vegetables and flowers. This structured garden is a spatial garden, an enclosed space that is the permanent frame for growing annual herbs, flowers, and vegetables. The plants change with the season and with the years. Each of the squares is edged with antique brick and is raised about 8 inches (20 cm). The squares are about 4 feet (1.2 m) wide, the perfect size to harvest and weed without stepping on the soil.

   This is a designed garden, a built garden. The drawing demonstrates how the produce changes through the year. It is a usable planting plan; but it will change every year. Each season varies; some plants will do well and some will not. It is unpredictable as growing food often is. Treat it as a guide to the possibilities of what to plant in each season. It is a rough guide as fluid as any planting scheme often is. We will see this garden again, in summer (page 126) and in fall (page 170).

Bed 1
22 'Sorbet Yesterday, Today
   and Tomorrow' viola
'Nelly Viner' sweet peas

Bed 2
22 'Bull's Blood' beet
'Petit Pois Precoville' climbing
   peas

Bed 3
22 'Golden' beet
'Golden India Edible' pea pod

Bed 4
22 'Sorbet Yesterday, Today
   and Tomorrow' viola
'Dolly Varden' sweet pea

Bed 5
'America' spinach
'Red Russian' kale

Bed 6
'Red Rib' dandelion
arugula

Bed 7
4 'Green Magic' broccoli
'King Richard' leek

Bed 8
'King Midas' carrots
'Cherry Belle' radishes

Bed 9
4 'Windsor' fava bean
'Shunkyo Semi-Long' daikon
   radish

Bed 10
'De Ciccio' broccoli
'Deep Purple' scallion

Bed 11
8 'Super Red' cabbage (mini)
8 'Alaska' Savoy cabbage

Bed 12
'Lollo Rossa' lettuce
'Oak Leaf' lettuce
'Asian Red' lettuce

Bed 13
22 'Sorbet Yesterday, Today
   and Tomorrow' viola
'Old Spice Mix' sweet pea

Bed 14
'Purplette' onion
'Tall Telephone' English pea

Bed 15
mesclun mix
'Mr. Big' English pea

Bed 16
22 'Sorbet Yesterday, Today
   and Tomorrow' viola
'Old Spice Mix' sweet pea

SPRING PLANTING PLAN OF A FORMAL POTAGER

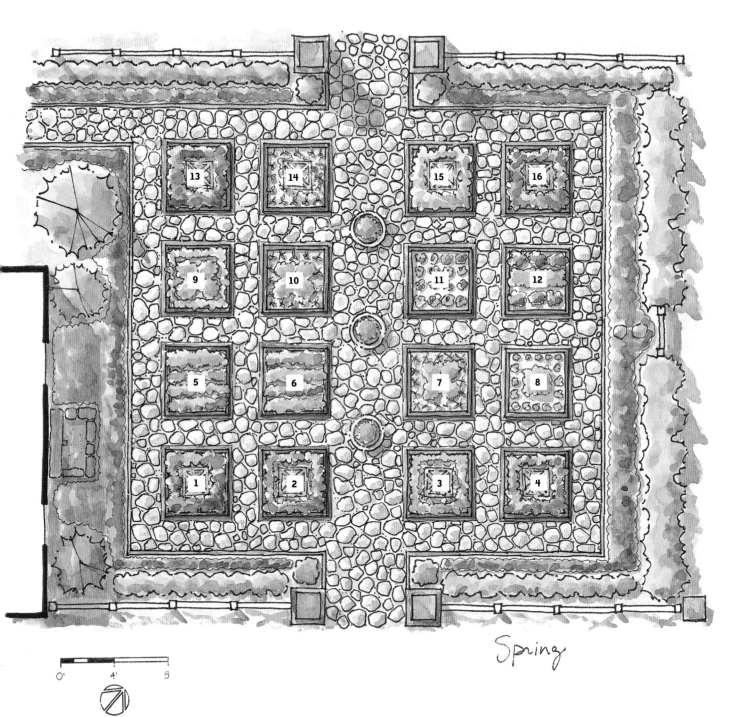

Spring

0' 4' 8

NORTH

WOODLAND GARDEN

An old hedgerow divides my residential lot from my neighbor's. The neighborhood used to be a farm. Some of my neighbors have eliminated the hedge-row and converted it to lawn. I prefer to let it grow wild, but have a plan to tame it over time. I am slowly adding trees, shrubs, and woodland perennials so there will be layers of screening between my house and my neighbor's. A canopy layer, a mid layer, and a groundcover layer, all with plants that will bloom or be attractive at different times of the year. This is a common issue in my design work. How do you create a useful, possibly edible, privacy screen with plants? The design presented here focuses on spring bloom, but really it is multiseasonal. It can be planted in stages. Trees first, shrubs and perennials added later.

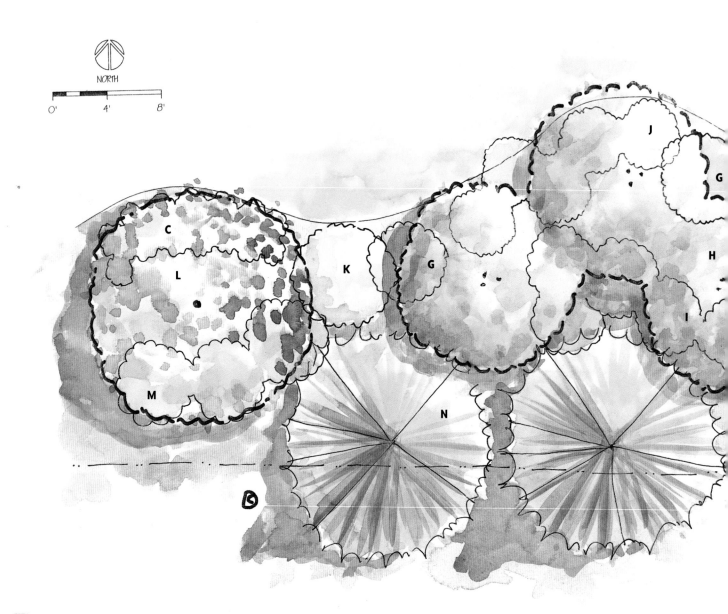

LABEL	NO. OF PLANTS	COMMON NAME	SCIENTIFIC NAME	ZONE	NOTES
A	1	common witch hazel	*Hamamelis virginiana*	4–8	eastern U.S. native; fall bloom
B	3	'Appalachian Spring' dogwood	*Cornus florida* 'Appalachian Spring'	5–9	resistant to dogwood anthracnose
C	28	ostrich fern	*Matteuccia struthiopteris*	4–7	has edible fiddleheads in spring
D	1	'Shasta' doublefile viburnum	*Viburnum plicatum* var. *tomentosum* 'Shasta'	4–8	late spring bloom
E	5	American elderberry	*Sambucus nigra* var. *canadensis* 'York' and 'Adams'	3–9	plant two varieties for pollination
F	3	'Ralph Senior' arrowwood viburnum	*Viburnum dentatum* 'Ralph Senior'	3–8	U.S. native; spring bloom
G	2	'Crandall' clove currant	*Ribes odoratum* 'Crandall'	3–7	plant one male and one female; black fruit on female plants in midsummer; U.S. native
H	3	'Ballerina' serviceberry	*Amelanchier* ×*grandiflora* 'Ballerina'	4–7	white flowers in spring; edible fruit in late summer
I	5	American cranberry bush viburnum	*Viburnum trilobum* 'Hahs'	2–7	late spring bloom; edible fruit in fall
J	5	'Kumson' forsythia	*Forsythia viridissima* var. *koreana* 'Kumson'	5–8	bright yellow flowers in spring
K	1	'Arnold Promise' witch hazel	*Hamamelis* ×*intermedia* 'Arnold Promise'	5–8	yellow flowers in early spring
L	1	redbud	*Cercis canadensis*	4b–9a	magenta-pink blooms in spring; U.S. native
M	3	spicebush	*Lindera benzoin*	4b–9a	yellow flowers in spring; U.S. native
N	2	Norway spruce	*Picea abies*	2b–7a	large evergreen screen

Plan view of a spring woodland edible and useful garden that has multiple layers of bloom and screening from the neighbor's property.

EDIBLE FRONT YARD: SPRING

The edible seasonal front yard garden in spring. The shrubs, flowers, and trees with interest or bloom at this time of year are highlighted in color.

This rendition of the edible front yard garden first shown on page 16 shows the useful or edible plants of spring. Sweet woodruff is in bloom and its flowers and young leaves can be used for May wine. Rhubarb and strawberries are ready to harvest. Peonies and fragrant viburnum and crabapple blossoms can be picked for the vase.

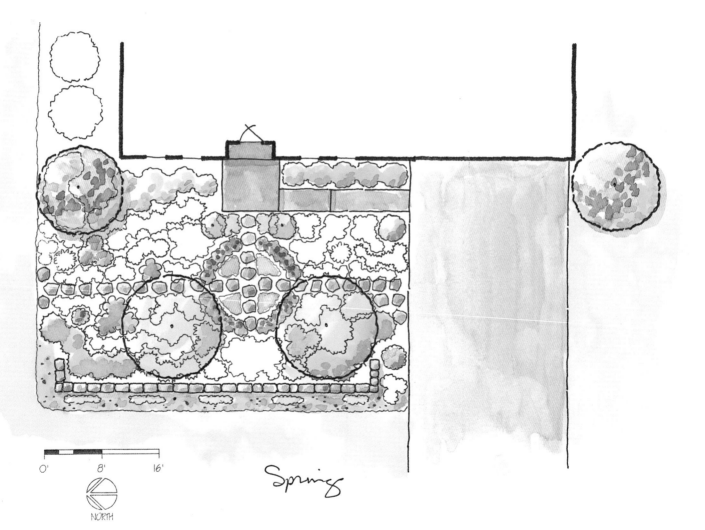

0'   8'   16'

NORTH

Spring

The edible seasonal front yard garden in spring. The shrubs, flowers, and trees with interest or bloom at this time of year are highlighted in color.

Spring Chores

✔ Plant fruit trees. Spring is a good time to plant additional fruit trees in the orchard or at the edge of the kitchen garden.

✔ Plant berries, shrubs, and perennials. Bareroot plants like currants, blueberries, rhubarb, and asparagus can be planted now. Container-grown plants can be planted any time the ground is not frozen.

✔ Prepare vegetable beds. Add 1 or 2 inches (2.5–5 cm) of compost to existing beds that were not prepared in the fall. Turn the compost into the soil with a shovel, breaking up large clods. There is no need to use a rototiller; the job can be done by hand.

✔ Assemble climbing structures for climbing peas, beans, vines, and tomatoes. Use bamboo poles, wood tuteurs, stakes, or metal cages.

✔ Start warm-season flower and vegetable seeds indoors. Sow seeds of peppers, tomatoes, eggplants, parsley, and marjoram under lights six to eight weeks before the frost-free date for your area.

✔ Sow cool-season seeds outdoors in the garden in early spring. These include carrots, peas, sweet peas, greens, kale, and lettuces. The crops will be ready for harvest by late spring or early summer. Set out transplants of cabbage and broccoli.

✔ Harvest fiddleheads, morels, ramps, shallots, green garlic, asparagus, strawberries, and salad greens.

✔ Gather floral material. Selectively prune blossoms of cherry, crabapple, redbud, magnolia, forsythia, pussy willow, and dogwood to bring indoors. Cut bouquets of peonies, iris, poppies, daffodils, and tulips.

SPRING MENUS

One
Spring Leek and Potato Soup
Ramp and Morel Quiche
Roasted Beet Salad
Asparagus
Strawberry-Chocolate Parfait
Bouquet of dogwood blossoms

Two
Grilled Lamb Kabobs
Mint Chutney
Dilly Heirloom Potato Salad
Spring Greens with Basic
    Vinaigrette or Creamy Green
    Goddess Dressing
Strawberry-Rhubarb Granola
    Crumble
May Wine
Bouquet of peonies, Siberian iris,
    and 'Giant Globe' allium

Three
Stuffed Trout with Green Garlic
    and Herbs
Quinoa Pilaf with Spring
    Vegetables
Spring Peas with Mint Cream
Rhubarb Custard Pie
Bouquet of tulips, viburnum, and
    asparagus fronds

Summer

FOR ME SUMMER BEGINS on the frost-free date for my area when it's safe to plant all the wonderful vegetables that taste of summer such as corn on the cob, tomatoes fresh from the vine, tender green beans, and basil for pesto. And it's not just the food. It's time to go barefoot and celebrate the sun. It's time to be outside. The days get longer and hotter. The soil warms up. The vegetables that require summer heat and warmth can be planted outside without worry of killing frost.

The beginning of summer is a time to harvest the cool-season vegetables that were sown in the spring. Harvest the last of the spring radishes and cool-season greens to make room for summer-heat-loving vegetables. The luscious greens that were seeds in the spring have matured to full-grown bok choy and lettuce heads. Cabbage, kale, lettuce, and broccoli will continue to grow at the beginning of the season until it gets really hot and they bolt.

The growing season is in transition and you may need to remove perfectly good cool-season plants to make room for the summer varieties. Go ahead and add a good amount of compost to the beds as you transition crops. It helps replenish the soil with nutrients.

A collection of perfectly ripened heirloom tomatoes.

A table setting in the garden.

Warm-Season Vegetables

BEANS (*Phaseolus*)
Annual
Seed to table: 46 to 65 days

There are many types of beans—bush beans, climbing beans, and runner beans—and they have different requirements. Bush beans do not need a trellis for climbing but the other varieties do. The trellis needs to be sturdy enough to support the vines. It can be as simple as bamboo poles stuck in the ground and lashed together at the top to make a teepee. Because the tiny growing bean tendrils need to attach to something small, I string natural twine between the poles. At the end of the season the dried vines and twine go in the compost.

Plant beans outdoors when all danger of frost is gone. They germinate best in warm soil. Plant seeds 5 to 6 inches (12.5–15 cm) apart for bush beans. Plant 3 or 4 seeds around each pole and then thin to 1 or 2 vines per pole.

There are many ways to enjoy beans. Sometimes it's fresh off the vine while you are in the garden. Pick them young at the *haricot vert* stage or when they are more mature. Runner beans have edible blossoms that can be put in salads. The beans should be eaten young when small and tender.

Shell beans can be used in recipes like other varieties by either eating the whole bean when they are young or waiting until the seeds mature in size, then shelling and cooking them like you would lima beans. Fresh shell beans are great in curries. Dried beans are the final stage; the bean should be left to

'Purple Podded' beans will retain their vivid coloring if used raw in salads or cook them and watch them turn to green.

Green Beans with Lemon

Serves 4
3 cups fresh, young green beans
Juice of ½ lemon
2 tablespoons extra virgin olive oil

Trim the ends of the green beans, leaving the beans whole. Steam them in a saucepan with a small amount of water until just cooked. Drain, then arrange the steamed beans on a serving platter. Squeeze lemon juice over beans and drizzle with olive oil. Serve immediately.

dry, then discard the dry shell and store the beans. (See Dried Beans in Winter chapter, page 184.)

Two of my favorite varieties are 'Purple Podded', which has bright purple beans, and 'Scarlet Emperor' runner bean with bright red flowers that attract hummingbirds.

Beans are part of the traditional "Three Sisters" garden and can be planted with corn and squash in a trio. Bean trellises also partner well with lettuce. The tall poles will provide needed shade for the summer lettuce.

Natural twine can be strung between bamboo poles so the tiny tendrils of beans have something to attach to. At the end of the season, twine and all go in the compost.

Homegrown carrots from the farmer's market.

CARROTS (*Daucus carota*)
Biennial grown as an annual
Seed to table 52 to 70 days

Carrots that were sown in the spring will be ready for harvest in summer. Harvest at the baby stage for small tender carrots and leave 2 to 3 inches (5–7.5 cm) of spacing between the others. Harvest when carrots have turned orange. Eat carrots raw or lightly steam and add lemon juice or a dash of maple syrup. Grated carrots add sweetness to baked muffins.

Continue to sow carrot seeds outside until midsummer. For a continuous supply of tasty, young tender carrots, sow every three weeks. See more on carrots in the Spring and Fall chapters (pages 25 and 136, respectively).

Spicy garden curry is served with rice and cool yogurt sauce and hot peach chutney for an outdoor dinner party.

Spicy Garden Curry

Serves 4
1 tablespoon ghee or butter
2 cups fresh green beans, ends trimmed
2 small potatoes with skins, cut into bite-sized pieces
6–8 green onions, sliced
2 garlic cloves, chopped
3–4 carrots, sliced
¾ cup fresh shelled beans
4 cups vegetable stock
1 can (14 ounces) coconut milk
2 teaspoons curry powder
Salt
3 tablespoons fresh Thai basil, sliced

Melt the ghee or butter in a large saucepan, then sauté the green beans, potatoes, onions, garlic, carrots, and shell beans for a few minutes until the onions are translucent. Add the vegetable stock and cook until the potatoes are soft and the vegetables are just cooked, but still firm (about 20 minutes).

Add the coconut milk, curry, and salt to taste. Cook until heated, stirring as the mixture thickens. Pour into a serving bowl and top with Thai basil. Serve immediately over cooked rice with cool yogurt sauce and hot peach chutney.

CORN (*Zea mays*)
Annual
Seed to table: 68 to 100 days

There is nothing like sweet corn from the American Midwest in the summer. Maybe it's the weather or the deep glacial till. I think it's the soil. Sweet corn just tastes better here.

Corn takes some room to grow. It is better to plant in multiple short rows rather than one long row because corn is pollinated by the wind. Corn will shade other plants around it, so keep that in mind. It's possible to plant with squash and beans. Plant corn when soil is warm. Dig trenches 4 to 6 inches (10–15 cm) deep and sow seeds about 10 inches (25 cm) apart, in rows 30 inches (75 cm) apart. Fill in the trenches with soil as the corn grows to support the stalk.

Corn is a heavy feeder and needs sufficient water through the growing season. Amend the soil with compost before planting. Corn will be knee-high by the Fourth of July, as the saying goes. Corn will cross pollinate with other varieties growing within 100 feet (30 m), even ornamental corn. See more on corn in the Fall chapter (page 164).

Three salsas for an outdoor Mexican meal: cilantro salsa, roasted red pepper and corn salsa, and pico de gallo.

Roasted Red Pepper and Corn Salsa

This is a mild corn salsa and is meant to be served with Cilantro Salsa (page 106) and Pico de Gallo (page 78) for extra spice.

Makes 4 cups
6 ears of fresh sweet corn in husk
4–6 red sweet peppers
3–4 green onions, chopped
3 tablespoons extra virgin olive oil
Juice of 1 lime
½ teaspoon salt
Freshly ground pepper

To prepare the corn for grilling, remove the outer husks and leave the remaining husks on. Soak the husked corn in water for about 20 minutes.

Place corn husks and red peppers on hot grill. Roast the peppers about 5 minutes on each side until they are soft and the skins begin to char. Remove the peppers and cover completely until cool. Roast the corn until the husks begin to char and corn is hot.

When peppers are cool enough to handle, peel off the skin and discard it; it will come off easily. Chop the peppers and put them in a serving bowl. Slice kernels of corn into the bowl and discard the cobs. Add green onions, olive oil, lime juice, salt, and pepper. Serve immediately or chill and reserve for later.

Grilled fresh sweet corn with cilantro butter may be a meal by itself.

Grilled Corn on the Cob with Cilantro Butter

Serves 6
6 ears of fresh sweet corn, husks removed
¼ cup butter, melted
½ cup fresh cilantro, coarsely chopped
Salt and freshly ground pepper

Place shucked corn directly on a hot grill. Heat until corn just starts to char. Place hot corn on serving platter. Drizzle with butter and cilantro. Add salt and pepper. Serve immediately.

CUCUMBER (*Cucumis sativus*)
Annual
Seed to table: 60 to 70 days

Cucumbers should be sown outdoors after all danger of frost is past. Plant the seeds 2 inches (5 cm) apart in hills 5 feet (1.5 m) apart and thin to 3 plants per hill. The vining plants will spread. Cucumbers can be trained to grow up a trellis when space is tight; use willow or bamboo tee-pees or a strong metal tomato cage. Pick the fruit when it's young and small to encourage the plant to produce more. Harvest by cutting the fruit instead of pulling. 'Lemon' produces round yellow cucumbers. 'White Wonder' is an heirloom variety with ivory fruits.

Tabbouleh is served with rosemary chicken, pita bread, and skordalia, a Greek garlicky potato dip.

Tabbouleh

Serves 6
1 cup boiling water
1 cup bulgur wheat
3–4 small cucumbers
2–3 small mixed tomatoes
2 cups fresh flat-leaf parsley
½ cup fresh mint leaves
6–8 green onions
Juice of 2 lemons
⅓–½ cup extra virgin olive oil
Salt and freshly ground pepper

Pour hot water over bulgur wheat and let sit until all water is absorbed, about 30 minutes. Chop cucumbers, tomatoes, parsley, mint, and green onions, then add to the bulgur. Add lemon juice and olive oil. Cover and allow to sit for 30 minutes for flavors to combine. Stir before serving.

Cucumbers will spread; train them up a trellis or give them room to sprawl on the ground.

Tzatziki

This yogurt sauce goes well with grilled vegetables or grilled meat. Use it in half a toasted pita with lettuce, carrots and tomatoes and some thin slices of hard cheese for a quick sandwich or as a dip for raw vegetables.

Serves 4–6
2 cups Greek yogurt (or your own yogurt cheese)
3–4 medium cucumbers
½ cup fresh dill, finely chopped
3–4 garlic cloves, finely chopped
2 tablespoons extra virgin olive oil
1 tablespoon honey (optional)
Salt to taste

To make yogurt cheese: Scoop some plain yogurt in a coffee filter and place in a strainer over a bowl. Put the bowl in the refrigerator for a few hours or overnight. This creates a thick yogurt cheese similar to the Greek-style yogurt and much better for tzatziki.

Peel, seed, and chop or shred the cucumbers. (I prefer to chop them instead of shredding them in the traditional Greek style.) Combine all the ingredients. Add a little honey if you need to make it a bit sweeter. Serve with pita bread or with grilled meat or vegetables.

(continued)

69

Pick eggplant at the baby stage and grill or sauté.

EGGPLANT (*Solanum melongena*)
Annual
Seed to table: 70 to 85 days

Eggplant should be set out as a plant when all danger of frost has passed and the soil has warmed. It is a true heat lover so make sure the days and soils have warmed up. The leaves are susceptible to leaf beetle, which causes them to look like they have been shot with a miniature pellet gun. Fortunately, a few holes in the leaves will not affect the fruit.

Eggplant is best picked young and tender. I don't fuss with it too much; it can go directly from the garden to the grill. Slice it in half lengthwise and place it on a hot outdoor grill. Brush each side with olive oil as it cooks. Serve with chopped fresh rosemary, parsley, cilantro, or tarragon.

Pasta with Eggplant and Herbs

Serves 6
1 pound Italian pasta, uncooked
½ cup extra virgin olive oil
4–5 small eggplants, diced
2 garlic cloves, finely chopped
1 cup fresh flat-leaf Italian parsley, chopped
1 cup fresh basil leaves, chopped
1 cup mixed tomatoes, chopped
Salt and freshly ground pepper
½ cup parmesan cheese, coarsely grated

Bring a large pot of water to a boil, add the pasta and cook to al dente stage. Drain, rinse, and keep warm while making the sauce.

Heat the olive oil in a large saucepan, then add the eggplant. Sauté until the eggplant is just cooked. Add the garlic but don't overcook. Next add the parsley, basil, and tomatoes, just heating through. Remove the pan from the heat.

Put the pasta in a serving bowl. Pour the sauce over it. Serve immediately with parmesan cheese.

Garlic harvested from the author's garden. Garlic is very easy to grow and needs to cure before long-term storage.

GARLIC (*Allium sativum*)
Annual bulb
Planting to table: 180 days

Garlic is planted in the fall and harvested in the spring as green, immature garlic or in the summer as plump, mature garlic bulbs. Sometime before they mature, hardneck varieties will send up a flowering stalk called a scape. Cut these off so that the plant uses all of its energy to produce fat bulbs instead of flowers. The scapes are edible and can be sautéed or used in salads.

Garlic flowers and stems have interesting shapes and I have used them in flower arrangements, although they only last a day or two. Keep the arrangement outside, on the patio or in the garden, as the scapes share every bit the garlic odor of the bulbs.

Mature garlic is ready to harvest when half of the leaves turn brown and begin to fall over. Dig up the bulbs with a shovel, taking care not to dig too close to the bulbs or you will slice them in half. Remove most of the dirt and allow the bulbs to dry for a few days. Inspect the bulbs carefully. Damaged bulbs will not store well, so set them aside to use immediately. Hang the remaining bulbs in a dry place out of direct sunlight for a couple of weeks.

For long-term storage, cut off the top of the bulb but leave the papery shell. Store the bulbs in a basket or mesh bag in a cool, dry place. Properly cured garlic can be stored for many months. David Cavagnaro of Decorah, Iowa, an expert gardener, cook,

Garlic is ready to harvest when about half the leaves have turned brown and have fallen over in midsummer (around the Fourth of July in the Midwest).

Grilled garlic: When you are cooking on the grill this summer, add some garlic to roast over the hot coals at the same time. Cut off the tops of whole garlic bulbs, just to reveal the tip of the garlic cloves. Place the bulbs on a sheet of foil and drizzle with olive oil and coarse salt. Wrap tightly and seal the edges. Place on the grill and roast for 35–40 minutes over hot coals. Serve on toasted bread or crackers.

and photographer who sits on the board of directors at Seed Savers Exchange, keeps his garlic for a year (pers. comm.). He prefers to use the previous year's garlic when making pesto in large batches to freeze and store because he finds the older garlic is easier to peel. See more on garlic in the Spring and Fall chapters (pages 26 and 138, respectively).

Garlic chicken skewers at a summer cookout.

Garlic Chicken Skewers

Serves 6–8
6 boneless chicken breasts
½ cup soy sauce
3 tablespoons honey
6 garlic cloves, finely chopped
Juice of 2 lemons

Pound the chicken breasts flat and cut into strips. Put in a large bowl and set aside. Mix the rest of the ingredients together in a small bowl. Pour the marinade over the chicken and let sit for 4 hours or longer. Lace marinated chicken onto wood skewers and grill over hot coals until chicken is cooked.

Ground cherries are surprisingly sweet and best eaten fresh from the garden.

GROUND CHERRIES (*Physalis*)
Annual
Seed to table: 60 to 80 days

Ground cherries are related to tomatillos. The fruit is a tasty, sweet golden berry covered in a papery husk. When the fruit is ripe the husks fall to the ground. The plant reseeds in the same place in the garden every year for me. It's not a tall plant, but it does need room to spread. Space it 24 inches (60 cm) apart. One or two plants is probably enough.

To harvest just stick your hand under the spreading leaves and grab some of the golden fruit. Peel off the papery thin husk to reveal the sweet berry. They are great in salads or used in salsas, but I enjoy them most fresh from the garden. Friends, guests, and children are usually amazed at the strange sight. Have visitors taste the sweet berry as you show them your garden.

OKRA (*Abelmoschus esculentus*)
Annual
Seed to table: 50 to 60 days

If you live in the southern United States, then you are already familiar with this delightful vegetable and probably adore it battered and fried or sliced in gumbo. This relative of the hibiscus family also has a beautiful flower but the real treat is the horn-shaped fruit.

Okra is easy to grow in warm weather. Sow seeds outdoors directly in the garden after the frost-free date when soil is warm. Space seeds 6 to 12 inches (15–30 cm) apart, and then thin to 18 inches (45 cm) when the seedlings develop. The plants grow about 4 feet (1.2 m) high and the fruits can be harvested over a period of time. Harvest regularly so plants continue to produce.

Eat okra fresh and raw in salads or batter and fry. When you slice okra for soup, stew, or gumbo, it produces the magical ingredient that makes gumbo, gumbo.

'Aunt Hettie's Red' is burgundy red from the stem to the pod and looks stunning in the garden. 'White Velvet' produces pale green pods that are smooth. 'Clemson Spineless' was an All American Selection winner in 1939 and has been a popular variety since then.

Onions are ready when the tops begin to fall over or they can be harvested at any stage for green onions.

ONIONS (*Allium*)
Biennial grown as an annual
Seed to table: 40 to 50 days for green onions, 90 to 120
    days for bulb onions

Bulb onions that were planted in the spring are ready for harvest when the tops have fallen over and died and the swollen bulb has broken the soil surface. On sunny, breezy days onions can be pulled and left in the garden for a few days to dry. To store onions, cure them in a warm well-ventilated area until the necks are thoroughly dry, a process that takes at least two weeks. Then store the onions in a cool dry area in ventilated containers. Freshly harvested onions can also be washed, sliced, and used immediately. See more on onions in the Spring and Fall chapters (pages 28 and 138, respectively).

Traditional Greek salad is often served with the feta left whole. No greens in this salad, just red onions, cucumbers, tomatoes and cheese.

Greek Salad

Order a salad at a restaurant in Greece and you may be surprised to find no lettuce in your bowl. This is the traditional way to serve Greek salad—with good olive oil and fresh lemon juice. Sweet red onions make it colorful.

Serves 4–6
4 medium cucumbers
1 large red onion, sliced
2 cups mixed tomatoes, coarsely chopped
½ cup extra-virgin olive oil
Juice of 2 lemons
8 ounces feta cheese, in blocks
Salt and freshly ground pepper
Fresh oregano, chopped

Peel, seed, and chop the cucumbers. Put them in a serving bowl with the onion and tomatoes; toss with olive oil and lemon juice. Top with blocks of feta. Add salt, pepper, and oregano to taste.

Braised brisket and red onion is served on tortillas with white cheddar cheese, roasted red pepper and corn salsa, cilantro salsa, and pico de gallo.

Braised Brisket and Red Onion Fajitas

Serves 6–8
2½ pounds beef brisket
Salt and freshly ground black pepper
2 teaspoons cumin
2 tablespoons extra virgin olive oil
1 large red onion, chopped
2–3 Anaheim peppers, chopped and seeded
4 garlic cloves, finely chopped
2 tablespoons fresh oregano, finely chopped
1 cup red wine
1 cup beef stock
16 corn tortillas

Preheat oven to 325°F. Season the meat with salt, pepper, and cumin. Heat the olive oil in a Dutch oven. Brown brisket on both sides. Transfer to a platter temporarily. Add onions and peppers to the pan and sauté until soft, about 8 minutes. Add garlic and oregano and cook for another minute. Add wine and stock and bring to simmer. Add the browned meat to the pan, cover it, and place the Dutch oven in the oven for 3½ to 4 hours.

When the meat is tender, remove it to a serving platter and slice. Bring the sauce to high heat and continue to cook it until it reduces. Add additional salt and pepper to taste.

Serve sliced brisket on tortillas with Grilled Summer Vegetables (page 82), grated cheddar cheese, and Roasted Red Pepper and Corn Salsa (page 67), Cilantro Salsa (page 106), and Pico de Gallo (page 78). For vegetarian fajitas, omit the beef.

PEPPERS (*Capsicum*)
Annual
Seed to table: 102 to 127 days

Green, yellow, and purple peppers from the farmer's market.

Set peppers out as transplants in warm soil after all danger of frost is past and when night temperatures stay above 50°F. The transplants can be ones you have grown indoors from seed or purchased from a garden center. Peppers require a long growing season, so it makes sense to start them outside as transplants. Of tropical origin, peppers require full sun and will take heat. Place the plants about 18 inches (45 cm) apart and water thoroughly when planted in the garden.

Peppers are easy to grow and the plants are relatively pest free. In very hot weather, when temperatures spike and stay over 90°F during the day, peppers won't set fruit or the fruit will be misshapen. The plant will return to producing when the temperatures moderate. Small fruited pungent peppers will do better in hot climates where the temperatures stay high.

All peppers can be dried in a dehydrator, but the thin-walled varieties will easily dry in the sun, especially if you live in a dry, warm climate. In New Mexico, where the state vegetable is the chile pepper, drying peppers is an art form. Ristras can be found hanging at entryways and back porches. The hanging peppers look decorative but are really a way of storing and drying peppers to create New Mexican red chile. In Ohio, ristras would be fun to make but the peppers would rot before they dried in the humidity; I have had success leaving the thin small cayenne peppers on the plants to dry naturally. Use

Medium hot yellow peppers are good for pickling.

(right) *'Kung Pao' cayenne peppers are hot. The walls are thin so the pepper dries easily and can be broken up into flakes. Stir-fry in oil to make hot oil for Asian cooking.*

a dehydrator to thoroughly and reliably dry peppers for the spice cupboard.

Peppers have a variety of uses for the cook with colors ranging from yellow to orange and red or green, white, purple or brown. Peppers range in shape, too. Thick blocky bell types are good fresh or stuffed and thin-walled, small and pointy cayenne peppers are best cooked quickly in hot oil to flavor Asian dishes.

Hot pepper lovers can choose habanero peppers. I discovered a few years ago I couldn't really use them—way too hot—way beyond my Scoville limit. (Bell peppers are rated at 0 on the Scoville scale, habanero peppers at 300,000 and higher). My brother just discovered this last year when he was trying to give me his harvest of the pretty, orange lethal fruits. He is not growing them again this year.

Here are four of my favorites. 'Holy Molé' is a pasilla-type pepper with a rich flavor and dark color and not too hot (700 Scoville units); it's great for drying or used fresh. 'Chocolate Beauty' is a sweet pepper that turns from deep green to chocolate brown. 'Corno di Toro' is an Italian heirloom sweet pepper; shaped like a bull's horn, it glows red when ripe. 'Purple Jalapeño' has all of the heat of a good jalapeño pepper (2000 to 5000 Scoville units) but turns purple when ripe.

Moments later the tomatoes and peppers are transformed into stuffed peppers with fresh marinara sauce.

Stuffed Peppers with Marinara Sauce

Makes 8 stuffed peppers
½ pound bulk Italian sausage
1–2 small zucchini, chopped
½ bulb fennel, chopped
3–4 baby eggplants, diced
4 green onions, chopped
8 green peppers
2 cups cooked brown rice
¼ cup fresh flat-leaf parsley, chopped
2 cups fresh marinara sauce (page 87)
½ cup parmesan cheese, freshly grated

Preheat oven to 350°F. Heat a small amount of oil in a large skillet; add crumbled sausage and cook until brown. Add zucchini, bulb fennel, and eggplant (or about 2 cups of mixed vegetables) to the pan. Add green onions. Cut off tops of peppers; set rest of peppers aside. Chop cut off pepper tops and add to pan. Continue to sauté the meat and vegetables until the vegetables are tender. Remove from heat. Add cooked brown rice and parsley to the meat mixture.

Remove the seeds from green peppers. Place the peppers in a baking dish and stuff with filling. Pour marinara sauce over the stuffed peppers. Top with cheese. Bake for 30 minutes until heated through and the cheese is melted.

Fresh pico de gallo can be adjusted for heat- add another jalapeno if you want it hotter. Great with chips or as an accompaniment to anything.

Pico de Gallo

Makes about 5 cups
10–12 medium yellow and orange tomatoes, coarsely chopped
1 medium sweet onion, chopped
2–3 hot peppers, such as jalapeño, chopped and seeded
1 sweet pepper, chopped
½ cup ground cherries cut in half (optional)
½ cup fresh cilantro, chopped
Juice of 1 lime
3 garlic cloves, chopped
½ teaspoon sea salt

Drain excess water from the chopped tomatoes. Combine with the remaining ingredients and serve immediately with corn chips or with Mexican dishes.

Harvested from the author's garden, a collection of hot and mild peppers, tomatoes including paste tomatoes, ground cherries and cilantro for pico de gallo.

(left) 'Amish' paste heirloom tomatoes for marinara sauce and sweet green peppers for stuffed peppers.

This is the visual recipe for the marinade for grilled flank steak with hot pepper and herb marinade. Right after the photograph we chopped up the ingredients for the marinade.

Flank steak over hot coals.

Grilled Flank Steak with Hot Pepper and Herb Marinade

Serves 4 to 6
1 cup fresh cilantro
12 garlic cloves (about 1 bulb)
3–4 hot peppers, such as poblano, serrano, or jalapeño
3–4 cipollini onions
Few sprigs of fresh thyme
1 teaspoon coarse salt
Freshly ground pepper
3 tablespoons extra virgin olive oil
2 pounds flank steak

Chop the herbs and vegetables and put in a large, flat pan. Add the salt, pepper, and olive oil and mix well. Coat the top and bottom of a flank steak with the marinade. Cover and refrigerate overnight. The next day grill the steaks over hot coals.

POTATOES (*Solanum tuberosum*)
Annual grown from a tuber
Planting to table: 50 to 120 days

Harvest early potatoes that were planted in the spring. Potatoes are ready when the foliage begins to die back. Continue to harvest early, mid, and late varieties until frost. See more on potatoes in the Spring and Fall chapters (pages 29 and 140, respectively).

Skordalia

Skordalia is a garlicky Greek dip served cold with pita or bread. It traditionally is served with salty fish or fried vegetables. It's like hummus in a way, although hummus is made with garbanzo beans and skordalia is made with potatoes. It's part of the summer menu and is served as an appetizer.

Makes 2 cups
3 medium potatoes
¼ cup extra virgin olive oil
8 garlic cloves, finely chopped
Juice of ½ lemon
Salt and freshly ground pepper

Wash and peel the potatoes before placing them in a sauce pan. Cover with water and boil until the potatoes are cooked and soft. Drain the water. Transfer the potatoes to a large bowl; mash them with a potato masher along with olive oil and garlic. Add lemon juice, salt and pepper. Thin with a little water if necessary to make a smooth, creamy consistency. Serve at room temperature.

Give vining squash a sturdy trellis to climb. Photo taken at the potager of personal chef, Jaclyn DeCourcey.

SQUASH (*Cucurbita*)

Annual

Seed to table: 48 to 68 days for summer squash, 80 to
   120 days for winter squash

What's summer without oodles of baseball-bat-size zucchini we either give away or receive from our neighbors? How much zucchini bread can you eat? The first word of advice is to pick the fruits young and small and eat them at the tender baby stage or pick a few of the blossoms and eat them. Stuff a few bright yellow blossoms with herb cheese, dip in tempura batter, and brown in butter on all sides.

There are so many different kinds of summer squashes to try. They are best cooked minutes from picking because they don't keep or store well. Try 'Trombocino', an heirloom Italian variety with bright green fruits that are long and skinny with a swollen bulb on one end. 'Ronde de Nice' is a round French variety that should be picked small or allowed to grow a little larger to stuff. All of the summer squashes are perfect for quick sautés or grilled.

Winter and summer squash are easily grown from seed and do well when sown directly in good garden soil after all danger of frost is past. Plant about 5 seeds on mounded soil 2 feet (60 cm) apart. Squash needs room to spread.

Grilled Summer Vegetables

Grill whatever vegetables are ripe and perfect in your garden. Use this as a guide for how to get started. This combination of grilled vegetables is wonderful and great to set aside for your vegetarian guests and family at your next cook out. Use it as the filling for roasted vegetable enchiladas with green tomatillo sauce or to serve with pita when you serve the meat eaters rosemary chicken.

Serves 6
2–3 summer squash
2–3 'Ping Tung Long' eggplants (or variety)
2 red sweet peppers, stemmed and seeded
2 sweet onions
Extra virgin olive oil
2 tablespoons fresh marjoram, chopped

Slice the squash, eggplant, and peppers in half. Slice the onions into rings. Place the vegetable pieces directly on a hot grill. Brush with olive oil. Sprinkle with marjoram. Cook until vegetables begin to char, turn, brush other side with olive oil and cook until done. Serve immediately as a side dish or use in recipes.

When the seedlings sprout and are doing well thin them to two plants per hill. Small varieties can be grown on a strong trellis. Gently tie the vines to the trellis for support. See more on squash in the Fall and Winter chapters (pages 142 and 186, respectively).

SWEET POTATOES (*Ipomoea batatas*)
Perennial grown as an annual from a tuber
Planting to table: 90 to 140 days

Sweet potatoes are warm-season tropical vining plants. They are in the morning glory family and related to the ornamental sweet potato vines that grow in containers like 'Blackie' or 'Margarita'. Order cuttings from a nursery and plant as soon as possible. These rooted plants are called slips. Plant the slips in late spring when the soil has warmed and all danger of frost has passed about 12 inches (30 cm) apart. Plant at the end of the day and water thoroughly so plants don't wilt. 'Beauregard' is one of the faster maturing varieties at 90 days. See more on sweet potatoes in the Fall chapter (page 142).

TOMATILLOS (*Physalis*)
Annual
Seed to table: 117 days

Tomatillos should be planted indoors under lights six weeks before the frost-free date. Tomatillos produce cherry-tomato-like fruits in a husk, similar to their relatives the ground cherries. The plants grow large and spread and do well supported with a cage or stake. 'De Milpa' is a purple and green Mexican heirloom. 'Toma Verde' is a green variety, excellent for sauces. Harvest when the fruit is plump and the papery husk splits, or when the fruit falls to the ground.

Fresh green tomatillos from the farmer's market. (Photo Sara Bartley)

Roasted veggie enchiladas with green tomatillo sauce are the bounty of the summer garden wrapped in corn tortillas and drenched with a spicy sauce.

Roasted Vegetable Enchiladas with Green Tomatillo Sauce

This recipe will satisfy vegetarians and non-vegetarians and is a great way to use the bounty of vegetables growing in your summer garden. Make an extra batch, wrap well and freeze before baking.

Serves 6
18 corn tortillas
Extra virgin olive oil
Grilled Summer Vegetables (see page 82)
½ cup sour cream
2 tablespoons fresh chives, finely chopped, plus more for garnish
Green Tomatillo Sauce (recipe follows)
8 ounces white cheddar cheese, grated, plus more for garnish

Preheat oven to 350°F. Place 6 tortillas on a cookie sheet and brush with a small amount of olive oil. Turn tortillas over and brush the other side. Heat the tortillas in the oven for a few minutes, turn them over, and heat the other side for a few more minutes. Tortillas should be hot and soft, not crispy. Wrap the tortillas in foil and keep warm until ready to use. Repeat for the other tortillas.

Cut the grilled mixed vegetables into bite-size pieces and place them in a bowl. In a separate bowl, combine the sour cream and chives.

To assemble the enchiladas, put ½ cup of green tomatillo sauce in the bottom of a casserole dish and set aside.

Take one tortilla and place some grilled vegetables on it. Sprinkle with white cheddar cheese. Add 1 tablespoon of the sour cream mixture. Roll up the tortilla and place it in the casserole dish. Repeat with the other tortillas, lining them up snugly in the dish.

Pour tomatillo sauce over all; add additional cheese and chives on top. Bake for 25–30 minutes until hot and cheese is bubbly. Serve immediately.

Green Tomatillo Sauce

You will be surprised how easy this green tomatillo sauce is to make. Tomatillos as they cook transform into a chunky tangy sauce. Add more jalapeños if you want it spicier. If you have an abundance of tomatillos in the garden double the recipe and freeze half.

Makes 2 cups
1 tablespoon butter or olive oil
1 small white or yellow onion, chopped
2–3 jalapeño peppers, chopped and seeded
16–20 tomatillos, quartered
3 garlic cloves, finely chopped
½ cup fresh cilantro, chopped
Juice of ½ lime
Salt and freshly ground pepper

Melt butter (or heat oil) in a large heavy pan over medium-high heat. Add the onion and jalapeños and cook until the onions are translucent. Add the tomatillos and garlic and cook until the tomatillos are soft and begin to break down. Continue to cook stirring periodically until everything breaks down into a nice sauce. Add the cilantro and lime juice and cook until the sauce is reduced and not watery. Add salt and pepper to taste.

(continued)

83

Greek heirloom tomatoes with no name, brought back from Greece thirty years ago by Dr. George Chatos and carefully grown every year since then, with the seeds meticulously harvested and saved for the next year. George's son now grows these tasty tomatoes in his garden with his family, and I am growing and saving the seeds as well.

TOMATOES (*Lycopersicum*)
Annual
Seed to table: 107 to 142 days

Tomato plants should be placed in the garden after all danger of frost is past. The transplants can be special varieties you grew from seed or potted seedlings purchased from a garden center. Place the tomato plant deep in the soil so that some of the stem is buried; this will give the plant added support. The stem will produce additional rootlets and help anchor the plant.

Indeterminate varieties keep growing and branching, producing leaves, suckers, and flower clusters until frost or disease stops them. The rambling vines need support. so either stake or cage the little plants when you set them out. If you use

Heirloom cherry and pear tomatoes are perfect for roasting.

Roasted cherry tomatoes are sweet and delicious on good bread or in a salad as the dressing.

Roasted Cherry Tomatoes with Thyme

This method roasts the tomatoes quickly at high heat but gives a slow-roasted flavor. Start with cherry tomatoes or cut up paste tomatoes. This dipping sauce is addictive and goes on any good bread or crackers. Serve it over fresh greens with goat cheese for a summer salad.

Serves 4–6
1½ quarts mixed cherry or pear tomatoes
4 tablespoons extra virgin olive oil, divided
1 teaspoon coarse salt
Freshly ground pepper
½ teaspoon dried thyme
Juice of 1 lemon
2 teaspoons fresh lemon or lime thyme

Preheat oven to 450°F. Cut cherry tomatoes in half and combine with 2 tablespoons olive oil, salt, pepper, and dried thyme. Place in a single layer in a jelly roll pan or oven-proof dish. Bake for 20–25 minutes. Turn off the oven and let dish remain in the oven until cool, about 2 hours, or leave overnight. Before serving, mix the remaining 2 tablespoons olive oil, the lemon juice, and fresh thyme into the roasted tomatoes. Serve immediately or refrigerate to serve later.

a wooden stake, select a sturdy one 6 feet (1.8 m) long. Pound it into the ground and plant the tomato beside it. This method requires pruning the plant so that you have one main stem. Tie the plant to the stake as it grows.

Sturdy cages work well, not the flimsy, tiny ones you see. You can build your own using a roll of wire mesh and rebar. I have used branches from fallen limbs to create rustic tomato cages as I just can't bear the aesthetic of the cheap metal cages. I put sturdy branches in the ground to form a tripod, then use twine to lash the tops together and to support the growing vines. The goal is to keep the tomato branches and leaves off the ground, away from the soil to prevent disease.

There are infinite varieties of tomatoes to grow. Everyone has their favorite. Choose what you want based on how you intend to use them. Roma or paste tomatoes are thick and excellent for making sauces. 'Amish Paste' is an heirloom variety with good flavor and bright red color. 'Principe Borghese' is an Italian heirloom that is excellent for drying. See more on tomatoes in the Fall and Winter chapters (pages 144 and 186, respectively).

Use paste tomatoes and fresh basil to make tomato and basil quiche.

Tomato and Basil Quiche

Makes 1 (10-inch) quiche
½ cup cold butter, cut in 8 pieces
1½ cups unbleached flour
½ teaspoon salt
2–3 tablespoons cold water
1 tablespoon butter
3–4 green onions, chopped
3 eggs
½ cup milk
2 small zucchini, sliced
2 small paste tomatoes, sliced
½ cup fresh basil leaves, chopped
½ cup fresh flat-leaf parsley, chopped
¾ cup Swiss cheese, grated
2 tablespoons parmesan cheese, coarsely grated

Preheat oven to 350°F. Process ½ cup butter with the flour and salt in a food processor until crumbly. With processor running, slowly add cold water a tablespoon at a time; sometimes the amount of water needed depends on the humidity of the day. Process in pulses just until the dough clings together. Roll the dough out on a floured board to the size of your quiche pan. Place the dough in the bottom and sides of pan. Straighten out the crust and crimp the edges as desired. Set aside.

Melt 1 tablespoon butter in a medium saucepan. Sauté the onions, zucchini, and tomatoes until the onions are translucent. In a separate bowl whisk the eggs and milk together until well blended. Add the sautéed vegetables, stirring to blend. Add the basil and parsley. Stir in the cheeses. Pour the mixture into the prepared pie crust. Bake for 35–40 minutes until the filling is set.

Start with the basic ingredients for quick oven cheese tacos, then embellish with leftover vegetables, meat or beans you may have on hand.

Quick Oven Cheese Tacos

Makes 6 tacos
6 soft corn tortillas
Extra virgin olive oil
¾ cup sharp white cheddar cheese, grated
½ cup fresh cilantro, chopped
1 cup ripe tomatoes, chopped

Preheat oven to 350°F. Lightly brush a cookie sheet with olive oil. Place the tortillas on the cookie sheet. Cover each tortilla with cheese, cilantro, and tomatoes. Bake in the oven for 7–10 minutes, until the cheese is melted and the tortillas begin to crisp. Remove the tacos from the oven and fold each in half to serve.

Summer garden gazpacho with a fresh basil leaf garnish is a great way to use the surplus of tomatoes and summer vegetables growing in the garden.

Summer Garden Gazpacho

Gazpacho is a fresh tomato soup traditionally served cold with cucumbers, peppers, and herbs. The flavorful soup is perfect for the hot days of summer, when you don't want to heat up the kitchen. It's best when you use the tomatoes, herbs, and vegetables at the peak of their ripeness, fresh from the garden or farmer's market, in season.

Serves 6–8
10–12 red paste tomatoes
1 cup fresh marinara sauce (recipe follows)
1 small cucumber, peeled and seeded
½ cup sweet corn, cooked
1 small zucchini
1 New Mexican chile or Anaheim pepper, stemmed and seeded
3 green onions
2 garlic cloves
Juice of ½ lime
½ cup fresh basil leaves, plus more for garnish
2 tablespoons fresh dill leaves
2 tablespoons fresh flat-leaf parsley
Salt and freshly ground pepper

Place fresh paste tomatoes in boiling water for about 30 seconds and then quickly place them in cold water to remove skins. Coarsely cut up the tomatoes and remove the cores and peels.

(continued)

Place half of the raw tomatoes, the fresh marinara sauce, and half of the cucumber in a food processor and process until smooth. Remove to large glass serving pitcher.

Place the rest of the tomatoes, the vegetables, and the herbs in the food processor and process until coarsely chopped. Pour the coarsely chopped vegetables into the pureed tomatoes and stir will. Add salt and pepper to taste. Chill for two hours and serve cold with a basil leaf garnish.

Fresh Marinara Sauce

Makes 3 cups
2 quarts (about 12 large) fresh paste tomatoes, such as 'Amish Paste'
3 garlic cloves, chopped
1 small onion, chopped
1 tablespoon extra virgin olive oil
½ teaspoon sea salt
Freshly ground pepper
1 teaspoon dried basil

Place the unpeeled, uncut tomatoes in boiling water for about 30 seconds, then plunge them in ice cold water to remove skins. Skins will easily peel off when you cut through the tomato. Core, peel, and coarsely chop tomatoes.

Sauté the garlic and onion in olive oil until the onion is translucent. Add the tomatoes, dried basil, salt, and pepper. Cook until sauce is thickened and reduced, about 1 hour.

This is an excellent tomato sauce for any dish from pasta and lasagna to stuffed peppers (see page 78) or garden gazpacho (this page).

Summer Fruits

BLACKBERRIES AND RASPBERRIES (*Rubus*)
Deciduous shrubs
Zones 4 to 9

Don't tell my childhood next door neighbor, but I used to sneak a few plump red raspberries from his berry patch when I was a young girl. They controlled the brambles by planting them in a 6 foot × 6 foot (1.8 m × 1.8 m) raised bed, which was very effective in keeping the roaming brambles in check.

(top) *Red raspberries are ripe and ready for picking.*

(left) *Black raspberries are a treat of summer.*

Simple, elegant and perfect. Fresh blackberries and summer local, just picked peaches are wonderful with mint cream.

Blackberries and Peaches with Mint Cream

Serves 4
½ cup heavy cream
1 tablespoon sugar
2–3 fresh mint leaves, plus more for garnish
Juice of ½ lime
3 peaches, peeled, pitted, and sliced
1 cup fresh blackberries

In a small saucepan, heat together the cream, sugar, and mint leaves. Stir well, crushing the mint with a wooden spoon as you stir. Add the lime juice and heat until scalding. Remove from the heat and chill until cool. To serve, remove the mint leaves and discard. Place the prepared fresh fruit in 4 individual serving dishes, pour the mint cream over the fruit. Garnish with fresh mint leaves.

This black raspberry cobbler can be put together very easily, no need to worry about a crust. Gather some berries and within minutes you will have a homemade cobbler.

Black Raspberry Cobbler

Makes 1 (10-inch) cobbler
1½ cups all-purpose flour
½ cup butter
1½ cups sugar, divided
½ teaspoon salt
5–6 cups fresh black raspberries or blackberries

Preheat oven to 375°F. Blend the flour, butter, ½ cup sugar, and salt in a food processor until crumbly. Set aside.

Butter the bottom of a large 10-inch quiche pan. Add the berries and 1 cup sugar. Pour the crumbled mixture on top of the berries, spreading evenly. Press down. Bake for 45 minutes. Serve warm.

Blackberries and raspberries need plenty of room. They require pruning and maintenance yearly, although currently my method is to let the native brambles grow up as they will at the edges of my property. The fruit they produce is enough to provide a pie or two every season. The hedgerow gives cover to wildlife and screening from the neighbors. Both the native blackberries and black raspberries grow for me.

Eventually, when I plant named varieties I will put posts in the ground with wire for trellising. The experts tell me I will need to cut down the wild types to reduce spread of disease. For now I like the screening the wild berries provide at my property line and the handfuls of berries I am able to gather. Some erect types of red and purple raspberries do not need trellising.

Yogurt pound cake with red raspberry coulis looks like a fancy dessert for a summer party, but it's easy to make. The pound cakes and coulis can be made the day before. Photographed in the garden of Dean and Sally Schmitt.

Yogurt Pound Cake with Red Raspberry Coulis

This moist, rich pound cake can be served with any fruit topping. It's also great with fresh strawberries and whipped cream for strawberry shortcake.

Makes 2 loaves or 1 (10-inch) Bundt pan or 6 small Bundt pans

1 cup butter, softened, plus more for pan
2½ cups sugar
6 eggs
1 teaspoon vanilla
3 cups all-purpose flour, plus more for pan
¼ teaspoon baking soda
½ teaspoon salt
1 cup plain yogurt, divided
1 pint fresh red raspberries
2 tablespoons sugar
Juice of ½ lime
1 ounce orange-flavored liquor, such as Cointreau

To make the cake, preheat oven to 300°F. Butter and flour the bottom and sides of 2 loaf pans *or* one 10-inch Bundt pan *or* 6 small Bundt pans.

Cream 1 cup butter and 2½ cups sugar until well blended and light. Using a mixer, beat in the eggs, one at a time, blending well after each addition. Add the vanilla.

In a separate bowl, combine the flour, baking soda, and salt.

(continued)

With the mixer on medium speed, add the flour mixture, alternately with the yogurt, to the butter mixture. Blend well, scraping the sides of bowl. Pour the batter into the prepared pans. Bake for 55–60 minutes or until the cake is done.

Remove the cake from the oven, allow it to cool on a wire rack for about 10 minutes, then remove the cake from the pan and allow it to cool completely.

To prepare the sauce, cook the berries, 2 tablespoons sugar, and the lime juice over medium-high heat in a saucepan. Stir and mash the raspberries to release the juices. Cook the berries until they reduce by half. Run the cooked berries through a food mill to remove the seeds and return the sauce to the saucepan. Add 1 ounce orange-flavored liquor. Stir until well blended. Cool.

To serve, cut pound cake, placing each slice on a serving platter. Pour some of the coulis over each slice.

To freeze fresh blackberries, raspberries, or blueberries, place unwashed berries in a single layer on a cookie sheet and set in the freezer. When berries are frozen, remove them from the pan and place them in bags, seal, date, and return back to the freezer. The berries will stay individually separated. When you are ready to use the berries, wash them in a colander, drain, and serve.

Fresh blueberries at the farmers market.

BLUEBERRIES (*Vaccinium*)
Deciduous shrubs
Zones 4 to 10 (varies with cultivar)

Blueberry shrubs are ornamental with three seasons of color, even if you don't eat the berries. The 4- to 5-foot (1.2- to 1.5-m) shrubs have tiny white flowers in the spring, luscious berries in the summer, and foliage that turns vibrant orange to scarlet in the fall before dropping to the ground. Blueberries like acid soil so you may need to amend the soil accordingly. For bigger berries and higher yields, it is recommended to plant two cultivars. In the midwestern United States, 'Bluejay', 'Collins', 'Elliot', and 'Herbert' are recommended. Local nurseries can suggest varieties suitable for other areas. Blueberries make an excellent shrub for any residential landscape planting, even a nonedible one.

The only time to make the world's best blueberry pie is in the middle of summer when the local blueberries are ripe. Even if you don't grow your own, this is the time when they are abundant and relatively inexpensive at the farmer's market.

World's Best Blueberry Pie

Makes 1 (9-inch) pie
5 cups fresh blueberries
1 cup sugar
Juice of ½ lemon
Dash of cinnamon
Dash of salt, plus ½ teaspoon, divided
2¾ cups unbleached flour, divided
¾ cup cold butter, cut into pieces
4 ounces cream cheese, at room temperature
1 tablespoon butter, softened
½ cup confectioners' sugar
Dash of cinnamon
2 tablespoons milk or cream

Preheat oven to 375°F.

To make the filling, mix together the blueberries, 1 cup sugar, the lemon juice, a dash of cinnamon and a dash of salt with ¼ cup flour. Set aside.

To make the crust, process ¾ cup butter with the cream cheese in a food processor until well blended and smooth. Add 2½ cups flour and ½ teaspoon salt and continue to process just until the dough sticks together well.

Remove the dough from the food processor and place it on a floured board. Divide in two. Wrap half the dough (for the top crust) in plastic and place it in refrigerator while you roll out the other half to make the bottom crust.

To assemble the pie, pour the blueberry mixture into the bottom crust. Roll out the top crust and place it on the pie. Seal the edges and slit the top to let steam escape. Bake for 40–50 minutes until the crust is lightly browned

and filling is bubbly. If the top crust begins to get too brown, cover it with a circle of aluminum foil.

To make the glaze, mix 1 tablespoon butter, the confectioners' sugar, a dash of cinnamon, and 2 tablespoons milk in a small bowl and blend well with a fork. Brush on warm pie. Serve the pie warm or cool.

Fresh blueberries and peaches drizzled with honey fill fruit meringue cups. Meringues are not difficult to make and they travel surprisingly well. Just wrap with the fruit filling and take for picnics or packed lunches.

Fruit Meringue Cups

Makes 8 large meringue shells
3 egg whites
½ cup sugar
8 cups fresh fruit
Honey for drizzle

Preheat oven to 200°F. Line a cookie sheet with parchment paper.

Beat the egg whites in a stainless steel mixing bowl at high speed until soft peaks form. With mixer running, add in the sugar, a tablespoon at a time. Continue to mix at high speed until stiff peaks form. Plop a heaping spoonful of meringue on the parchment and use the back of the spoon to create a depression.

Bake in the center of the oven for two hours. Turn off oven and allow the meringues to remain in the oven for two more hours.

To serve, fill the cooled, crisp shells with strawberries, blueberries, blackberries, raspberries, or peaches. Drizzle with honey.

Fresh sour cherries picked from the North Star cherry trees of Dr. Dede McGehee are ready for cherry pies, tarts, or jam.

CHERRIES (*Prunus*)
Deciduous fruit tree
Zones 4 to 8

The best cherries for pies, jams, and tarts are sour cherries (*Prunus cerasus*). Recommended varieties are 'Montmorency' or 'North Star'. Sour cherries are self-fertile so they don't require two varieties for pollination. Plant one-year-old whips on well-drained soil in full sun.

Most sweet cherries (*Prunus avium*) need two varieties to set fruit. When selecting the varieties, make sure they have the same bloom time and thus are compatible for pollination. The fruit of sweet cherries is good to eat fresh.

Cherries, like most fruit trees, are grafted onto rootstocks to ensure the variety is true to type. Select the rootstock that is suitable in size and hardiness for your climate.

Rustic cherry tarts can be made with any fruit. These were made with a combination of sour cherries, peaches, and blackberries. They are meant to be served informally so guests can help make them.

Rustic Cherry Tarts

Serves 8–16
⅓ cup slivered almonds
1 cup cold butter, cut into 16 pieces
2⅓ cups unbleached flour, plus 3 tablespoons
½ teaspoon salt
2–3 tablespoons cold water
3 cups sour cherries, pitted
¾ cup sugar
4 teaspoons butter, divided

Preheat oven to 375°F. To make the tart shells, process almonds in a food processor until finely ground. Add the 16 pieces of butter, 2⅓ cups flour, and salt and process in pulses until the butter is in small pieces. Add the cold water a tablespoon at a time until the dough just clings together.

Divide the dough into four pieces. On a floured surface, roll out each piece into a circle. Set aside.

To prepare the filling, put the cherries, sugar, and 3 tablespoons flour in a large bowl. Stir until blended.

To assemble the tarts, place ¼ of the cherry mixture on each rolled out circle of dough. Place a teaspoon of butter on top of each. Fold up sides of tart, pressing together. Leave an opening at the top. Place each tart on a cookie sheet. Bake for 35–40 minutes or until crust is brown and filling is bubbly. Cut each tart in half or fourths to serve.

Native 'Crandall' black currants grown by Janell Baran, owner of Blue Owl Garden Emporium, a small herb farm, and sold at the farmer's market in Granville, Ohio.

CURRANTS (*Ribes*)
Deciduous shrub
Zones 4 to 9 (varies)

Currants make excellent hedges; even the non-edible variety is known as a dependable shrub in the landscape for its low-maintenance requirements and tolerance of urban conditions. Choose shrubs that bear fruit and they become doubly utilitarian. Currant shrubs are hardy and attractive and produce clusters of small white, pink, red, or black fruits.

Black currants are widely popular in Europe where you find the strong flavoring in everything from gum to soft drinks. Black currants are the alternate host to white pine blister rust and in many states the European black currant (*Ribes nigra*) is banned. In 1966 the federal ban on black currants in the United States was lifted, but check local requirements in your state. 'Crandall' clove currant (*Ribes odoratum* 'Crandall'), which produces black fruit and is not susceptible to white pine blister rust, is native to North America.

Fresh black currant jam is now my favorite jam. This is made from native North American 'Crandall' black currants. Lovely served on toast or on pancakes.

Fresh Black Currant Jam

When you have your own currant bushes, sometimes you pick in small amounts. This jam uses whatever berries you have. It's a delectable treat when made with Crandall black currants. Because this jam is made without pectin, it is necessary to cook the jam to the right consistency.

Makes about 2 cups
1 cup black currants
¾ cup sugar
Small amount of water

For every 1 cup of black currants, use ¾ cup sugar. In a saucepan, bring the currants and sugar to boil with a small amount of water. Continue to cook the jam until the syrup sheets off a spoon. Pour into jars and store in refrigerator. Serve over pancakes or on toast.

Space plants 2 to 4 feet (60–120 cm) apart for a hedge. Currants grow 3 to 6 feet (90–180 cm) tall. The fruit usually ripens at one time on each plant, but mature fruits can hang for a few weeks on the plant.

'Red Lake' and 'Jonkeer Van Tets' are red, 'White Imperial' and 'Primus' are white. Jostaberry (*Ribes nidigrolaria*) is a cross between a black currant and a gooseberry.

ELDERBERRIES (*Sambucus nigra*)
Deciduous shrub or small tree
Zones 3 to 9

The common American elderberry (*Sambucus nigra* subsp. *canadensis*) is native to the eastern United States and can be found growing at the edges of woods and in old hedgerows. It is practically a weed but a useful and beautiful one at that. Along the edge of my property, I have allowed the old fence-row to grow naturally with little intervention. The birds have seeded a few wild elderberry bushes here where they grow quite happily nestled in a partly sunny spot.

Elderberries are a nice addition to the back of the garden. The multistemmed shrubs grow to 12 feet (3.6 m) high and have attractive, serrated leaves. The small reddish drupes turn black when ripe in the fall and make wonderful jelly. 'Adams', 'Kent', 'Nova', 'Scotia', 'Victoria', and 'York' produce large, abundant fruits. 'Maxima' was selected for its large flowers. For best fruit production, plant two varieties.

American elderberry is a subspecies of the European elderberry (*Sambucus nigra*), so popular for elder flower cordial in England. The infused drink can just as easily be made from the flowers of the native American variety. Elderberry flowers are a good source of nectar for butterflies.

Elderberry shrubs produce a burst of showy umbrella-like white flowers in early summer. These can be gathered for drinks or fried for fritters. Don't harvest all the flowers on the shrub; you will want to make elderberry jam from the berries in the fall. Elderberry is truly a marker plant for the season: you can celebrate summer's beginning with elderflower cordial and summer's end with elderberry jam. See more on elderberries in the Fall chapter (page 149).

Elderberry flowers in the spring are used to make elder flower cordial.

Elder Flower Cordial

Makes 6 cups
12–15 large elder flower heads
3 lemons
4 cups sugar
3 cups water

Select flowers at the peak of their bloom; the tiny flowers will be fragrant and white. Remove flowers from the stems and place in a crock pot or ceramic bowl. Zest the three lemons and add it to the flowers; then slice the lemons very thinly and add them to the bowl with the sugar.

In a saucepan, heat the water until it's just boiling. Pour it over the flower-lemon mixture and stir until the sugar is dissolved. (The purpose of heating the water is to help dissolve the sugar.) Cover and let steep in the refrigerator for 2 to 4 days, stirring periodically.

Strain the liquid through a muslin cloth and place in saucepan. Bring the mixture to a hard boil, cool, and pour into glass jars that have been sterilized. Attach lids and store in the refrigerator for 1 to 2 months. Serve with 3 parts of sparkling water or sparkling champagne to one part elder flower cordial for a refreshing summer drink.

Melon fizz is refreshing on a summer day. Keep some melon chunks in the freezer to make this cool drink anytime.

Melon Fizz

Serves 4–6
1 small (about 2 cups) fresh melon
Sparkling wine or champagne
Mint leaves (optional)

Peel fresh melon and cut into chunks. Place the chunks in plastic bags, seal, and freeze two hours or overnight. Puree frozen melon in a blender adding a small amount of sparkling wine or champagne to make it easy to process. Add additional sparkling wine and stir by hand, to preserve the effervescence, until mixture is slushy and easy to pour. Pour into chilled glasses. Serve immediately with garnish of mint leaves. Use sparkling grape juice for a non-alcoholic version.

A variety of fresh melons at the farmer's market.

MELONS (*Cucumis melo*)
Annual
Seed to table: 75 to 115 days

Melons require room to spread in the garden. They also need a long growing season, so it's best to start plants from seed indoors under lights 4 weeks before the frost-free date or buy plants from a nursery. Choose a sandy soil with southern exposure and full sun. For short growing seasons, try 'Sweet Granite' cantaloupe. Watermelons need lots of room and may do best on the compost pile where they have room to expand. Some varieties take 100 days or more from seed to harvest.

Fresh peaches picked from the garden of Joyce and E. John Bartley.

PEACHES (*Prunus persica*)
Deciduous fruit tree
Zones 5 to 9

Peaches are self-fertile so you don't need two cultivars for pollination. Plant a few different varieties and you can harvest fresh peaches from late summer to early fall.

The incomparable sweet taste of peaches only develops when the peaches ripen on the tree. Peaches picked before they ripen so they can travel in a truck to your grocery store shelf won't get any sweeter sitting in a bowl on your countertop.

Select freestone varieties for your home orchard; it's so much easier when the fruit doesn't cling to the pits. Peach trees, like most fruit trees, should be planted at the crest of a hill, not at the bottom. Cold air flows downward and can pool at the bottom causing freeze damage in the spring when blossoms are forming. 'Red Haven' is an early freestone variety excellent for desserts. 'Belle of Georgia' is a late freestone variety with sweet, white flesh.

The hotness of the jalapeños blends perfectly with the sweetness of fresh peaches.

Hot Peach Chutney

This should be called spicy peach chutney. The jalapeños make it hot. It's not served warm, but it makes a good counterpoint to cool yogurt sauce.

Makes 4 cups
4 peaches, pitted and peeled
3–4 jalapeño peppers, stemmed and seeded
3–4 green onions
3 tablespoons fresh cilantro
1 tablespoon rice wine vinegar
1 tablespoon extra virgin olive oil
1 tablespoon honey

Chop peaches, jalapeños, green onions, and cilantro. Add to a serving dish. In a separate bowl, combine the rice wine vinegar, olive oil, and honey until well mixed. Pour the mixture over the chopped ingredients and stir well. Serve with spicy garden curry (see page 66) and cool yogurt sauce (see page 111).

Peach halves with three cheeses is served with a drizzle of balsamic vinegar. Serve this as an appetizer or a dessert.

Peach Halves with Three Cheeses

Serves 8
4 peaches, pitted and halved
8 ounces cream cheese, at room temperature
8 ounces sharp white cheddar cheese, grated
2 ounces blue cheese
3 green onions, finely chopped
3 tablespoons fresh flat-leaf parsley, chopped
Splash of balsamic vinegar
Fresh mint leaves (optional)

Place a peach half, cut side up, on each serving platter. Combine the three cheeses in a food processor and blend until well mixed. Add the green onions and parsley and process just until blended. To serve, put a scoop of the cheese mixture in each peach half, drizzle with some balsamic vinegar, and garnish with fresh mint leaves.

The crust of these tarts is made with cookie dough. Fresh peaches on top have a drizzle of honey.

Peach Cookie Crust Tarts

This buttery, blonde-brownie type of crust is great with any fresh fruit that you have on hand. It's simple to make but looks elegant with fruit piled high and glazed with honey. Add whipped cream for a special occasion. We have served these tarts for my daughter's birthday instead of cake.

Makes 4 (4-inch) tarts
½ cup butter
½ cup sugar
1 egg
⅛ cup honey, plus more for drizzle
1 teaspoon real vanilla
1 cup unbleached flour
½ cup whole oats
¼ cup whole wheat flour
½ teaspoon baking soda
½ teaspoon baking powder
4 peaches, peeled, pitted, and sliced

Preheat oven to 350°F. Cream the butter and sugar together in a mixer at medium speed. Add the egg and mix well. Add in the honey and vanilla and mix well. In a separate bowl, combine the dry ingredients and stir to mix. With the mixer running, slowly add the dry ingredients into the batter and mix well.

Press ¼ of the batter into a 4-inch spring form pan. Repeat for the rest of the batter and the pans. If you don't have small spring form pans, you can make four large cookies on a cookie sheet. Bake the tarts (cookies) for 20–25 minutes. Remove from the oven and cool.

To serve, place slices of fresh peaches on the top of each tart (cookie) and drizzle with honey.

Decadent peach ice cream may be the best ice cream you will ever eat. It's served with mint leaves and daisies on the plate which are in bloom when the peaches are ripe.

Decadent Peach Ice Cream

Serves 6
4 cups peaches, peeled, pitted, and chopped
½ cup sugar
2 cups heavy cream
½ cup brown sugar
6 egg yolks
⅛ teaspoon salt
2 tablespoons sugar

To prepare the fruit, place the peaches in a saucepan with ½ cup sugar. Bring the mixture to a boil over moderately high heat, stirring. Simmer for about 5 minutes. Set aside while you make the custard. The fruit can be prepared a day or two ahead of time, covered and stored in the refrigerator until you are ready to make the ice cream.

To prepare the custard base, place the cream and brown sugar in a heavy saucepan and heat, stirring constantly until the sugar is dissolved. Heat until the mixture almost boils, but doesn't. Remove from heat and cover.

In a separate mixing bowl, beat the egg yolks, salt, and 2 tablespoons sugar at medium-high speed until slightly thickened and the sugar is dissolved. Reduce speed to slow and add the hot cream mixture in a slow stream until well blended. Return the custard to saucepan and cook, stirring constantly until scalding. Custard will begin to thicken. Do *not* boil. Remove the custard from heat. Add the peach mixture and stir well.

Chill completely in refrigerator, at least 4 hours or overnight. Freeze custard in ice cream maker according to manufacturer directions. The ice cream is pretty soft at this point. Store it in an airtight container to harden in freezer.

Freshly picked yellow and purple Japanese plums.

Serve up some colorful plum tarts. Easy to make and fun to eat.

Plum Tarts

Makes 1 dozen tarts
½ cup butter
4 ounces cream cheese, at room temperature
1½ cups unbleached flour
1 egg
Juice of 1 lemon
½ teaspoon vanilla
Dash of salt
6 plums, pitted and halved

Preheat oven to 350°F. Blend the butter and cream cheese in a food processor until well mixed. Add the flour and process until the dough clings together. Divide and press the dough into the bottom and sides of 12 tart shells.

In a small bowl, combine the egg, lemon juice, vanilla, and salt. To assemble the tarts, place one plum half in each tart shell. Pour some of the filling over each plum. Bake for 20–25 minutes. Serve warm or cool.

PLUMS (*Prunus*)
Deciduous fruit tree
Zones 5 to 10 (varies)

European plums (*Prunus domestica*) are the most cold tolerant plum and recommended for growing in the northern and midwestern United States, where the fruit ripens late summer and early autumn (late August to September). The trees are hardy in zones 5 to 9.

Damson plums (*Prunus insititia*) are ancient blue plums originating in Damascus. Mirabelle plums are yellow and date to medieval times in France. Japanese plums (*Prunus salicina*) are the plums sold in the grocery store. The trees are hardy in zones 6 to 10. Some varieties are self-fertile and don't need another pollinator; others will need two varieties for pollination. 'Shiro' is an early ripening Japanese variety excellent for baking and eating; the yellow fruit ripens in late summer (July).

North American native plums (*Prunus americana* and *Prunus angustifolia*) have potential for the residential garden, especially if you are interested in native fruit. The trees can be grafted and grown as a single tree, but otherwise grow as large shrubs producing thickets. The fruit is small and suitable for jams and jellies.

A container planting of variegated horseradish (Armoracia rusticana 'Variegata') at the Bourton House Garden in Gloucestershire, England, is both ornamental and edible. The young leaves are eaten in salads while the roots are grated and used in recipes.

Summer Greens

Lettuces and cool-season greens like mustards and kale will bolt when it gets too hot. Remove cool-season greens like dandelion and arugula. Try sowing lettuce seeds in the shade of bean or flower trellises and water consistently. Some greens tolerate heat better than others; check for varieties that are adapted to summer. There are some greens that prefer warm weather.

A rustic tomato cage supports sprawling tomato vines. Red cabbage planted in the cool of spring is ready to eat in the summer. Moments after I took this photo I harvested the cabbage to make fresh mint picnic coleslaw to serve at a family get together.

AMARANTH (*Amaranthus*)
Annual
Seed to table: 39 days

Amaranth is a tropical grain with edible leaves although you may have seen relatives of this plant at the nursery and not known it. Love-lies-bleeding (*Amaranthus caudatus*), a striking ornamental with drooping burgundy red flowers is in the same family as is celosia (*Celosia argentea*).

'Hopi Red Dye' is an heirloom ornamental with red stems and feathery, upright bracts; the leaves are edible and can be cooked like spinach or used raw in salads. 'Tricolor' is a heat-loving edible with striking poinsettia-type glowing red leaves.

CABBAGE (*Brassica oleracea* Capitata Group)
Biennial grown as an annual
Seed to table: 60 to 95 days

Cabbage heads planted in the spring will be ready to harvest now. Check regularly for cabbage worms, or rather have your eight-year-old check for them. Look closely between the leaves; you might spy a small lime green caterpillar munching holes in the leaves. Pick the worms off by hand and squish them under your shoe. It takes daily diligence to control by hand but is the best way for small crops.

Harvest cabbage heads at any size when the heads are firm and the leaves haven't begun to spread out too much. Cut at the base and remove outer leaves. Dig up the root and place it in the compost pile. See more on cabbage in the Spring and Fall chapters (pages 38 and 156, respectively).

MALABAR SPINACH (*Basella alba*)
Perennial grown as an annual
Seed to table: 70 days

Malabar spinach, sometimes called climbing spinach, is not spinach at all but a tropical climbing vine. The leaves are edible and a substitute for spinach;

Fresh Mint Picnic Coleslaw

Serves 6 to 8

Apple cider vinegar
Juice of 1 lemon
½ cup extra-virgin olive oil
2 tablespoons honey
Salt
1 small head cabbage
4–5 green onions, sliced
4–5 carrots, shredded
1–2 jalapeño peppers, finely chopped
½ cup fresh flat-leaf parsley, chopped
¼ cup fresh mint leaves, chopped
½ cup sliced almonds, toasted
½ cup dried cherries or cranberries

To make the dressing, add apple cider vinegar to the lemon juice to make ½ cup liquid. Add the oil, honey, and salt to taste. Stir well. Set aside

Slice cabbage into bite-size pieces and put in a large serving bowl. Mix in the remaining ingredients.

Pour the dressing over the vegetables and serve immediately.

they can be cooked or served in salads. The plant loves heat and does not tolerate frost or cool temperatures. It does need trellising. 'Rubra' has red ornamental stems and red venation in the leaves which makes it not only stunning in the kitchen garden but pretty on a plate.

ORACH (*Atriplex*)
Annual
Seed to table: 38 days

Also called mountain spinach, orach is a heat loving annual with deep red leaves. The leaves can be cooked like spinach or use the baby tender leaves for salad mixes.

SHISO (*Perilla frutescens*)
Perennial grown as an annual
Seed to table: 80 to 85 days

The first time I saw the beautiful burgundy serrated leaf of shiso was not in the garden but on my plate—dipped in tempura batter and deep fried. It's beautiful in the garden as well and slightly fragrant with an anise scent. The leaves can be used in salads or chopped to add flavor. They are used in Japanese cooking. At the end of the summer the plant produces tiny edible flowers. There is a green variety as well. Sow outside after all danger of frost is past.

Summer Herbs

BASIL (*Ocimum basilicum*)
Annual
Seed to table: 60 to 70 days

Basil is one of the easiest herbs to grow, but it has one special requirement: it likes it warm. It does not tolerate cold or frost so delay planting until the soil is warm and there is no chance of frost. Every year I try and speed up the season by planting too early. Here is what I've learned: the basil you plant by seed in the garden a full week after the frost-free date, when the soil is warm, will surpass the plants you set out when it's a little chilly. It's fast growing so you can sow it later in the season after you harvest late spring cool-season crops. Ornamental varieties can be left to flower, otherwise be diligent about culinary basil; keep pinching off the flowers to keep the plant bushy and full.

The best ornamental varieties are 'African Blue', 'Magical Michael', 'Ebony Wonder', 'Thai', 'Red Rubin', and 'Purple Ruffles'. The best varieties for cooking are 'Sweet Genovese', 'Spicy Globe' (Greek basil), 'Mrs. Burns' (lemon basil), and 'Thai'. The best variety for pesto is 'Sweet Genovese'.

Pesto is a magic combination of these few ingredients. Tweak the recipe to your taste. A good olive oil is essential. I prefer extra virgin olive oil from Greece, made with kalamata olives.

Classic Pesto

Use this recipe as a beginning point; everyone has their special preferences. When my son John comes to visit he adds a small green or jalapeño pepper, and substitutes toasted pine nuts for the walnuts. Short on 'Genovese' basil? Add some flat-leaf Italian parsley or substitute other basils.

Makes about 3 cups
8 cups fresh basil leaves
½ cup parmesan cheese, coarsely grated
¼ cup walnuts
2 garlic cloves, peeled
½ teaspoon sea salt
Juice of ½ lemon
¾ cup extra virgin olive oil, divided

Process the basil, parmesan cheese, walnuts, garlic, salt, and lemon juice in a food processor with some of the olive oil. With the processor running, slowly add in the rest of the olive oil. Process until smooth. Serve over pasta or use as a dip with fresh bread.

Basil Bruschetta

This is a simple and flexible dish; the combination of ingredients depends on what is growing in the garden. It takes just a few minutes to make. Have your guests gather the ingredients from the garden.

Makes 16 to 18 appetizers
2 cups fresh basil leaves
1 cup cherry tomatoes
½ cup ground cherries (optional)
1–2 small sweet peppers
2 garlic cloves, finely chopped
¾ cup extra virgin olive oil
½ cup parmesan cheese, coarsely grated
Salt
1 loaf Italian or French bread, sliced

Coarsely chop by hand the basil, tomatoes, ground cherries, and peppers. Put the chopped vegetables in a bowl with the garlic. Add the olive oil. Stir in the cheese. Salt to taste.

Spoon the mixture over sliced bread and broil until the cheese melts and the bread is toasted. The mixture can also be served at room temperature as a dip with fresh bread.

(opposite top) *A collection of freshly picked herbs including flat leaf parsley, Thai basil, dill, and cutting celery.*

(bottom) *Culinary and ornamental basils look lovely even if you don't make pesto. 'Genovese', 'Cinnamon', and 'Red Rubin' grow side by side.*

Cilantro Salsa

Makes about a cup
2 cups fresh cilantro
4–5 green onions
3–4 jalapeño peppers
2 garlic cloves
Juice of 1 lime
2 teaspoons extra virgin olive oil
Salt

Chop the cilantro, onions, peppers, and garlic. Put in a bowl. Add the lime juice, olive oil, and salt to taste. Mix well.

CILANTRO (*Coriandrum sativum*)
Annual
Seed to table: 50 to 55 for leaf, 90 to 105 for seed

Cilantro will reseed in the same place every year, so find a permanent place in the garden for it. To establish a clump, sow seeds every two weeks in the summer. When the plant does go to seed allow some to fall to the ground; the rest can be harvested and used in cooking. The seeds are called coriander and add a different flavor when roasted and crushed. Cilantro is essential for Mexican cooking. The spicy leaf is perfect to flavor salsas or to marinade pork, beef, or chicken.

CHERVIL (*Anthriscus cereifolium*)
Annual
Seed to table: 60 days

Chervil has a mild anise flavor and is a traditional herb for French cooking. The leaves look similar to flat parsley and can be used for marinades or to garnish soups. Sow seeds outdoors after danger of frost is past. The herb is an excellent addition to soups.

CHIVES (*Allium schoenoprasum*)
Perennial in zones 3 to 11
Planting to table: 40 to 50 days

The pink flowers blossom in the spring but will rebloom sporadically throughout the summer if you deadhead the spent flowers by cutting out or pulling the brown spent blooms and stalks. Continue to harvest the oniony leaves for dips, garnishes, and omelets through fall. See more on chives in the Spring chapter (page 42).

CUTTING CELERY (*Apium graveolens*)
Perennial grown as an annual
Seed to table: 80 to 85 days

Cutting celery looks like flat-leaf Italian parsley but has a biting celery flavor. It can be started indoors like parsley and then transplanted outdoors to the garden after all danger of frost is past. Cutting celery is frost tolerant once established and I have had it survive in my garden over the winter.

This herb is grown for the flavorful leaves and not for the stems. It's delicious in soups and stews. Plant some now so you have an abundant supply in the fall. It's also a great addition to recipes that call for flat-leaf parsley. This is a great herb for the edible garden.

DILL (*Anethum graveolens*)
Annual
Seed to table: 40 to 55 days for leaf, 85 to 105 days for seed

Dill is an attractive feathery plant that grows to 3 feet (90 cm) tall. It is self-seeding, so find a permanent place for it in the garden and allow it to reseed every year. You may find it likes to move about the garden; just pick the unwanted seedlings and use them in the kitchen. Dill is excellent for flavoring fish, pasta, sauces, and pickles. It's easily grown from seed; sprinkle seed on the ground, cover it lightly with soil, and water regularly.

An informal summer arrangement of whatever was in bloom at the time of the family get-together:
flowering dill, anise hyssop, 'Little Lamb' hydrangea, and 'Canary' helenium.

FENNEL (*Foeniculum vulgare*)

Annual as bulb fennel; perennial in zones 4 to 9 as
   herb fennel

Seed to table: 70 to 80 days for bulb fennel, 50 to 60
   days for herb fennel

There are two kinds of fennel—the herb grown for its fragrant foliage and the vegetable grown for its bulbous root stalk. Both are very easy to grow from seed. Fennel looks like dill and will create a feathery cloud to 4 feet (1.2 m) high. Bronze fennel (*Foeniculum vulgare* 'Purpurascens') has coppery purple foliage. See more on fennel in the Fall chapter (page 136).

'Munstead' lavender borders one edge of the raised bed in the author's potager. It does not require as much water or nutrients as the vegetables growing next to it. Since I water the garden by hand, this is no problem. The yellow flowers are calendula which reseeds every year.

LAVENDER (*Lavandula*)

Perennial

Zones 5 to 9

Lavender, like many herbs, is native to the Mediterranean so it prefers those climatic conditions, namely, full sun and well-drained soil. In fact, herbs like lavender and thyme prefer slightly sandy, alkaline loam soil. They don't like it rich. Lavender can be difficult to grow in humid climates with heavy clay soil, like the midwestern United States. The plant is so valuable in the herb garden for its fragrance and light purple flowers that bloom all summer that it's worth growing and replacing those plants that succumb to cold, wet winters. The flowers are edible, but better for garnishes as the flavor is strong. Use the blossoms for cut arrangements all summer. The flowers last long in the vase and are easy to dry.

MARJORAM (*Origanum marjorana*)
Perennial in zone 9, grown elsewhere as an annual
Seed to table: 80 to 95 days

Marjoram is an annual herb for me; it's actually a perennial hardy in zone 9. I set out plants in the summer to create a fragrant gray-green border in the potager. Marjoram can also be grown from seed planted outside after danger of frost. The leaves have the flavor and fragrance of oregano, but milder. Use them fresh in any recipe that calls for oregano and in making marinades. I allow the plant to flower, because the flowers are white, attractive, and edible but the flavor of the leaves does diminish.

MINT (*Mentha*)
Perennial in zones 4 to 9 (varies)
Planting to table: 75 days

Plant a variety of mints in containers or sink the container in the soil to keep boisterous mint in check. Yes, mint will take over your garden, if you don't set its boundaries. I am still pulling up mint I planted a decade ago in my garden. Mint can also be planted in garden spaces that are surrounded by pavement. Driveways and walkways create an edge that prevents the runners from spreading through the garden.

Thirsty for a mint julep or a mojito in the middle of the hot summer? The classic mint for mint julep is *Mentha spicata* 'Kentucky Colonel' because of its intense spearmint flavor. Corsican mint (*Mentha requienii*) is low growing with tiny leaves and is suitable for growing between stones in a walkway. Habek mint (*Mentha longifolia*) is a Middle Eastern variety to try in tabbouleh. There are a multitude of flavored mints—chocolate, banana, pineapple, lime, and orange—so have fun.

OREGANO (*Origanum vulgarum*)
Perennial in zones 4 to 8
Seed to table: 35 to 45 days

Oregano is the classic spice for pizza and Italian sauces. Fresh oregano is very fragrant, and a few snips can be gathered to flavor fish or tomato dishes. The herb goes well with squash sautéed in butter. It has a stronger flavor than its cousin, sweet marjoram. I find it does seed itself around the garden if left to flower. 'Aureum' has pretty gold foliage.

PARSLEY (*Petroselinum crispum*)
Biennial grown as an annual
Seed to table: 75 to 85 days

Grow parsley from seed under lights indoors 8 weeks before you set them out in the garden after the frost-free date. Soak seeds in warm water for twenty-four hours for better germination. Parsley is notoriously slow to germinate. Be patient.

In my zone 5 climate, I treat parsley as an annual. It is actually a biennial that is hardy in mild winters; it goes to seed the second year. If I have any parsley that does survive the winter, I allow it to flower and go to seed because the flowers attract beneficial insects.

Flat-leaf Italian parsley is the best for cooking. It also is excellent as an edging plant in the potager or even the perennial border. It looks great all season, even if you don't harvest the leaves for cooking. It will take shady conditions, and in very warm climates may require some shade.

Parsley is an essential herb for tabbouleh, quiche, and pasta dishes. 'Giante d'Italia' has large dark green flavorful leaves.

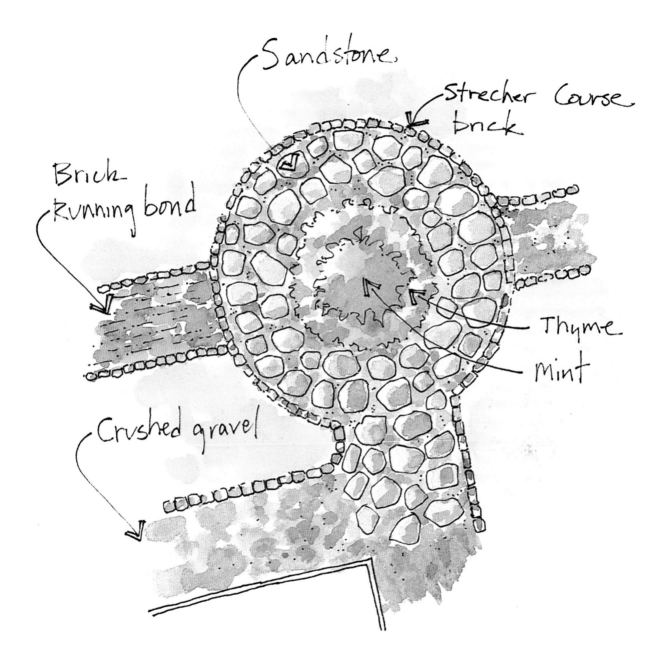

Sandstone

Strecher Course brick

Brick Running bond

Thyme

Mint

Crushed gravel

Mint should be planted in containers to avoid its spread through your garden. Another option is to plant it where it is surrounded by pavement. This drawing shows a plan for a pathway leading to a formal potager. Thyme is also planted among the mint.

ROSEMARY (*Rosmarinus officinalis*)
Perennial in zone 8, grown as an annual elsewhere
Seed to table: 85 days

Rosemary is treated as an annual in colder climates. It does well in containers or in the vegetable or flower garden. The small fragrant leaves are wonderful for marinades, or sprinkled on top of focaccia. Golden rain ('Joyce DeBaggio') is a chartreuse variegated variety. 'Blue Spire' is a good culinary variety, but any rosemary variety is suitable for cooking. You only need a small amount; the flavor can be intense. The fragrance is divine. Throw some sprigs on anything you may be grilling. See more about rosemary in the Winter chapter (page 192).

SAGE (*Salvia officinalis*)
Perennial in zones 5 to 9
Seed to table: 75 days

Culinary sage is a short-lived herb. It can be gray-green, multicolored, or purple. Golden variegated sage ('Icterina') is hardy in zones 7 to 8. 'Berggarten' sage is a compact plant with broad, oval leaves; it is very attractive and hardy. Garden dwarf sage ('Compacta') is hardy to zone 4b and is neater and more compact than common sage. See more about sage in the Winter chapter (page 192).

TARRAGON (*Artemisia dracunculus*)
Perennial in zones 4 to 8
Seed to table: 90 days

French tarragon will grow 2 to 3 feet (60–90 cm) high with a 15-inch (38-cm) spread. Cut sprigs for flavoring poultry or fish or for flavoring vinegars for salad dressings. Tarragon, along with shallots, is used to flavor the classic emulsion of butter and egg yolks called Béarnaise sauce. Be diligent about weeding around tarragon. I find that the open leaves

allow the perfect light for weeds to grow under the plant. Grass intermingled with tarragon will have you pulling up the entire plant to get rid of the entwined grass. I speak from experience.

Rosemary Chicken Gyros

Serves 6
6 boneless chicken breasts
Salt and freshly ground pepper
2 tablespoons olive oil
Juice of 1 lemon
¼ cup white wine vinegar
2 garlic cloves, finely chopped
3 tablespoons fresh rosemary, chopped
2 tablespoons fresh Greek basil leaves, chopped

Place chicken breasts in casserole dish. Sprinkle with salt and pepper to taste. In a small bowl, combine the remaining ingredients to make the marinade. Pour the sauce over the chicken, coating each piece. Cover the dish and marinate for 4 hours or longer. Discard the marinade and grill the chicken over hot coals until done. Slice the grilled chicken and serve with pitas, Grilled Summer Vegetables (page 82), and Tzatziki sauce (page 69). For a vegetarian gyro, omit the chicken.

Cool Yogurt Sauce

Makes 2 cups
4–5 green onions
½ cup fresh flat-leaf Italian parsley
3 tablespoons fresh cilantro
3 tablespoons fresh Thai basil
5–6 fresh mint leaves
1 garlic clove
2 cups plain yogurt, drained

Finely chop the onions, herbs, and garlic. Put in bowl with the yogurt and mix. Serve immediately or let flavors meld by storing in the refrigerator and serving the next day. Serve with Indian food.

Thyme will fill in cracks between stone in the garden because it will grow in lean soil.

Herb Cream Cheese can be made the day before you need it. It makes a quick appetizer with crackers. It's also great on fresh crusty bread or bagels.

Herb Cream Cheese

Makes about 1 cup
2 garlic cloves
1 small green sweet pepper, seeded and stemmed
½ cup fresh flat-leaf parsley
2 tablespoons fresh dill
8 ounces cream cheese or goat cheese, at room
    temperature

Place the garlic, pepper, and herbs in a food processor and process briefly until chopped. Add the cheese and process until blended. Chill overnight for flavors to blend, and then serve at room temperature with an assortment of crackers or raw vegetables.

THYME (*Thymus vulgaris*)
Perennial in zones 5 to 9 (varies)
Seed to table: 70 days

Thyme can be grown in containers or between stones along pathways. It is native to the Mediterranean so prefers sandy, well-drained soil. Thyme can be used to flavor soups, stews, tomato dishes, potatoes, or salad dressings. I find a little goes a long way. To add variety to recipes, use both dried thyme and fresh thyme; each brings a different flavor. There are many varieties: coconut, golden lemon, green lemon, or lime. One of my favorites is *Thymus* 'Doone Valley'. *Thymus vulgaris* 'Argenteus' has pale gray, leaves.

An arrangement of early summer flowers grown and put together by the talented members of the Little Garden Club of Woodford County near Lexington, Kentucky.

Shrubs and Flowers for the Table

ALYSSUM (*Lobularia maritima*)
Annual
Site conditions: Full sun

Alyssum is an annual flower that should be in every vegetable garden. The tiny flowers aren't for picking nor are they for eating, but they will attract beneficial insects, specifically nectar-seeking hover flies. Plant alyssum next to beans and the hover flies might munch the aphids before they suck the tender leaves of the beans. Alyssum, or sweet alyssum, blooms all season and is heat and drought tolerant. 'Carpet of Snow' is white. 'Wonderland Purple' is purple.

The plant grows 6 to 8 inches (15–20 cm)) high so it's a great height for edging the raised beds in the kitchen garden. Plant flats outdoors after dan-

ger of frost or sow directly in the garden. Alyssum will self-sow and come up on its own, and this is a very lucky thing. Allow it to be a living mulch in the kitchen garden; as a low ground cover it covers the soil while cutting down weeds and providing nectar for beneficials.

ANISE HYSSOP (*Agastache foeniculum*)
Perennial in zones 6 to 9
Site conditions: Prefers full sun

This is a useful perennial to plant right outside the formal potager. The tall purple blue flowers bloom in mid summer. The fragrant blossoms attract beneficials, are edible, and are great for cut flower arrangements. The leaves can be dried and used for tea.

I grow anise hyssop among my peonies along the fence surrounding my raised beds in the kitchen garden. When the peonies are done blooming, the blue spikes of anise hyssop take over the show.

BLACK-EYED SUSAN (*Rudbeckia*)
Perennial in zones 3 to 10
Site conditions: Prefers full sun, tolerates part sun;
 drought tolerant

This is not a fancy plant. It's seen everywhere, but it's easy to grow and the flowers brighten the midsummer to fall garden. The twenty-five species of *Rudbeckia* are native to North America. *Rudbeckia fulgida* var. *sullivantii* 'Goldsturm' is a popular plant. It is easy to grow and is long lived in the garden. *Rudbeckia fulgida* var. *fulgida* is similar to 'Goldsturm' but has smaller flowers and longer lasting blooms. *Rudbeckia hirta* 'Prairie Sun' grows has greenish eyes and lemon yellow petals. One of my new favorites is quilled sweet coneflower, *Rudbeckia subtomentosa* 'Henry Eilers'; it has pale yellow quilled petals and grows to about 4 feet (1.2 m) tall. See more on black-eyed Susan in the Fall chapter (page 161).

Anise hyssop attracts bees for pollination of fruit trees that may be growing nearby. The plant is fragrant and the flowers make lovely arrangements.

(opposite) Annuals like sweet alyssum and signet marigolds attract beneficial insects and look good planted as a border or in among the vegetables. They are very useful for the kitchen garden.

CALENDULA (*Calendula officinalis*)
Annual
Site conditions: Full sun to part shade

Calendula is perfect for the kitchen garden. The edible flowers were once grown in monastic medicinal gardens and are still valued as a medicinal plant. I enjoy calendula because it's edible, has bright cheery flowers that bloom summer through fall, and it attracts beneficial insects to the garden. It is easy to grow from seed and the sunny flowers will reseed every year. Treat it as an annual and grow from seed every year or find a permanent place and allow it to reseed there. It will even reseed in pots that are left outdoors all winter.

The variety growing in my garden is yellow, and the seeds came from a Shaker kitchen garden in Kentucky. Calendula also comes in shades of orange, rust, and even orangey pink. It makes an excellent cut flower for the vase because the flowers are long lasting. The flowers can also be dried.

CONEFLOWER (*Echinacea*)
Perennial in zones 3 to 8
Site conditions: Prefers full sun; drought tolerant

Echinacea is truly an American plant, native to much of North America. *Echinacea purpurea* is native to the central and eastern part of the country, while *Echinacea pallida* is native to the west. Early Native Americans used the plant to cure wounds, infections, and as a general cure all.

Years ago I purchased purple coneflower seeds and periodically I walk my wildflower meadow and scatter seeds to ensure more purple coneflowers. The hybrid varieties don't spread by seed but you can now get interesting varied colors. The choice is immense: pale yellow, electric yellow, white, lime green, orange, pale pink, and variances of magenta. *Echinacea purpurea* 'Ruby Star' is vivid pink with the petals held horizontally. *Echinacea* 'Tiki Torch' has an intense orange color. *Echinacea purpurea*

'Hope' is pale pink and a portion of proceeds from purchase of this plant goes to the Susan G. Komen Foundation to benefit cancer research.

Coneflowers belong in the perennial border planted near the kitchen garden because they attract beneficial insects and birds to the summer garden. They prefer full sun and are drought tolerant. The stiff, upright flowers make excellent cut flowers for the vase. They are long lasting and provide cut blooms for the table from mid to late summer.

I enjoy the combination of Shasta daisies and 'White Swan' coneflower (*Echinacea purpurea*). The daisies bloom early and when they begin to fade the white daisy-like coneflowers bloom, so there is a continuation of cheery white flowers with yellow centers blooming in the garden. The uninitiated would think I had daisies blooming all summer. Different flower, same look.

DAYLILY (*Hemerocallis*)
Perennial in zones 3 to 9
Site conditions: Prefers full sun, tolerates some shade

Daylilies will grow just about anywhere, and the flowers come in every imaginable hue. Some rebloom for a long season of color, others bloom in one flush early, mid, or late in the season. In the southern United States some varieties are evergreen and so make a doubly useful plant in the border. Daylilies belong near the potager because each bloom, albeit only for a day, attracts beneficial insects to the garden. Of course, daylilies produce many blooms and the overall effect lasts many days. Daylilies in the border are part of a total scheme to have blooms for the table from spring through fall. Every now and then you may want to pop a blossom in your mouth or stuff it with herb cream cheese, dip it in batter, and fry it like a fritter. Just remove the stamen first; it will be more palatable.

Coneflowers like Echinacea *'Tiki Torch' make great cut flowers and belong in the perennial border planted near the kitchen garden, where they attract beneficial insects and birds in summer and fall.*

*(left) A single daylily flower of 'Buttered Popcorn' shares a vase with orange butterfly weed (*Asclepias tuberosa*). Daylilies attract beneficial insects in the garden, are edible, and can be cut for flower arrangements.*

Kate Pettegrew enjoys a cool summer drink with crushed mint and limes. The table is set with a vase of 'Little Lamb' hydrangeas gathered from the garden moments before we sat down in the garden to eat.

HYDRANGEA (*Hydrangea*)

Deciduous flowering shrub in zones 4 to 7 (varies with variety)

Site conditions: Shade to sun (depending on the variety)

Hydrangeas are some of the most valuable shrubs for the border inside or outside the home. These billowy, old fashioned blossoms brighten any corner, create space, and provide cut fresh and dried flowers for the table (see dried hydrangeas in the Winter chapter on page 200). *Hydrangea macrophylla* is hardy in zones 6 to 9. It is the most popular hydrangea and has colors ranging from bright pink to dark blue. Part of the color depends on the acidity of the soil. Acidic soil produces blue flowers, and alkaline soil, pink. This hydrangea is the same plant that florists use in containers. Most plants require shade and plenty of moisture. 'Beauté Vendômoise' is a cultivar of this species with lacecap blue flowers.

Hydrangea paniculata will take full sun conditions if it receives sufficient water until it is estab-lished. The plant will talk to you when it is thirsty; you will see it droop. This species is the most cold hardy hydrangea, from zone 4 to 7. 'Little Lamb' and 'Zwijnenburg' (Limelight) are two selections with creamy white flowers.

Oakleaf hydrangea (*Hydrangea quercifolia*) is native to the United States and produces white flowers with attractive leaves that turn red in fall. 'Alice' is a selection.

MARIGOLD (*Tagetes*)

Annual

Site conditions: Full sun

Marigolds are easy to grow from seed, add color to the kitchen garden, help repel pests, make excellent cut flowers, and some varieties are edible. Signet marigolds (*Tagetes tenuifolia*) produce tiny, color-ful, fragrant and edible flowers over lacy, fragrant foliage. The plants grow about a foot (30 cm) high, so make an excellent edger for the kitchen garden. 'Lemon Gem' and 'Tangerine Gem' each bear the fra-grance and color of their names. 'Starfire' is a range of orange and yellow. There is also a red variety, 'Red Gem'. Mexican mint marigold (*Tagetes lucida*) has tiny bright yellow flowers and aromatic leaves. It's also edible. French marigolds (*Tagetes patula*) have been effective at controlling nematodes in the soil.

NASTURTIUM (*Tropaeolum majus*)

Annual

Site conditions: Full sun; poor soil

This cheery flower comes in an array of colors and is easy to grow. It prefers cool weather and may languish in the heat of summer. The low-growing annual fits nicely in and among the vegetables in the kitchen garden. All parts of the flowers are edible. 'Empress of India' is still one of my favorite varieties and I find myself planting it again and again for its deep blue-green foliage and scarlet red flower.

ROSES (*Rosa*)
Perennial in zones 2 to 9 (depending on variety)
Site conditions: Full sun

I like to incorporate roses into mixed perennial and flowering shrub borders to add color and a few blossoms to cut and bring inside. It can be as simple as tucking a few plants in the perennial border. I confess I am not a rose aficionado. I just don't have the patience to coddle a plant so prone to leaf diseases, and for this reason I prefer the hardy shrub roses. They are disease resistant, cold hardy, grow on their own rootstocks, and have a long period of bloom. I get the joy of roses without the commitment. 'Therese Bugnet' (zones 3 to 7) has clear pink double, fragrant flowers. 'Nearly Wild' is a worry-free, heavy blooming small shrub rose with fragrant pink and white blossoms.

RUSSIAN SAGE (*Perovskia atriplicifolia*)
Perennial in zones 5 to 9
Site conditions: Prefers full sun; average soil; drought
    tolerant

I have a gardener friend who has difficulty growing Russian sage. It's not because she's a bad gardener. On the contrary, she can't grow this plant because her soil is too rich; she amends her soil too well. Russian sage grows on lean clay soil and takes little care and fussing. The plants are billowy, have a pleasant fragrance, and the blue flowers can be cut for arrangements. The feathery flowers will dry easily to extend your indoor arrangement.

SHASTA DAISY (*Leucanthemum*)
Perennial in zones 5 to 8
Site conditions: Prefers full sun

Shasta daisies bloom in early to mid summer. They are easy to grow and make excellent cut flowers for the vase. Are you planning a June wedding? Shasta daisies will probably be in bloom and can be cut for

Russian sage is the centerpiece for a summer meal at the home of Dean and Sally Schmitt.

bouquets or for table decorations. For my daughter's wedding we picked baskets full for informal flower arrangements at the back of the church. Shasta daisies are easily propagated every year; just divide the clump in early spring. 'Becky' grows larger than most cultivars topping out at 3 to 3 ½ feet (90–100 cm). 'Crazy Daisy' has a frilly double row of petals and multiple blossoms per stem.

STONECROP (*Sedum*)
Perennial in zones 3 to 10
Site conditions: Prefers full sun; drought tolerant

Sedum is a drought-tolerant and easy-to-grow perennial that likes full sun. 'Autumn Joy' looks good in the garden all year and every part of the plant can be used in the vase (see "Dried Flowers and Grasses" in the Winter chapter page 199). In the summer the flowers of this sedum transition from pale pink to deep rosy red. The light green succulent leaves

Dark purple, black, and lime green make a nice combination in this arrangement composed of the seed heads of Penstemon digitalis *'Huskers Red', the flowers of Thai basil, the pale flowers of* Sedum *'Autumn Joy', and the dark leaves of* Sedum *'Postman's Pride'.*

and broccoli-like flowers make interesting flower arrangements.

There are a number of dark-leafed varieties with color variations from dark red purple to black. 'Postman's Pride' is a hybrid with dark purple, almost black leaves. The flowers are a bright pink, but not the most interesting part of the plant. 'Black Jack' emerges with green and light purple leaves in the spring that darken to a deep purple-black.

SUNFLOWER (*Helianthus annuus*)
Annual
Site conditions: Full sun; well-drained soil

Sunflowers are easy to grow in and around the kitchen garden. Just for the fun of it plant one of the towering 10-foot (3-m) tall varieties and create a jungle for the little ones in your life. Native Americans cultivated sunflowers for the edible seed. Sunflowers attract birds to the garden. See also perennial sunflowers in the Fall chapter (page 164).

YARROW (*Achillea*)
Perennial in zones 3 to 10
Site conditions: Prefers full sun; drought tolerant

Yarrow is an all-around excellent flower in the border or in the vase. The tall bright blossoms with fragrant gray green leaves bloom in mid to late summer and both flowers and foliage can be used to make arrangements or wreaths. Yarrow is drought tolerant and the flowers are excellent for drying. Just cut some stems and put them in a vase with or without water. They will dry indoors and hold the vibrant color all winter.

Yarrow blooms in a variety of colors from pink and pale cream to brick red and variations of yellow. 'Coronation Gold' has been growing in my garden for years; the bright gold yellow flat-topped flowers are attractive. I prefer it to 'Moonshine'. 'Walter Funke' has flowers that emerge bright red with yellow and fades to shades of copper and peach.

Hover flies like to sip nectar from the tiny blooms of yarrow. It's good to attract these insects to the kitchen garden because their larvae are voracious eaters. One of their favorite snacks is aphids.

ZINNIA (*Zinnia*)
Annual
Site conditions: Full sun

Zinnias come in an array of colors and sizes and belong in and among the vegetables in the kitchen garden. Browse a catalog and choose your favorite. Zinnias attract butterflies and beneficial insects, so are part of strategy for growing without the use of pesticides. And they look pretty. This is an easy-to-grow annual for every garden.

Yellow yarrow, purple coneflowers, and blue Russian sage are the perfect trifecta of summer. They each are easy to grow and look great in the garden or in a vase.

Design for Summer

CULINARY HERB GARDEN

In early medieval drawings of kitchen gardens the medicinal herb garden, or garden of simples, is located separately from the vegetable garden. You see this separation at the recreated medieval garden at the Château de Villandry in France, one of the most monumental kitchen gardens in the world. It's brilliant really. It just makes sense to dedicate a special place for those herbs that come up year after year or in mild climates are evergreen.

I have adopted this concept in my own designs not because of any symbolism but because it's practical. It's easier to maintain the garden when you separate edible perennials and edible annuals. Many of the culinary herbs are perennial or they act like perennials because they reseed and come up in the same place.

The themed culinary garden is the new medicinal garden so dedicate a permanent space in your landscape for perennial herbs. It doesn't hurt to tuck in a few annual herbs as well. In my garden that would be basil, parsley, chervil, and marjoram. These annuals belong everywhere—in the herb garden, the mixed border, and in the vegetable garden.

The design shown here is at the entrance to a fenced-in kitchen garden. The culinary herbs are outside the fence. The stone pathway is in a bed of thyme. The design also features some flowering and fruiting shrubs. 'Hahs' American cranberry bush viburnum is one of the best native viburnums for edible fruit; the shrub provides year-round interest and structure to this bed.

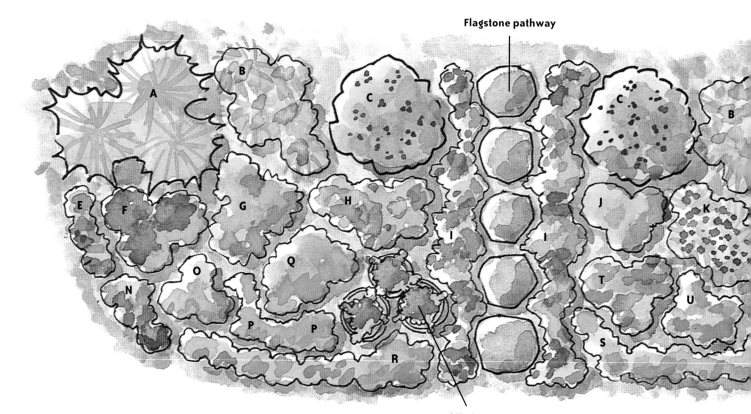

Flagstone pathway

Pots filled with mint and herbs

LABEL	NO. OF PLANTS	COMMON NAME	SCIENTIFIC NAME
A	3	'Northwind' switchgrass	*Panicum* 'Northwind'
B	10	'Rocket City' daylily	*Hemerocallis* 'Rocket City'
C	2	'Hahs' American cranberry bush viburnum	*Viburnum trilobum* 'Hahs'
D	1	'Wentworth' American cranberry bush viburnum	*Viburnum trilobum* 'Wentworth'
E	3	'Siam Queen' Thai basil	*Ocimum basilicum* 'Siam Queen'
F	3	Spanish lavender	*Lavandula stoechas*
G	3	'Tuscan Blue' rosemary	*Rosmarinus officinalis* 'Tuscan Blue'
H	6	'Tricolor' sage	*Salvia officinalis* 'Tricolor'
I	21	thyme (plant variety)	*Thymus* spp.
J	3	summer savory	*Satureja hortensis*
K	7	chives	*Allium schoenoprasum*
L	5	dill	*Anethum graveolens*
M	3	'Provence' lavender	*Lavandula ×intermedia* 'Provence'
N	6	'Osmin' purple basil	*Ocimum basilicum* 'Osmin'
O	3	cutting celery	*Apium graveolens*
P	7	'Genovese' basil	*Ocimum basilicum* 'Genovese'
Q	7	cilantro	*Coriandrum sativum*
R	10	flat leaf Italian parsley	*Petroselinum crispum* var. *neapolitanum*
S	9	marjoram	*Origanum marjorana*
T	3	'African Blue' basil	*Ocimum basilicum* 'African Blue'
U	5	'Cinnamon' basil	*Ocimum basilicum* 'Cinnamon'
V	5	tarragon	*Artemisia dracunculus*
W	3	shiso	*Perilla frutescens*
X	5	'Berggarten' sage	*Salvia officinalis* 'Berggarten'

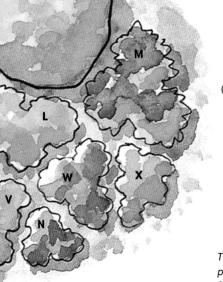

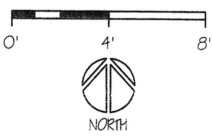

This culinary herb garden is at the entrance to a formal kitchen garden; it makes sense to separate the perennial herbs from the annual vegetables. There are a few flowering shrubs and perennials mixed up for variety in this herb garden.

PERENNIALS NEAR THE POTAGER

One of the most exciting things to me as a designer is incorporating flowers, grasses, and shrubs into the landscape because of the diversity they bring to the kitchen garden. The goal is to plan a garden with perennials and shrubs that bloom in succession and meet the habitat needs of beneficial insects the entire growing season. Plant a garden where something is always blooming. What a wonderful coincidence: the flowers we love to look at and pick for arrangements are often the plants that predatory insects seek for nectar and pollen.

Our vegetable gardens should not be isolated at the edge of our lawns. Rather, they should be integrated with a diverse system of plants. This is the vision: to transform our residential landscapes into havens that sustain a variety of insects and wildlife.

Pest management may be as simple as enlarging your mixed borders and planting them near the annual vegetable garden. It may help to add annual flowers to the vegetable garden. Biological pest control is more complex than that and beyond the scope of this book, but much is being discovered on that topic. Scientific research does show that attracting beneficial insects helps to control the insects that eat our beans and cabbage leaves.

Perennials can be planted near the vegetable garden. They add beauty and fragrance while providing pretty petals to snip for the vase. I find it most convenient to plant perennial flowers with perennial edibles and annual flowers with the annual vegetables.

This design for a formal potager demonstrates how the mixed perennial and flowering shrub border is related to the kitchen garden. The flowers selected for the plan attract beneficial insects or are used for cut flowers. The flowers and shrubs help define the space of the garden, as does the raised hedge of pleached trees.

This vignette is part of a mixed border of shrubs and perennials with multiseason bloom. The flowers either attract beneficial insects or are cut for use indoors. The design of flowering shrubs, perennials, and grasses complements the formal kitchen garden which is on the other side of the fence. The sketch illustrates how to bring color to the working garden. The goal is to integrate the vegetable garden to the rest of the landscape and that is done best by bordering the kitchen garden with shrubs, grasses, and perennials. The shrubs and perennials follow a general order of tall in the back, medium in the middle, and shortest in the front of the border. The bloom time is also staggered with the goal of something in bloom through the season.

Mixed border near the potager to attract beneficial insects or for cut flowers throughout the season.

LABEL	NO. OF PLANTS	COMMON NAME	SCIENTIFIC NAME	ZONE	NOTES
A	2	'Northwind' switchgrass	*Panicum* 'Northwind'	5–9	ornamental grass with year-round interest
B	1	'Winterthur' viburnum	*Viburnum nudum* 'Winterthur'	5–9	spring flowers; fall color and fruit; attracts butterflies
C	1	Autumn Sun black-eyed Susan	*Rudbeckia nitida* 'Herbstsonne'	4–9	tall plant, 5–8 ft.; attracts monarchs and beneficial insects summer–winter; fall bloom
D	3	'Husker Red' beardtongue	*Penstemon digitalis* 'Husker Red'	3–8	bronze foliage spring–fall; white summer flowers
E	3	'Fragrant Angel' coneflower	*Echinacea purpurea* 'Fragrant Angel'	3–8	white flowers summer–fall; U.S. native; winter interest
F	3	chives	*Allium schoenoprasum*	3–11	spring bloom; edible leaves and flowers in summer

FORMAL POTAGER: SUMMER

This is the summer planting plan for the formal potager introduced in spring (page 56). The plan shows the vegetables, herbs, and flowers suitable for a zone 8 garden in summer, all safe to plant after the frost-free date. The garden in the summer overflows with color. Annual flowers like 'Wonderland Blue' alyssum, 'Profusion Orange' zinnia, and 'Tangerine Gem' marigold (*Tagetes tenuifolia*) add bright splashes of color but they are tucked in as edgers because they attract beneficial insects to the garden. 'Orange Porcupine' calendula is also edible.

Willow tee pees provide the structure for the warm-season vines like 'Purple Podded' pole beans and 'Dragon Tongue' pole bean. There is enough room for tomatoes, eggplant, and several kinds of basil. The sprawling squash can be trained up a trellis or left to flow into the walkways. We will see this garden again, in fall (page 56).

Bed 1
22 'Wonderland Blue' alyssum
'Kentucky Wonder' pole bean

Bed 2
3 'Pomme d'Or' squash
22 'Tangerine Gem' marigold
3 ground cherry

Bed 3
22 'Tangerine Gem' marigold
4 'Cinnamon' basil
3 'Lemon' cucumber

Bed 4
22 'Wonderland Blue' alyssum
'Dragon Tongue' pole bean

Bed 5
22 'Profusion Orange' zinnia
4 'Aunt Hettie's Red' okra

Bed 6
1 'Green Zebra' tomato
4 'Red Rubin' basil
9 'Sweet Genovese' basil

Bed 7
1 'Dr. Wyche's Yellow' tomato
4 curly parsley
9 sweet marjoram

Bed 8
22 'Profusion Orange' zinnia
4 'Long Purple' eggplant

Bed 9
22 'Profusion Orange' zinnia
4 'Toma Verde' tomatillo

Bed 10
1 'Amish Paste' tomato
4 'Mrs. Burns' lemon' basil
9 flat leaf Italian parsley

Bed 11
4 'African Blue' basil
9 'Sweet Genovese' basil
1 'Principe Borghese' plum tomato

Bed 12
4 peppers
22 'Profusion Orange' zinnia

Bed 13
22 'Wonderland Blue' alyssum
scarlet runner beans

Bed 14
3 'Lemon' squash
3 'Red' shiso
18 'Orange Porcupine' calendula

Bed 15
3 'White' acorn squash
18 'Orange Porcupine' calendula

Bed 16
'Purple Podded' pole bean
22 'Wonderland Blue' alyssum

SUMMER PLANTING PLAN OF A FORMAL POTAGER

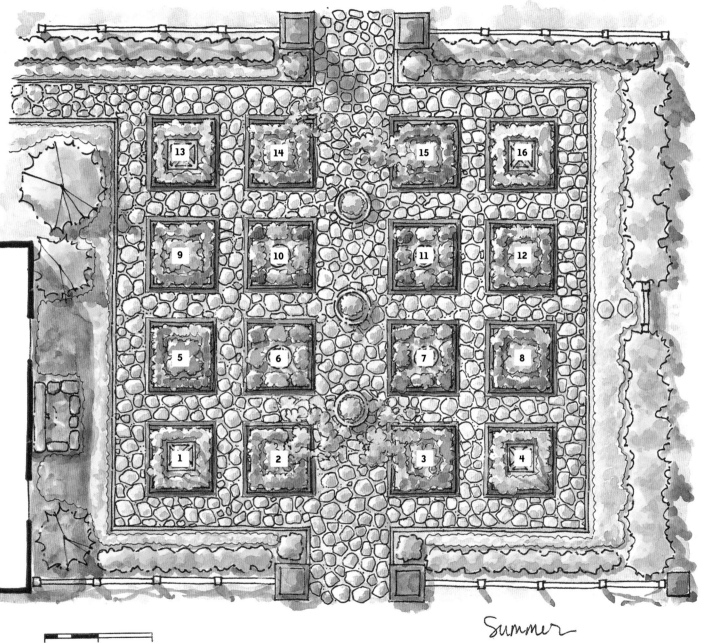

Summer

0' 4' 8'

NORTH

EDIBLE FRONT YARD: SUMMER

In summer the seasonal front-yard garden (first shown on page 60) features shrubs, grasses, perennials, and more edibles. Strawberries that were blooming in the spring now form a nice groundcover for the rest of the season. Rhubarb continues to look good in the garden even though it has passed the time for harvesting. Shasta daisies are in bloom followed by the coneflowers which will continue into the fall. Anise hyssop begins its bloom of bright blue-purple flowers that attract bees. The daylilies bloom in orange in this garden. Catmint continues to bloom and surrounds the spot for the annual herbs and vegetables in the center of the garden. Basil and other culinary annuals can be planted after the frost-free date. There is room for tomato or pepper plants as well.

0'   8'   16'

NORTH

Summer

Summer Chores

☑ Feed plants regularly with an organic or slow-release fertilizer.

☑ Check plants for disease and damage from insects. Hand pick cabbage worms. Kill Japanese beetles by picking them off and placing them in soapy water. Use a mild soap solution to kill aphids.

☑ Remove cool-season plants that have gone to seed and toss them in the compost.

☑ Deadhead perennials that have finished blooming. Some of these perennials will rebloom. Remove spent flowers and leaves of chives; they will rebloom sporadically through the summer.

☑ Keep a garden journal. Record keeping can be as simple as placing tags of perennials and annuals in a box; at least you have a record of the varieties. It can be a sketch and date book with notes of when things bloom and planting plans. I have a friend who staples tags on the inside of a journal. For me, currently my camera is my best tool. I photograph plants as they grow. It's an accurate record of bloom times with dates.

☑ Sow seeds of cool-season vegetables that have a long growing season. Plant cauliflower, parsnips, Brussels sprouts, Swiss chard, cabbage, and broccoli in midsummer so that they are near maturity by frost.

SUMMER MENUS

One
Grilled Flank Steak with Hot Pepper and Herb Marinade or Grilled Summer Vegetable Enchiladas with Green Tomatillo Sauce
Grilled Corn on the Cob with Cilantro Butter
Summer Greens and Roasted Cherry Tomatoes with Thyme
World's Best Blueberry Pie
Bouquet of sunflowers, Russian sage, and black-eyed Susans

Two
Rosemary Chicken or Grilled Summer Vegetable Gyros
Tzatziki
Skordalia
Tabbouleh
Greek Salad
Green Beans with Lemon
Blackberries and Peaches with Mint Cream
Bouquet of white hydrangeas

Three
Braised Brisket and Red Onion Fajitas or Grilled Summer Vegetable Fajitas
Roasted Red Pepper and Corn Salsa
Cilantro Salsa
Pico de Gallo
Decadent Peach Ice Cream
Bouquet of pink hydrangeas, anise hyssop, dill, and helenium

Four
Garlic Chicken Skewers
Spicy Garden Curry on Rice
Cool Yogurt Sauce
Hot Peach Chutney
Yogurt Pound Cake with Red Raspberry Coulis
Bouquet of purple coneflowers, yarrow, sunflowers, Russian sage

Fall

F ALL IS A BOUNTIFUL TIME of the year. The summer fruits and vegetables are still abundant but the tinges of vibrant orange appearing on the sugar maple signal shorter days and cooler nights. It is a transition time. Harvest the last of the warm-season produce and set out the plants of the cool-season vegetables.

If tomatoes or peppers are languishing or are diseased, pull them out to plant the cool-season vegetables and greens. Sometimes it is difficult to pull out perfectly good heat-loving, producing plants, but it has to be done to give enough time for the new plants to grow before the weather is too cold.

Fall is a time for family and celebration—Halloween, apple butter parties, harvest festivities, and finally Thanksgiving. Cabbages and kale, carrots and cucurbits, the colors of the season are purple and orange.

Purple artichokes are grown as an annual in cooler zones and need a long growing season. In zone 8 climates artichokes are perennial.

Cool-Season Vegetables

Cabbages growing in the Bolen potager in Oklahoma. Garden design by John Fluitt.

Vegetables and greens that prefer cool weather are back on the menu. The difference between spring cool-season vegetables and fall cool-season vegetables is the length of time they happily stay in the garden. In the spring cool days are waning with the onset of longer and progressively warmer summer days. Now the days are getting shorter and cooler; vegetables like broccoli, cauliflower and Brussels sprouts that have a long growing season can stay for a while with out bolting or withering. These crops are frost tolerant and even get sweeter when tinged with a few frosts. Kale and mustards bolt when the days get warm. Now, with the days getting cooler they are less likely to do so.

(opposite) Fall is a transition time in the author's potager; frost has killed the basil and heat-loving vegetables but the calendula flowers are still blooming. Cabbages, kale, lettuce, beets, Swiss chard, and cutting celery are thriving.

132

ARTICHOKE (*Cynara scolymus*)
Perennial in zone 8; annual in cooler climates
Seed to table: 85 to 100 days

Harvest artichokes that were grown as annual plants when the buds are still tightly closed. When you eat an artichoke you are actually consuming the immature flower. See more on artichoke in the Spring chapter (page 22).

BEETS (*Beta vulgaris*)
Biennial grown as an annual
Seed to table: 45 to 58 days

Sow beet seeds outdoors at the beginning of fall for a second crop of beets. Try and get the seeds planted about eight weeks before the expected frost. Beets are frost tolerant and even the seedlings will do fine in cool weather. Cover with cloches for late-fall protection.

Beets planted in the fall should be allowed to grow to maturity and left in the ground until then. They will store for a longer period of time.

Harvested beets will keep in the refrigerator for a few weeks. Remove all of the leaves and stem before storing. See more on beets in the Spring chapter (page 23).

BROCCOLI (*Brassica oleracea* Italica Group)
Annual
Seed to table: 45 to 95 days

Late summer is a good time to plant broccoli seeds outdoors in the garden so that the heads mature in the cool weather. Broccoli is frost tolerant, so in mild climates some varieties can be planted in the fall, left in the garden through the winter, and harvested in the early spring.

'Early Purple Sprouting' broccoli is an English heirloom that has been bred for overwintering. It produces a small central head with numerous purple sprouts and side shoots. If you live in the northern

Artichoke and Spinach Pizza

Makes 2 (12-inch) pizzas
1 cup unbleached flour
1 cup whole wheat flour
2½ teaspoons yeast
½ teaspoon salt
¼ cup extra virgin olive oil, plus more
¾ cup very warm water
4 small artichoke hearts
Lemon juice
3 garlic cloves, chopped
4 cups fresh spinach, chopped
Salt and freshly ground pepper
1 cup mozzarella cheese, grated
1 cup parmesan cheese, coarsely grated

To make the pizza crust, combine the flours, yeast, salt, ¼ cup olive oil, and water in a mixer at a moderate speed until well blended. Knead with a dough hook for 10 minutes. Sometimes weather effects the amount of flour required so adjust as needed. The dough should be soft and pliable but not overly sticky. Place additional olive oil at the bottom of a bowl, place the ball of dough in and swirl to coat. Cover and let rise in a warm place for an hour.

To prepare the artichoke hearts, cut off bottom stem and tip of artichokes. Place in a pot of water and add enough water to halfway cover the artichokes. Squeeze some lemon juice into the water. Cover with a lid and cook over high heat until artichokes are tender, about 20 minutes, depending on the size. Cool and remove leaves. Eat the sweet artichoke from the bottom of each leaf, or save them for another time. Remove choke and discard. Scrape away all chokes from the heart. Chop the heart into small pieces. Set aside.

Place a skillet over medium-high heat and add a drizzle of olive oil. Add the chopped artichoke hearts, garlic, and spinach, cooking just until the spinach is wilted. Add salt and pepper to taste. Set aside.

To assemble the pizzas, preheat oven to 375°F. Flatten risen dough into two circles on a cookie sheet that has been lightly oiled with olive oil. Spread the spinach and artichoke mixture on top of the pizza dough; sprinkle with the cheeses and bake for 20–25 minutes until the cheese is melted and bubbly and the crust is browned. Serve immediately.

Cut through a 'Chioggia' beet to reveal the candylike stripes.

Harvest Brussels sprouts after a few light frosts, but before the ground freezes in early winter.

half of the United States, plant 'Early Purple Sprouting' in late summer (at the end of August) to harvest in midautumn (at the end of October). This variety takes 60 days from seed to harvest.

'Natalino' is a Romanesco variety that produces conical, chartreuse, spiral heads and is excellent for fall harvest. It takes 90 days to mature; plant in midsummer (mid July) to harvest in midautumn (mid October).

Broccoli florets and small leaves are best eaten raw, but if you must cook it, do so quickly—lightly sautéed with good olive oil or steamed. See more on broccoli in the Spring chapter (page 25).

BRUSSELS SPROUTS (*Brassica oleracea* Gemmifera Group)
Annual
Seed to table: 85 to 105 days

Plant Brussels sprouts in the garden about 2 feet (60 cm) apart. They are a cool weather crop with a long growing season, so they do best as a fall crop. Plant

Simply Roasted Brussels Sprouts

Roasting at high heat brings out the flavor. The key to the sweet taste is using fresh sprouts that are harvested young in cool weather after a few frosts and then cooking them quickly.

Serves 4–6
3 tablespoons olive oil
1 pound fresh Brussels sprouts
Few sprigs of fresh thyme, chopped
Coarse salt

Preheat oven to 425°F. Cut the Brussels sprouts in half so that they cook evenly. Drizzle the olive oil in a heavy Dutch oven, add the Brussels sprouts, stirring them around so they are coated with the oil. Add the thyme and salt to taste. Stir a few more minutes before placing the pan in the oven. Roast uncovered for 25–30 minutes. Serve immediately with pasta or as a side dish.

'Violet Queen' cauliflower turns green when cooked and tastes like broccoli.

them in midsummer and harvest them in the fall. Their flavor is best when they are harvested after a few light frosts to bring out the natural sweetness. Harvest a few at a time from the plant or pull up the entire plant and slice the individual baby cabbages into a dish.

CARROTS (*Daucus carota*)
Biennial grown as an annual
Seed to table: 52 to 70 days

Harvest carrots that were sown in midsummer before the ground freezes. In mild climates carrots can be covered with mulch and left in the ground over the winter. See more on carrots in the Spring and Summer chapters (pages 25 and 66, respectively).

CAULIFLOWER (*Brassica oleracea* Botrytis Group)
Annual
Seed to table: 54 to 80 days

Cauliflower seeds can be directly sown in the garden in midsummer so the cauliflower head matures before it gets too cold. Cauliflower tolerates some

frost and has the best flavor when it matures in cool weather. Thin the seedlings so the plants are about 24 inches (60 cm) apart.

When the cauliflower head begins to form and is about the size of a golf ball, tie the outer leaves around the head with twine or secure with rubber bands or clothes pins to protect it from light. The heads will be ready for harvesting one to two weeks later when they are still firm and about 6 inches (15 cm) in diameter.

'Violet Queen' is a purple variety; it looks like purple broccoli and turns green when cooked. 'Cheddar' is an orange cauliflower. White varieties need blanching to keep them white and sweet. See more on cauliflower in the Spring chapter (page 25).

FENNEL (*Foeniculum vulgare*)
Annual as bulb fennel; perennial in zones 4 to 9 as herb fennel
Seed to table: 70 to 80 days for bulb fennel, 50 to 60 days for herb fennel

Herb fennel is grown for its feathery fernlike licorice leaves and Florence fennel is grown for its bulbous stem. The white bulbs are overlapping layers that transition to a pale green stalk with dill-like feathery aromatic leaves. All parts of the plant are edible but the crunchy licorice-flavored bulb is great cooked in a variety of ways, including stir-fried with Asian vegetables, sautéed with butter, or braised in the oven. Sometimes it's the secret ingredient in soups or chopped raw in salads.

'Zefa Fino' is an Italian variety. 'Trieste' is a French hybrid that is bolt resistant and bred for sweet anise flavor.

Fennel grows best in cool conditions. It can be planted in spring or in midsummer for fall harvest. Seed directly in the garden and thin seedlings to 12 to 18 inches (30–45 cm) apart. Fennel is a heavy feeder so add fertilizer or fish emulsion every three weeks. See more on fennel in the Summer chapter (page 108).

Fennel Pickles

The crispy licorice taste of fennel is preserved in these refrigerator pickles. They are best served cold after a week of marinating and keep up to three months in the refrigerator. Use with sandwiches or as a relish to accompany other dishes.

Makes 2 quart or 4 pint jars
4 cups bulb fennel
2 cups (1 large) sweet onion, sliced
2 small hot peppers, halved
2 garlic cloves, halved
4 cups cider vinegar (5% acidity)
2 cups sugar
1 teaspoon turmeric
1 teaspoon celery seed

(continued)

Bulb fennel is grown for the licorice flavored bulb, which can be roasted or cut up raw to add crunchiness to salads.

1 tablespoon coriander seed
½ teaspoon ground mustard

Sterilize 2 quart jars *or* 4 pint jars and set aside.

Slice the white fennel bulb with some of the green stem and feathery leaves; discard the rest of the stems and leaves. Place the fennel, onion, peppers, and garlic in a large bowl and mix well. Divide the vegetables between sterilized jars, packing them to within ½ inch (12 mm) of the top.

In a stainless steel pot, heat the vinegar, sugar, and spices to boiling. Boil for about 5 minutes. Pour into packed jars. Screw on metal lids. Bring to room temperature then refrigerate.

Plant garlic in the fall at the same time you plant daffodil and tulip bulbs. Be sure the pointy tip faces up.

GARLIC (*Allium sativum*)
Annual bulb
Seed to table: 6 months

Plant garlic in the fall anytime before the ground freezes. It is really easy to do. Break seed heads into individual cloves just before planting. Insert one clove into the soil with the pointy end at the top. Plant each clove about 6 inches (15 cm) apart in rich soil 3 to 4 inches (7.5–10 cm) deep. The garlic will be fully ripe and ready for harvest next summer, although immature (green) garlic can be harvested earlier, in spring (see page 26).

Try varieties that are suitable for your climate. This year I planted 'New York White', a softneck variety, and 'German Extra Hardy', a hardneck variety. Both of these do well in northern climates. See more on garlic in the Summer chapter (page 72).

JERUSALEM ARTICHOKE (*Helianthus tuberosus*)
Perennial in zones 3 to 9, grown from a tuber
Planting to table: 120 days or more

Jerusalem artichokes are perennial sunflowers native to central and eastern North America. The tall plant produces sunny yellow daisylike flowers in late summer and fall. In the fall it also produces edible tubers. The tubers are best dug after a few frosts. Dig up the roots like you would potatoes. The tubers can be peeled and chopped for stir-fries, roasted or eaten raw in salads. The starch in the tubers can be tolerated by diabetics.

Plant Jerusalem artichokes in a place where they can spread, because they will. Grow the 6- to 8-foot (1.8- to 2.4-m) plants around a compost area to help screen the view.

LEEKS (*Allium ampeloprasum* Porrum Group)
Annual
Planting to table: 120 to 150 days

Harvest leeks when young for thin slender stalks and use like green onions or leave leeks in the garden through the winter for large thick stems. Recommended heirloom varieties to overwinter are 'American Flag' and 'Musselburgh'. Thoroughly wash leeks after you pluck them from the ground. The multiple layers of leaves are notorious for trapping bits of dirt. The entire leek can be used from the green tops to the white stalk. See more on leeks in the Spring chapter (page 27).

ONIONS (*Allium*)
Biennial grown as an annual
Seed to table: 40 to 50 days for green onions, 90 to 120 days for bulb onions

In warm climates sow seeds outdoors from late summer to midautumn (the end of August to the beginning of October) for winter bulb onions. In warm climates onions will remain in the garden all

Plant Jerusalem artichokes at the edge of your property where the tall plants have room to spread.

(left) Jerusalem artichoke tubers have been enjoyed as a food staple in this country for centuries. The crunchy roots can be roasted or stir-fried.

The best varieties of pumpkins for baking are small and stringless. Try the heirloom variety 'New England Pie'.

winter. A favorite mini-onion for fall planting is *Allium cepa* 'Bianca di Maggio' cipollini. Try planting seeds of *Allium fistulosum* 'Evergreen Hardy White', a cold hardy Welsh onion. See more on onions in the Spring and Summer chapters (pages 28 and 74, respectively).

POTATOES (*Solanum tuberosum*)
Annual grown from a tuber
Planting to table: 50 to 120 days

Continue to dig up potatoes when the foliage dies back. By early fall, harvest the last of the late-variety potatoes. First cut back any remaining foliage and compost it. Leave the potatoes in the ground as long as possible for storage potatoes. Gather them just before the ground freezes. Use a pitch fork to dig up all of the potatoes. Don't wash them for storage. Allow them to dry in a single layer in a dark place. Store them in boxes in a cool, dark place, like a basement. See more on potatoes in the Spring and Summer chapters (pages 29 and 80, respectively).

PUMPKIN (*Cucurbita*)
Annual
Seed to table: 110 to 120 days

Harvest pumpkins by cutting the stem with a knife. Make sure you leave enough on the pumpkin so you have a handle. Pumpkins can be left in the garden as the vines die back. Bring them into the house before it frosts.

Roasted potatoes with rosemary and herbs will heat up a cool kitchen.

Crispy Roasted Potatoes with Rosemary and Herbs

Serves 4
6–8 potatoes with skins
Extra virgin olive oil
Coarse salt
2–3 tablespoons fresh rosemary, chopped
2 tablespoons fresh thyme, chopped
Salt and freshly ground pepper

Preheat oven to 400°F. Wash the potatoes and cut off any green or bad spots. Cut into bite-size pieces but do not peel. Swirl a little olive oil in a roasting pan and add the potatoes. Stir to coat. Add the fresh herbs and stir well. Sprinkle generously with salt and pepper to taste. Roast in a hot oven for 25–30 minutes or until potatoes are hot and crispy. Serve immediately.

RADISHES (*Raphanus sativus*)
Annual
Seed to table: 22 to 40 days

Everything that makes pumpkin pie creamy, sweet, and spicy is baked inside the shell for inside out pumpkin pie. The filling and pumpkin are baked together.

Inside-Out Pumpkin Pie

Serves 8
3 small pie pumpkins
1 cup sugar
3 eggs
1 can (12 ounces) evaporated milk
1 teaspoon vanilla
2 teaspoons ground cinnamon
½ teaspoon ground ginger
½ teaspoon fresh ginger root, grated
3 tablespoons butter, melted

Preheat oven to 350°F. Prepare the pumpkins by cutting off their tops. Scoop out and discard the strings and seeds. In a mixing bowl, whisk together the sugar and eggs until well mixed. Beat in evaporated milk, vanilla, spices and melted butter. Blend well.

Pour the filling mixture into the prepared pumpkins, dividing evenly between the pumpkins. Bake filled pumpkins for 45–60 minutes.

Radishes are back in the garden in the fall. You can plant again the small round quick-growing radishes of spring or try some specialty varieties that mature best in the fall. These need to mature into the cool fall weather. Watermelon radish is a large radish with pink flesh and good flavor. Black radishes from northern Europe are large and can be sliced and served with multigrain bread for a quick meal. The black radishes store well. German beer radishes are long and white and can be served up with salt and your favorite fall brew. See more on radishes in the Spring chapter (page 30).

SHALLOTS (*Allium cepa* Aggreatum Group)
Annual grown from a bulb
Planting to table: 80 to 90 days

Plant shallots in fall in fertile soil about 6 inches (15 cm) apart and 4 inches (10 cm) deep. Place the root end down in the soil. One bulb will multiply into numerous clusters next spring. See more on shallots in the Spring chapter (page 32).

SQUASH (*Cucurbita*)
Annual
Seed to table: 48 to 68 days for summer squash, 80 to
    120 days for winter squash

Continue to harvest summer squash when the fruits are small before the first frost. Winter varieties are harvested at the mature stage and should be allowed to ripen outside until the first frost. See more on squash in the Summer and Winter chapters (pages 81 and 186, respectively).

SWEET POTATOES (*Ipomoea batatas*)
Perennial grown as an annual from a tuber
Planting to table: 90 to 140 days

Harvest sweet potato tubers when the leaves begin to turn yellow and die back before frost. If there is a light frost, the vines will be instantly killed but the tubers will be fine. Use a shovel or large fork and be careful not to damage the tubers as you dig them up.

Cure the sweet potatoes indoors in a warm (65 to 75°F) and humid room for two to three weeks. Curing helps to increase sugar content; the skin forms a coating at this time that will improve the long-term storage potential. Move to a dark location for long storage that stays above 50°F, or cook and freeze. See more on sweet potatoes in the Summer chapter (page 82).

A stack of heirloom pumpkins and squashes create a colorful display at the front door.

Cook squash including pumpkin by cutting into slices and roasting until soft, then remove the rind.

Squash soup with chopped leaves of cutting celery for garnish.

Squash Soup

Serves 6
1 Blue Hubbard or other winter squash
2 leeks, white part only, chopped
6–8 green onions, white and green parts chopped
    separately
2 tablespoons butter, melted
1½ quarts chicken stock
Cutting celery, chopped (optional)

Preheat oven to 325°F. Prepare the squash by slicing into large chunks. Remove the seeds and discard. Place the pieces on a cookie sheet and roast in the oven for 1 hour. When the squash is done cooking, remove and discard the rind; cut into smaller chunks and set aside.

In a large soup pot, melt the butter and sauté the leeks and the white part of the onions. Add the cooked squash and the chicken broth. Cook until the squash is soft, about an hour, adding more stock if necessary. Puree in a blender until smooth. Serve with a garnish of green onion tops and cutting celery.

Sweet Potato Muffins

This is a great way to use sweet potatoes. This muffin is perfect to make in the fall and is great to make on a blustery day. Make a double batch and serve for breakfast or a snack. The simple sweet potato flavor is not covered up with spices or added flavorings. The puree can be prepared a few days ahead of time and stored in the refrigerator. It can also be frozen in small batches to make muffins another day.

Make 1 dozen muffins
1¼ cup sweet potato, cooked and pureed (2 small sweet
    potatoes)
½ cup butter
1 cup sugar
½ cup brown sugar
2 tablespoons molasses
2 eggs
1½ cups unbleached flour
2 teaspoons baking powder
½ teaspoon salt

To make the puree, preheat oven to 350°F. Wrap sweet potatoes in foil. If using one large potato, cut it in half before wrapping each half in foil. Bake for 45–60 minutes or until the sweet potatoes are soft. When potatoes are cool enough to handle, remove the skins by cutting them away with a knife. Place the sweet potato in a food processor and puree. Cool completely before proceeding.

On the day the muffins are made, preheat oven to 350°F. Thoroughly cream butter and sugars in a mixer until light. Add in the molasses and continue blending. Add in the eggs one at a time and mix well. Add the sweet potato puree and blend well. In a separate bowl, combine the flour, baking powder, and salt; stir by hand to mix. Pour the dry ingredients into the batter and mix just enough to combine everything. Pour into a prepared muffin pan. Bake for 30 minutes or until done.

Harvest the Last of Summer

Basil retains its color and flavor when it is dried quickly in the microwave. Basil will turn black at the first freeze so the bounty needs to either be made into pesto and frozen or be dried for soups and stews in the winter.

WARM-SEASON VEGGIES

Many of summer's vegetables and herbs will continue to grow into fall, albeit much more slowly, and can be harvested up until the first frost.

TOMATOES (*Lycopersicum*)

Gather the last of the tomatoes before the first frost to make sauce or to freeze for use later. To prepare tomatoes for freezing, wash and core them, then place them whole on cookie sheets and set in the freezer. Don't worry about peeling the tomatoes; the skins can be removed later as you cook with them . Place the frozen tomatoes in glass jars or sealable plastic bags and store in the freezer.

Cherry and paste tomatoes are excellent dried. If you live in a very dry, hot climate like the U.S. South-

The last summer vegetables in the garden are put to good use in tofu kabobs for the vegetarians and sirloin kabobs for the meat eaters, accompanied by Béarnaise sauce for dipping.

Tofu or Sirloin Kabobs with Béarnaise Sauce

This recipe makes two kinds of kabobs—tofu for the vegetarians and steak for the meat eaters. I always make and cook each separately. Add the bounty from the last of the summer garden to the skewers, including onions, peppers, summer squash, and eggplant. The marinade makes use of summer herbs, and the Béarnaise sauce with fresh tarragon blends perfectly with the meat and grilled tofu.

Makes 6 tofu skewers and 6 steak skewers

¼ cup extra-virgin olive oil
Juice of 1 lemon
3 garlic cloves, minced
2 tablespoons fresh cilantro, finely chopped
2 tablespoons fresh tarragon leaves, finely chopped
Salt and freshly ground pepper
1–1½ pounds sirloin, cut in large cubes
1 package (16 ounces) very firm tofu, drained and cut in cubes
1 red sweet pepper, stemmed
1 large sweet onion
8 ounces portobello mushrooms
Béarnaise Sauce (recipe follows)

(continued)

In a large bowl, combine the oil, lemon juice, garlic, cilantro, tarragon, and salt and pepper to taste. Mix well. Pour half of the marinade in another large bowl. In one bowl add the steak chunks and half the vegetables. In the second bowl add the tofu and the other half of the vegetables. Cover both bowls and refrigerate for 15 minutes.

Cut the sweet pepper, onion, and mushrooms into large pieces. To assemble kabobs, lace the vegetables and steak or tofu on separate skewers, being careful to keep the tofu skewers separate from the steak skewers. Grill until done and vegetables are just cooked. Serve with Béarnaise sauce on the side.

Béarnaise Sauce

The classic sauce is made from tarragon and this recipe is no exception. It's so convenient when the herb is picked fresh from your garden. The sauce can be made in a double boiler but for convenience I make it in a saucepan on low heat. The secret is to whisk constantly with a wire whisk as you cook.

3 tablespoons white wine vinegar
1 tablespoon fresh tarragon leaves, chopped
1 green onion, minced
2 egg yolks
Juice of ½ lemon
½ cup cold butter, cut into pieces
1 tablespoon fresh tarragon leaves, chopped (optional)
1 teaspoon fresh chives, chopped (optional)

In a sauce pan over medium-heat cook the vinegar, tarragon, and green onion until the mixture is reduced by half. Remove from heat and strain. Whisk the egg yolks in a separate bowl; continue to whisk while slowly adding the vinegar mixture and the lemon juice. Pour the egg mixture in a clean saucepan and whisk over low, low heat until it begins to thicken. Add in butter, 1 tablespoon at a time, and cook until smooth and thick. Serve with a garnish of tarragon leaves or chives on top.

west or Southern California, by all means dry them in the sun. Elsewhere you'll need to use a dehydrator. Cut the cherry tomatoes in half and slice the paste tomatoes. Follow the directions on your dehydrator. When dried, store in containers in the freezer. Home-grown (sun-) dried tomatoes taste as sweet as candy so make enough for snacking. See more on tomatoes in the Summer and Winter chapters (pages 84 and 186, respectively).

DRYING HERBS

Some perennial herbs will tolerate frost and can be left in the garden. Thyme, sage, parsley, and cutting celery are frost tolerant. Basil will turn black the instant the weather hints at frost. During a glorious sunny fall day harvest the last of the basil and make batches of pesto to freeze or dry the leaves whole to crumble into soups and stews.

Gather the leaves and remove the stems. Rinse the leaves and pat dry. Place the leaves on a paper towel and microwave on high for a minute. Turn and continue microwaving at 30 second intervals until the leaves are dry. Quick drying in the microwave retains the color and aroma of the herbs. It works very well for basil at this time of year.

Many herbs can be dried this way but the best time to harvest herbs is before they flower. Microwave drying works for oregano, thyme, tarragon, and marjoram. Store the dried herbs in a light-proof air tight container and use throughout the fall and winter.

Fall Fruits

APPLE (*Malus*)
Deciduous fruit tree
Zones 3 to 10 (varies)

Harvest time for apples lasts from early to late autumn (early September to late October in my region), depending on the variety. The best varieties for pies are tart and hold their shape without turning to mush. Try peeled, cored, and sliced 'Jonathan', 'Jonagold', 'Melrose', or 'Suncrisp' wrapped in a crust or plopped in a baking dish and covered with a concoction of oats, nuts, and butter for an apple crisp. 'McIntosh', 'Cortland', and 'Melrose' varieties make great applesauce.

Smooth Applesauce

The easiest way to make applesauce is with a food mill. No need to peel or core them. Red apples will make pink applesauce.

Makes about 2 cups
6 apples with peel, cored and quartered
½ cup sugar
Dash of cinnamon

Put the quartered apples in a saucepan. Just cover with water and boil until the apples are soft. Run the mixture through the food mill; add sugar and a sprinkle of cinnamon to taste. Serve warm.

Chunky Stewed Apples

Makes about 2 cups
6 apples, cored, peeled, and sliced
½ cup sugar

Put sliced apples in a saucepan. Just cover with water and boil until soft. Add sugar and continue to cook until the mixture reaches the desired consistency. Slightly mash some of the apples as you cook. Serve immediately.

Freshly picked apples from the author's garden.

Bob Reynold's Apple Butter

We have been lucky enough to be invited to the annual Rimelspach family apple butter celebration for a few of the twenty-five years they have been gathering to make apple butter. It's an all-day affair with the family peeling, chopping, and pressing apples. They press their own cider then make the apple butter. Some of the apples are made into cider; some are sliced thin for the apple butter. The apple butter is cooked over an open fire in a copper-coated kettle outside. The recipe given here is an adaptation for indoors.

Makes about 2 quarts
5 pounds (20–25) apples, peeled, cored, and quartered
½ gallon apple cider

(continued)

2 cups sugar
2 teaspoons ground cinnamon
½ tablespoon ground ginger

Put the quartered apples in a large heavy kettle. Add the apple cider and sugar and cook over low heat for a few hours. Stir periodically so the sauce doesn't burn, breaking up the soft apples as you stir. Apples will soften and sauce will begin to thicken. Add more cider if necessary. When apples are thoroughly cooked and the mixture has reduced by half, add the spices and stir well. Continue cooking until desired thickness and dark brown. Pour into sterilized jars and place in canner and process in a boiling water bath for 10 minutes. Remove, cool, and store.

Sweet, rich, and easy to make, Mrs. Foster's crusty baked apples don't need additions. If you must, cinnamon ice cream is the perfect match.

Mrs. Foster's Crusty Baked Apples

Serves 6
6 apples
2 cups sugar, plus 2 tablespoons
2 cups water
½ teaspoon ground cinnamon, plus ¼ teaspoon
Juice of ½ lime
¼ cup butter, plus ¾ cup
¼ cup walnuts, chopped
½ cup golden raisins
2 cups all-purpose flour
½ teaspoon salt
2 teaspoons baking powder
¼ cup cold milk

To prepare the apples: core and peel them and leave whole. Set aside while you make the syrup, filling, and crust.

To prepare the syrup, combine 2 cups sugar, 2 cups water, ¼ teaspoon cinnamon, and the lime juice in a saucepan. Bring to a boil and add ¼ cup butter. Remove from heat and set aside.

To prepare the filling, mix the walnuts, raisins, 2 tablespoons sugar, and ¼ teaspoon cinnamon in a small bowl. Set aside.

To prepare the crust, blend the flour, salt, baking powder, and ¾ cup butter in a food processor until the butter is evenly distributed but still coarse. Add the milk and process until the dough sticks to the sides. Divide the dough into six pieces. Roll each into a 5-inch square, trimming the sides.

(continued)

To assemble the apples, preheat oven to 375°F. Place an apple in the center of each dough square and fill the core with the raisin mixture. Wrap dough around the apple and the seal edges. Repeat for all of the apples. Place in a baking dish. Pour the reserved syrup mixture around the apples. Bake for 35 minutes, periodically basting apples with the syrup. Serve warm or cool.

Pork tenderloin with crushed apples and cider gravy is perfect for a cool fall evening.

Pork Tenderloin with Apple and Onion Gravy

Serves 6 to 8
3 pounds pork tenderloins
2 tablespoons olive oil
Salt and freshly ground pepper
2 tart apples, cored, peeled, and chopped
2 small sweet onions, chopped
1 cup apple cider
1 cup chicken stock

Preheat oven to 350°F. In a large skillet, sear tenderloins, on all sides, in hot olive oil until brown. Remove meat and place in roasting pan. Salt and pepper generously. Sauté apples and onions in drippings until slightly browned. Pour over meat and roast uncovered in the oven for 35 minutes. When meat is done, cover and let rest for 10 minutes.

Meanwhile, add cider and chicken stock to drippings and deglaze. Reduce by half. Add the fruit and onions to cider and broth, stir well.

To serve, arrange the meat on a serving platter and pour the gravy over it.

CRANBERRIES (*Vaccinium*)
Perennial creeping shrub
Zones 4 to 8

Cranberries can be grown in the home garden by preparing the soil with peat moss to approximate the native growing conditions. Cranberries prefer acidic soil in a cool climate. Harvest the cranberries before a hard frost. Plant additional cranberries in the fall.

ELDERBERRIES (*Sambucus nigra*)
Deciduous shrub or small tree
Zones 3 to 9

The umbrella-like drupes turn purple-black when they ripen in late summer or early fall. The fruits are edible when cooked and good for making jelly. Elderberry shrubs attract a variety of wildlife that also enjoy the purple drupes, so keep an eye on the ripening fruits so the branches aren't picked clean.

The berries are eaten by birds as soon as they ripen, sometimes before. The fruit is considered to be a choice food of songbirds, such as the eastern bluebird, cardinal, yellow-breasted chat, rose-breasted grosbeak, blue jay, yellow-bellied sapsucker, white-throated sparrow, starling, brown thrasher, gray-cheeked thrush, Swainson's thrush, wood thrush, rufous-sided towhee, veery, cedar waxwing, red-bellied woodpecker, and red-headed woodpecker. The shrubs provide shelter for other wildlife as well; the shrubs massed together help to provide wildlife corridors. That's another reason to plant elderberries; the birds and wildlife will thank you.

The newer varieties of European elderberry (*Sambucus nigra*) are grown for the ornamental serrated black or chartreuse leaf. These fruits are also edible and like the American variety (*Sambucus nigra* subsp. *canadensis*) need to be cooked first. Elderberry jelly is very easy to make; it is really satisfying using what you grow yourself or have on hand. See more on elderberries in the Summer chapter (page 95).

Wild cranberries at the Cranberry Bog State Nature Preserve in Licking County, Ohio. This fragile remnant ecosystem of the boreal landscape is a reminder that the soil dictates the crops.

One of the black ornamental varieties of elderberry, Sambucus nigra, grown for the decorative cut leaf. The berries are edible when cooked.

Strain cooked elderberries through a muslin bag hanging on a wooden spoon to obtain the syrup for elderberry jelly or juice.

Elderberry Jelly

Because elderberries are very low in natural pectin necessary for the jelling process, you will need to partner with a fruit high in pectin or use a commercial pectin such as Sure-Jell or Certo. Crabapples, which are tart and high in pectin will be ready at the same time as the ripe elderberries and make a good complement. Elderberries also need a tart fruit to enhance the taste and improve jelling. For these two reasons choose crabapples or tart apples.

Crabapples or tart apples, uncored, unpeeled, but sliced
Fresh elderberries, stemmed
Water to cover
Jelly bag or 15-inch muslin square
Sugar
Juice of 1 lemon

Place an equal amount of apples or crabapples with the elderberries in a large stainless steel kettle . Add just enough water to cover the fruit and boil until the apples and elderberries are completely soft (about 45 minutes). Mash during cooking to extract all of the fruit juice.

Place the mixture into a jelly bag to filter away all but the juice. You can easily make your own jelly bag by cutting a piece of clean undyed cotton muslin into a 15-inch square. Tie the cloth around the fruit and attach it to a wooden spoon placed over a bowl. Allow the juice to drain into the bowl for a few hours, periodically twisting the cloth to extract more juice. You will have a beautiful purple-red thin syrup.

(continued)

Pour the strained juice back into the rinsed kettle, adding one cup of sugar for every cup of elderberry/apple juice. Add lemon juice for additional tartness. Boil until the syrup sheets off a cooled spoon. This may take a half an hour or so.

Pour into clean jelly jars and seal with metal cap and lid. Place jars in a canner of hot water, making sure jars are completely covered with water. Boil for 10 minutes. Remove jars and cool.

To harvest elderberries, clip the clusters of drupes with pruners and place them into a basket to take into the kitchen. Remove the berries from the stems and put into a colander to wash. Discard the branches and stems.

PAWPAWS (*Asimina triloba*)
Deciduous small tree
Zones 5 to 8

Harvest pawpaws when they are ripe enough to fall from the tree but be quick about it. Other creatures, such as raccoons and groundhogs, also love the fruit so it doesn't last long on the ground.

Pawpaws are a delectable and rare treat. The fruit tastes like a mild mango with a hint of vanilla. The texture is like an avocado. The fruit itself is fragile, ripening very quickly and not suitable for being transported long distances; this is the reason they have not been commercialized and why you won't find them at the grocery store.

The fruit is best to use when it is not too firm and not too soft. When the outside turns black and mushy, the fruit is fine to eat but it has passed its peak of usability in recipes. Pawpaws can turn from underripe to overripe in a matter of two days. Gather ripe fruit and use it immediately or refrigerate to keep longer.

Pawpaw trees are native to the American Midwest. They can be grown in full sun, but in such situ-

Pawpaw-Apple Cake

This is a great cake to make in the fall when you have an abundance of apples. Try using pawpaws if you can find them at the farmer's market or if you are lucky enough to have your own tree. You can substitute applesauce for the pawpaws. See photo of cake on page 163.

Makes 1 Bundt cake
1 cup pawpaw puree or applesauce
1½ cups sugar
1 cup butter, plus more for the pan
3 eggs
3 cups unbleached flour
1 teaspoon baking powder
1 teaspoon baking soda
Dash of salt
1 teaspoon vanilla
1 cup walnuts, chopped
2 cups apples, cored, peeled, and chopped

Glaze
½ cup brown sugar
½ cup water
2 tablespoons butter

Preheat oven to 350°F. Coat the bottom and sides of a Bundt pan with butter. Dust lightly with flour. Set aside.

To make the pawpaw puree, slice pawpaws in half, remove the seeds, and scoop out the fruit. Discard the skin. Puree the fruit in a food processor until smooth. Set aside.

In a large bowl, beat the sugar and butter together until light and well mixed. Beat in the eggs, one at a time until incorporated. In a separate bowl combine the flour, baking powder, baking soda, and salt. Add to the wet mixture along with the vanilla, nuts, apples, and pawpaw puree. Stir at low speed until everything is blended together. Pour into the prepared Bundt pan. Bake for 50–60 minutes or until done. Cool cake slightly then turn onto serving cake plate.

For glaze, bring brown sugar and water to a boil over medium heat. Continue to simmer for about 10 minutes, stirring frequently until syrup is reduced. Turn heat to low and add butter, stirring until incorporated and smooth. Remove from heat. Pour warm glaze over warm cake.

Pawpaws are a delicate fruit that Native Americans and early settlers enjoyed in the early fall. The men of the Lewis and Clark expedition were very fond of pawpaws and thought they could survive on them when out of provisions on the return trek in September of 1806.

A perfectly ripe pawpaw ready to eat fresh or to mash for pawpaw-apple cake. Try saving and planting the seeds by first chilling them in the refrigerator for three to four months.

Fall pears can be mashed into pear butter, baked whole, or sliced and put in tarts or served fresh in salads.

ations need to be watered frequently. In the woods they are an understory tree and prefer some shade. They prefer slightly acidic soil. Two trees of different varieties are required for cross pollination and fruit set. The flowers have a slightly fetid odor to attract flies and beetles, the primary pollinators.

PEARS (*Pyrus*)
Deciduous fruit tree
Zones 5 to 10 (varies with cultivar and rootstock)

There are two types of pears. European pears (*Pyrus communis*) are the pears most often in the grocery stores. They are known as the melting type. They are best picked a little green to ripen off the tree when they become soft and juicy. Popular varieties are 'Anjou', 'Bartlett', and 'Bosc' but many of these are susceptible to fire blight. Newer varieties may have some resistance and less grittiness. 'Seckel' is known as sugar pear and is hardier and more blight resistant than many. Pear trees bloom earlier than apple trees and are more susceptible to spring freezes that kill the blossoms.

Asian pears (*Pyrus pyrifolia*) produce fruit that is round, crisp and juicy. The fruit is best when left to fully ripen on the tree. Asian pears may be more suitable for warmer climates as they need less chill hours, or hours when the temperature needs to be between 45° and 32°F.

It is necessary to plant two different varieties of pears that bloom at the same time for pollination. Like all fruit trees, pears should be planted on a hill and not in a valley so cold air can move beyond the trees and not pool where it can cause freeze damage (see "Design for Spring" for more information on planting fruit trees). Hardiness varies with the cultivar and the rootstock.

Fall salad with fresh pears is made from the lettuces and greens abundant in the fall then topped with sugared walnuts, goat cheese and pears.

Fall Salad with Fresh Pears

This salad is simple with fresh greens and lettuce from the cool-season garden. Goat cheese adds some saltiness, and the slightly sweet balsamic vinegar and sugared walnuts complement the pear. The salad looks fancy, but it's thrown together in minutes.

Serves 4–6
1 teaspoon butter
1 cup walnuts
2 tablespoons sugar
4 tablespoons water
¼ cup extra-virgin olive oil
½ cup balsamic vinegar
6–8 cups of mixed fall greens, such as lettuce, kale, spinach, mustards, or cabbage
4–5 ounces soft goat cheese, divided into teaspoons
4 pears, peeled, cored, and sliced
Salt and freshly ground pepper

To toast the walnuts, place butter and walnuts in a heavy skillet over medium-high heat. Stir constantly for about 5 minutes, making sure the butter does not burn. Continue stirring until the walnuts are toasted. Add sugar and water and stir constantly so it doesn't burn. The water will evaporate leaving the nuts with a sugar coating. Remove from heat. Cool and store.

To prepare the fall salad dressing, mix the olive oil and vinegar. Set aside.

Toss the greens together. Assemble salads on individual plates. Add greens, goat cheese, walnuts, and pears. Pass the fall salad dressing. Salt and pepper to taste.

Pear Baklava

Baklava is very easy to make when you use premade thin pastry sheets. This version is topped with fresh pears which are baked along with the thin crispy layers of dough, butter, and walnuts.

Serves 8
4 cups walnuts
2½ cups sugar plus 2 tablespoons, divided
1 teaspoon ground cinnamon
¾ cup butter, melted
1 box (16 ounces) phyllo dough, thawed according to package directions
3–5 pears, cored and thinly sliced, peeling optional
Dash of salt
Juice of ½ lemon
Water to make 1 cup of liquid
¼ cup honey

Preheat oven to 350°F. To prepare the filling, place the walnuts, ½ cup sugar, and cinnamon in a food processor and chop until the nuts are finely ground. Divide into four parts and set aside.

Using a pastry brush, coat the bottom of a 9- by 13-inch pan with a tiny bit of melted butter. Divide the thawed phyllo dough (about 40 sheets) into four sections. (It is not necessary to count individual sheets.) Working with one stack, lay a single sheet on the prepared pan, brush with a small amount of butter. Place another sheet on top, brush it with butter, and repeat until the stack is used. Sprinkle ¼ of the walnut mixture over the buttered stack.

Repeat with the remaining three stacks of phyllo sheets and the walnut mixture until all is used. You will end this baklava with the walnuts on top.

(continued next page)

Lay the pears on top of the walnuts in any arrangement you desire. Overlap the pear slices slightly. Sprinkle 2 tablespoons sugar on top of the pears and a dash of salt.

Bake for 45–50 minutes until the pears are browned and baklava is done.

While the baklava is baking, make the syrup. Put the lemon juice in a measuring cup, then fill with water to 1 cup. Pour the liquid into a heavy saucepan with 2 cups sugar and ¼ cup honey. Bring to boil over medium-high heat. Continue boiling, stirring often for 10 minutes until the syrup is reduced. You have to watch it so it doesn't boil over. Set aside to cool.

When the baklava is done baking but still hot, pour the syrup over it. Let the baklava cool for a few hours. The syrup will be absorbed into the pastry layers and you will have a perfect dessert for guests. Slice into diamonds to serve.

American persimmon trees are very cold hardy. Make sure the fruit fully ripens on the tree or it will make your mouth pucker.

PERSIMMON (*Diospyros virginiana*)
Deciduous fruit tree
Zones 5 to 11

The American persimmon is native to eastern North America. The small ornamental tree produces lovely orange-yellow fruits in the fall. It is attractive in the landscape even if you don't eat the fruit.

American persimmons are astringent, which means the underripe fruit leaves a puckering, unpalatable aftertaste if you bite into one, the kind of "don't take another bite, spit it out of your mouth" taste that leaves you questioning whether the fruit is edible at all. Patience is required. To enjoy the literal translation of the name, food of the gods, wait until the fruit is soft and ripe before eating. You will be rewarded with the true flavor and sweetness. It takes time, sun, and a few light frosts to break down the astringent tannins. Of course, by this time you will be competing with wildlife for the sweet treats which can remain on the tree through winter.

The main reason to grow these delectable, rare, native fruits at home is that you cannot find them at the grocery store. You will need to plant two cultivars with the same bloom period for pollination. Persimmons prefer full sun and well-drained soil.

American persimmons are very cold hardy. 'Meader' is hardy in zones 4 to 8 and is a seedless, self-fertile variety. Asian persimmons (*Diospyros kaki*) are the variety most often seen in grocery stores and the fruit can be either astringent or non-astringent. Asian persimmons are hardy in zones 7 to 11.

Ornamental cabbage is usually grown as decoration in the garden but it is edible. In warm climates it will remain through the winter.

Fall Greens

Cool-season lettuces, kales, and Asian greens can be sown in the garden when the temperatures cool. Greens planted in the early fall should be allowed to mature, so let some grow without cutting them for leaf salads. Bok choy and cabbages and romaine lettuces mature well in cool weather. This is the subtle difference between the spring crops you eat at the baby stage and the fall crops you let grow up. Mature kales and cabbages tolerate cold temperatures better than the tender young crops. Continue to sow seeds of lettuce, kale, Asian greens, and mustards.

BROCCOLI RAAB (*Brassica rapa* Ruvo Group)
Biennial grown as an annual
Seed to table: 28 to 60 days

Continue to sow seeds outdoors every few weeks. Broccoli raab is frost tolerant and fast growing. Leaves and florets are ready to harvest in 35 to 42 days. Harvest just the buds for cut-and-come-again harvesting. May overwinter in mild climates. See more on broccoli raab in the Spring chapter (page 37).

155

CABBAGE (*Brassica oleracea* Capitata Group)
Biennial grown as an annual
Seed to table: 60 to 95 days

Cabbage is frost tolerant and can stay in the fall garden. Begin to harvest the heads that were sown in late summer. Harvest small, young heads for long-term storage. Plant transplants of ornamental cabbage into the garden or in containers for fall and winter color. See more on cabbage in the Spring and Summer chapters (pages 38 and 102, respectively).

Fall-garden spring rolls can be made with the cabbages and Asian greens that are abundant in the fall garden. Here they are served with three dipping sauces.

Fall-Garden Spring Rolls with Three Dipping Sauces

This is a great recipe to use all of the Asian greens that have matured into perfect white crispy stalks with flavorful leaves. You can use any combination of Asian bok choy or cabbage or any greens that are ready to harvest. Swiss chard, bok choy, mustard greens, celery, cutting celery, and mizuna are possibilities. Use all parts of the plant—the stems and the leaves. Try adding some grated daikon radish or even kohlrabi if you have an abundance in the garden.

Makes 20 to 24 spring rolls
2 tablespoons peanut oil, plus 3 cups for deep frying
4–6 cups bok choy, chopped
2 cups mixed greens, such as kale, mizuna, cabbage, cutting celery leaves
2 carrots, finely chopped or grated
8 ounces fresh mung bean sprouts
4 garlic cloves, minced
3–4 Hungarian hot peppers, chopped
1 small piece (1 inch) fresh ginger root, minced
6–8 green onions, chopped
8 ounces fresh mushrooms, sliced
3 tablespoons soy sauce
Freshly ground pepper
1 package (20 to 24 pieces) egg roll wrappers
Bowl of water
Hot Mustard Dipping Sauce (recipe follows)
Spicy Sweet and Sour Dipping Sauce (recipe follows)
Cucumber and Melon Dipping Sauce (recipe follows)

Add a small amount (2 tablespoons) of oil to a large skillet or wok and turn heat to medium high. Quickly cook bok choy, greens, carrots, bean sprouts, garlic, hot peppers, ginger, green onions, and mushrooms until crisp tender and greens just wilt. Add the soy sauce and stir well. Remove from heat. Sprinkle with pepper to taste.

To assemble spring rolls, set up a work area so the wrappers, filling, and paper for drying the egg rolls are all in one place. Place the pan with the cooked vegetables on a trivet with one end slightly raised so the filling drains. The secret to rolling successful spring rolls is to make sure the filling is not oozing with liquid. Roll out a sheet of freezer paper or use a paper sack to roll the spring rolls. Fill a bowl with water and place nearby to seal edges.

Lay out a wrapper and fill with a few tablespoons of well-drained filling. Roll up the wrapper beginning with a corner. Fold sides over filling and continue to roll. Dip your finger in the water and dampen the corner of the wrapper to seal it. Make sure there are no gaps. Place the roll on dry freezer paper or paper towels. Repeat with the rest of the wrappers and filling. Be sure none of the spring rolls touch each other as you roll the remainder.

Heat 3 cups peanut oil in wok until hot. Deep fry the egg rolls in the oil until one side is brown; turn with a wooden spoon to brown the other side. Remove and drain well. Serve immediately with three sauces.

Savoy cabbage is ready for harvest.

Hot Mustard Dipping Sauce

2 tablespoons ground mustard
2 tablespoons water

Mix the mustard and water to a smooth consistency. The resulting hot mustard is perfect for spring rolls.

Spicy Sweet and Sour Dipping Sauce

½ cup peach marmalade
1 teaspoon orange zest
3 tablespoons rice vinegar
1 tablespoon soy sauce
2 teaspoons hot pepper flakes

Combine all ingredients and serve immediately.

Cucumber and Melon Dipping Sauce

½ cup cucumber
½ cup melon
Juice of 1 lime
1 tablespoon fresh Thai basil, finely chopped
1 green onion, chopped
1 jalapeño pepper, chopped
Dash of salt

Peel and shred the cucumber and melon. Combine all ingredients and serve immediately.

'Red Russian' kale was picked from the garden, washed, quickly cooked with a little green onion, broth and then topped with crisp bacon.

Braised Fresh Kale with Bacon and Onions

Serves 3 or 4
4 strips lean bacon
6–8 green onions, sliced
6–8 cups kale, chopped
½ cup chicken stock

Cook bacon until crisp and remove to drain. Sauté onions in pan. Add kale and chicken stock. Braise until tender and broth is reduced. Crumble bacon on top and serve.

'Red Russian' kale does well in cool weather in the late fall garden. It's very tasty raw in salads or cooked.

KALE (*Brassica oleracea* Acephala Group)
Biennial grown as an annual
Seed to table: 45 to 65 days

Harvest leaves of kale through the fall in a cut-and-come-again fashion. Continue to sow seeds every few weeks to harvest baby kale for salads. Kale is frost tolerant and will survive light frosts and mild winters. Cover with cloches when weather turns cold to extend the season.

Favorite varieties raw in salads are 'Red Russian' or 'White Russian'. These are best gathered and eaten at the baby stage. The flat leaf with a deeply serrated edge is sweet. Give enough time for larger varieties like 'Winterbor' and 'Nero di Toscano' to grow to full size before the weather turns cold. Kale tolerates frost and cold but doesn't actively grow during cold weather. See more on kale in the Spring chapter (page 38).

SPINACH (*Spinacia oleracea*)
Annual
Seed to table: 35 to 40 days

Harvest spinach by cutting leaves at the base. Continue to sow seeds outdoors every week for a continuous supply. Seeds sown after early autumn can be covered with cloches or grown in cold frames for a winter supply in mild climates. See more on spinach in the Spring and Winter chapters (pages 41 and 180, respectively).

Fresh spinach is the main ingredient in this easy spanakopita.

Quick Spanakopita

Serves 4–6
2 narrow loaves of French bread
6 cups fresh spinach, chopped
6–8 green onions, chopped
Handful of fresh flat-leaf parsley, chopped
2 eggs
8 ounces feta cheese
¼ teaspoon hot pepper flakes

Preheat oven to 350°F. Cut off top of French bread and hollow out the middle (reserve for making croutons another time). Set aside bread as you make the filling. Blend together the remaining ingredients and mix well. Place mixture in hollowed out bread. Bake for 20 minutes until filling is set. Serve immediately.

SWISS CHARD (*Beta vulgaris* Cicla Group)
Biennial grown as an annual
Seed to table: 50 days

Swiss chard will remain in the garden through many light frosts. In mild climates or with protection Swiss chard will last through the winter. Continue to harvest stems and leaves for Asian stir-fries or to sauté in olive oil and serve with pasta dishes. See more on Swiss chard in the Spring chapter (page 41).

Swiss Chard Lo Mein

Serves 6
8 ounces Chinese noodles, cooked according to package directions
½ cup chicken or vegetable stock
¼ cup soy sauce
1 teaspoon sesame oil
3 tablespoons brown sugar
1 teaspoon cornstarch
Small amount of oil
4 cups Swiss chard, stalks and leaves, sliced
4 cups mixed Asian greens, such as bok choy, mizuna, or kale, stalks and leaves, sliced
2 carrots, sliced
2 jalapeño peppers, chopped
6–8 green onions, sliced
1 small piece (¾ inch) fresh ginger root, minced
2 cups mushrooms, sliced
3 garlic cloves, minced
½ cup unsalted peanuts, chopped

While noodles are cooking, prepare the sauce. In a mixing bowl, combine stock, soy sauce, sesame oil, and brown sugar. Stir in cornstarch until dissolved. Set aside.

To prepare the stir-fry vegetables, heat a large pan or wok and add small amount of oil, just to coat. Add the Swiss chard, mixed greens, carrots, jalapeños, green onions, and ginger. Cook over high heat until softened. Add the mushrooms, garlic, and peanuts and cook until just done.

To assemble the dish, pour the sauce over the cooked vegetables and stir until slightly thickened, about 2 minutes. Add cooked noodles to the pan. Stir and heat until combined. Remove from heat. Serve hot or cold.

Sara Bartley gathered a bouquet of fall-blooming flowers for an informal arrangement at a family gathering.

Shrubs and Flowers for the Table

ANEMONE (*Anemone ×hybrida*)
Perennial in zones 4 to 8
Site conditions: Shade to part sun; rich, moist soil

Japanese anemones are late summer- and fall-blooming perennials that range in color from white to shades of pale to deep pink. They have an informal look that complements other fall-flowering shrubs and perennials in the border, and they make excellent cut flowers for fall arrangements. *Anemone ×hybrida* 'Honorine Jobert' is a white variety. *Anemone hupehensis* 'Prince Henry' grows to 3 feet (90 cm) tall and has clear pink petals with yellow centers in the fall.

ASTER (*Aster*)
Perennial in zones 3 to 8 (varies with the cultivar)
Site conditions: Full sun

Asters are the classic fall bloomer providing color in the late border and on the table in the home. They range in color from dark purple and blue to pale lavender and pale blue. When you clip for indoor arrangements, make note of places in the garden that need a color boost this time of year. Fall is a good time for planting additional perennials, so tuck a few plants where needed. *Aster oblongifolius* 'October Skies' is a cultivar of an eastern North American native. It creates a nice mound of color about 2 feet (60 cm) tall and is good for cut flowers.

Anemone ×hybrida 'Honorine Jobert' *brightens the shade garden with white blooms from early to mid autumn. The flowers can be cut to add to any fall arrangement.*

(below) 'Henry Eilers' *sweet coneflower (Rudbeckia subtomentosum) brings late summer and fall color to the border. It also makes a long-lasting cut flower indoors.*

BLACK-EYED SUSAN (*Rudbeckia*)

Perennial in zones 3 to 10
Site conditions: Prefers full sun, tolerates part shade; drought tolerant

Many *Rudbeckia* relatives extend their sunny daisy-like blooms into the fall. Some are tall like Autumn Sun black-eyed Susan (*Rudbeckia nitida* 'Herbstsonne') and belong in the back of the border where it can grow 5 to 8 feet (1.5–2.4 cm) tall. 'Henry Eilers' sweet coneflower (*Rudbeckia subtomentosum*) has quill-like petals around a brown center. The flowers are long-lasting in the vase. See more on black-eyed Susan in the Summer chapter (page 115).

Crabapples are edible and can be used in flower arrangements. Here red crabapples and yellow edible calendula flowers adorn pawpaw-apple cake. An informal arrangement of viburnum berries, beauty berry, and asters grown in the author's garden completes the table.

(right) A fall arrangement of goldenrod, yellow calendula, dill flowers, and Autumn Sun black-eyed Susan.

BLUE MIST SHRUB (*Caryopteris ×clandonensis*)
Deciduous flowering shrub in zones 5 to 9
Site condition: Full sun; well-drained soil

Blue mist shrub shines with vivid blue flowers at the end of the season when many perennials have already bloomed. It's a low maintenance plant for late season color in the border. It also attracts bees and butterflies. Once established, it is drought tolerant. Treat it like a subshrub and cut it down to the ground at the end of the season. 'Longwood Blue' has gray green foliage with deep blue flowers. 'Worcester Gold' has new gold foliage that becomes vivid yellow-green and sky blue flowers. The blue-yellow combination is striking in the border and in the vase.

CRABAPPLE (*Malus*)
Deciduous ornamental tree in zones 4 to 8
Site conditions: Full sun; moist, well-drained soil

Crabapples can be used in place of apples in fruit jam recipes. Yes, the fruits are edible, although a little tart, and are perfect for jellies. Apples and crabapples are a natural source of pectin if you choose to make jams or jellies without the store-bought pectin that comes in a box or foil pouch.

Selectively prune trees by removing suckers and branches that are too close to other branches. Bring these cut branches indoors for fall arrangements. See more on crabapple in the Spring chapter page 47.

GOLDENROD (*Solidago*)
Perennial in zones 2 to 9 (varies with the cultivar)
Site conditions: Full sun; well-drained soil; drought resistant

This prairie plant has hundreds of varieties many of which are native to North America. It's a carefree perennial that makes sense for modern gardens. Goldenrod adds color in the border and attracts beneficial insects so plant it near the potager. Mix it with other fall-blooming perennials like asters and grasses for a late-season arrangement. *Solidago rugosa* 'Fireworks' has bright yellow flowers on arching stems and stays under 5 feet (1.5 m). Little Lemon goldenrod (*Solidago* 'Dansolitlem') has pale yellow flowers and only grows about a foot (30 cm) high.

JOE PYE WEED (*Eupatorium*)
Perennial in zones 4 to 9 (depending on the variety)
Site conditions: Full sun to part shade; moist, well-drained soils

This native fall-blooming perennial should be planted in the back of the border or in the meadow. It can grow 7 feet (2.1 m) tall but there are smaller cultivars. The plant is relatively carefree and part of a strategy of removing lawn and replacing with low-maintenance plants that are useful and beautiful. Joe pye weed attracts butterflies, songbirds, and beneficial insects. It's also a good selection for rain gardens. *Eupatorium maculatum* 'Gateway' is a shorter and improved selection of the native species. It prefers moist soil. *Eupatorium rugosum* 'Chocolate' is one of my favorite plants. I love it for the dark foliage all season; a spray of tiny white flowers in the fall is a bonus.

ORNAMENTAL CORN (*Zea mays*)
Annual
Seed to table: 68 to 115 days

There are many beautiful colors of ornamental corn from blue-green to deep burgundy. Some varieties feature a multitude of colors. All can be ground into flour or harvested for fall decorations. 'Oaxacan Green' is an heirloom variety with emerald green kernels. 'Miniature Blue' has dark blue kernels on small ears.

Harvest ornamental corn when the husks begin to dry; no hurry, the ears can be left on the stalks through a few frosts. Cut the shocks with the ears down for decorations beginning in midautumn (early October). Then store in a garage or shelter to finish drying. See more on corn in the Summer chapter (page 67).

Colorful ornamental corn can be ground into corn meal or used for harvest decorations.

PERENNIAL SUNFLOWER (*Helianthus*)
Perennial in zones 3 to 9 (depending on the cultivar)
Site conditions: Full sun; well-drained soil

Helianthus 'Lemon Queen', a perennial sunflower, bursts with sunny daisy-like soft yellow flowers in late summer that last until frost. It's a native back-of-the-border plant. *Helianthus multiflorus* 'Flore Pleno' has bright yellow double flowers that make a good substitute for mums in the vase. See more on sunflowers in the Summer chapter (page 120).

SASSAFRAS (*Sassafras albidum*)
Deciduous ornamental tree in zones 4 to 9
Site conditions: Full sun or part shade; rich, well-
    drained soil

Sassafras is a native tree that brings back childhood memories of walking the woods looking for the root beer plant. If you have one growing in your yard, you're lucky. It is the first tree young naturalists learn to identify by the leaf. A tricky tree, it has three forms of the leaf on one plant—single leaf, mitten shape, and three lobes. Sassafras was the original flavoring for root beer. It is no longer recommended safe to use the aromatic bark for teas and flavoring because it contains safrole, which causes cancer in laboratory rats. The leaves do not contain safrole so it is possible to use the dried leaves for filé powder.

> ### Filé Powder
>
> Collect young sassafras branches with leaves in the fall before they change color. Rinse with water and hang to dry indoors. Remove the leaves. Process in a blender or coffee grinder to a fine powder. Store in an airtight container and use to flavor gumbo.

*An arrangement of flowers from the author's garden freshly cut for the fall table. Here is a combination of 'Chocolate' Joe pye weed (*Eupatorium rugosum*), goldenrod (*Solidago sp.*), 'Canary' sneezeweed (*Helenium*), and 'Snowbank' boltonia (*Boltonia asteroides*).*

SNEEZEWEED (*Helenium*)
Perennial in zones 3 to 8
Site conditions: Full sun; average to moist soils

I have heard that 'Canary' sneezeweed (*Helenium*) is grown commercially because the cut flowers last longer than ten days in a vase. This is a tall plant for the back of the border; it's native to south central and eastern United States. *Helenium autumnale* 'Moerheim Beauty' grows to 4 feet (1.2 m) and has bronze red petals.

VIBURNUM (*Viburnum*)
Deciduous flowering shrub in zones 5 to 8 (depending
    on the cultivar)
Site conditions: Full to part sun

Many of the viburnums produce berries in the fall so are a great addition to the back of the perennial border. Clip the fruits of viburnum for indoor arrangements. *Viburnum nudum* 'Winterthur' has blue fruit but needs a pollinator like *Viburnum nudum* 'Bulk' (Brandywine) for best fruit production.

The fruits of the American cranberry bush viburnum (*Viburnum trilobum*) produce edible red fruits that are fine for making jam or jelly. I much prefer the native cranberry bush viburnum over the European variety (*Viburnum opulus*). See more on viburnum in the Spring chapter (page 52).

Design for Fall

SHADED GARDEN

Fall is a good time to walk through your property and make an inventory of additional trees shrubs and flowers needed to create a continuously blooming or productive garden. The memory of the summer flowers or lack of them is not that far away. Fall is also a good time to plant new perennials, shrubs and trees, as there still is enough time for the roots to become established before the ground freezes in the winter. A trip to the nursery at this time of year will remind you of the possibility of vibrant color for fall—asters, black-eyed Susans, and goldenrod.

This garden plan for a large urban lot focuses on fall-blooming flowers, shrubs, and trees. The clients for whom I designed the garden travel abroad every summer for academic study and wanted an

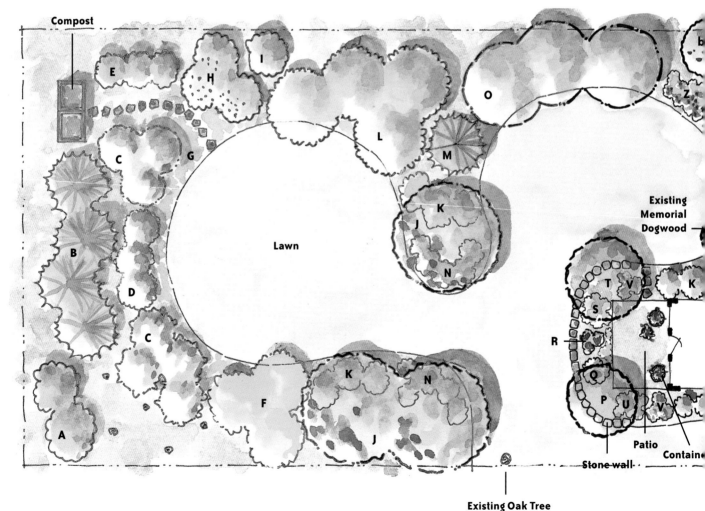

Plan view of an edible and useful garden on a shaded ¼-acre lot. The design focuses on fall-blooming ornamentals.

LABEL	NO. OF PLANTS	COMMON NAME	SCIENTIFIC NAME	ZONE	NOTES
A	2	spicebush	*Lindera benzoin*	4–9	leaves persist through winter
B	4	hemlock	*Tsuga canadensis*	3–7	evergreen screen
C	7	'Alice' oakleaf hydrangea	*Hydrangea quercifolia* 'Alice'	5–9	cut flowers; excellent fall color
D	3	'Annabelle' hydrangea	*Hydrangea arborescens* 'Annabelle'	3–9	good cut and dried flowers
E	3	American black elderberry	*Sambucus nigra* subsp. *canadensis*	3–11	flowers for cordial; berries for jelly
F	3	common witch hazel	*Hamamelis virginiana*	3–8	U.S. native; yellow flowers in fall
G	43	wintergreen groundcover	*Gaultheria procumbens*	3–7	evergreen fragrant groundcover; red berries in winter
H	3	'Winter Red' winterberry holly	*Ilex verticillata* 'Winter Red'	3–9	red berries in fall and winter
I	1	'Southern Gentleman' winterberry holly	*Ilex verticillata* 'Southern Gentleman'	3–9	pollinator for 'Winter Red'; red berries

(continued next page)

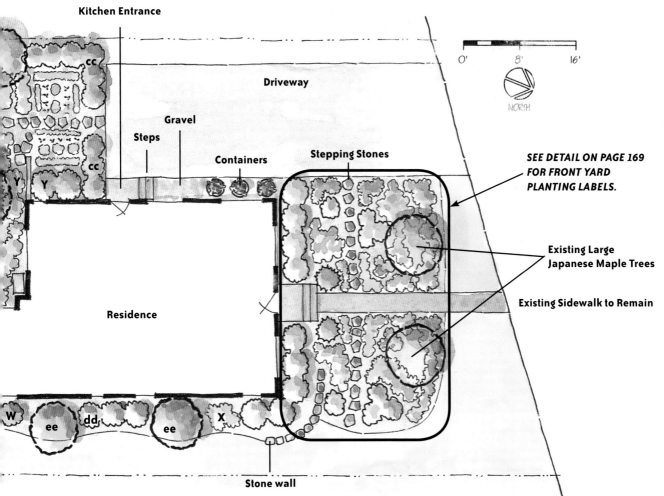

Kitchen Entrance

Driveway

Gravel

Steps

Containers

Stepping Stones

SEE DETAIL ON PAGE 169 FOR FRONT YARD PLANTING LABELS.

Existing Large Japanese Maple Trees

Existing Sidewalk to Remain

Residence

Stone wall

0'   8'   16'

NORTH

LABEL	NO. OF PLANTS	COMMON NAME	SCIENTIFIC NAME	ZONE	NOTES
J	3	redbud	*Cercis canadensis*	4–9	magenta flowers in spring
K	9	'Viking' black chokeberry	*Aronia melanocarpa* 'Viking'	3–7	edible black fruit in fall
L	4	Heart Throb kousa dogwood	*Cornus kousa* 'Schmred'	5–8	pink bracts
M	1	'Bakeri' blue spruce	*Picea pungens* 'Bakeri'	2–8	remains garden size; winter color
N	9	'Mount Airy' fothergilla	*Fothergilla gardenii* 'Mount Airy'	5–8	spring flowers; great fall color
O	3	Lamarck serviceberry	*Amelanchier lamarckii*	4–8	spring flowers; edible fruits in summer
P	1	sweet bay magnolia	*Magnolia virginiana*	5–9	fragrant white flowers in spring
Q	7	'Prairie Sun' black eyed Susan	*Rudbeckia hirta* 'Prairie Sun'	3–8	cut flowers summer–fall
R	3	'Autumn Joy' stonecrop	*Sedum* 'Autumn Joy'	5–9	leaves and flowers for arrangements spring–fall
S	7	'Tiny Dancer' sneezeweed	*Helenium flexuosum* 'Tiny Dancer'	4–10	yellow flowers midsummer to frost; good cut flower
T	2	Stellar Pink dogwood	*Cornus ×rutgersensis* 'Rutgan'	5–8	pink spring flowers
U	5	'Wood's Purple' aster	*Aster* 'Wood's Purple'	4–8	purple flowers in fall
V	6	'First Choice' blue mist shrub	*Caryopteris ×clandonensis* 'First Choice'	4–8	blue flowers in fall
W	5	'Green Mountain' boxwood	*Buxus* 'Green Mountain'	4–8	use cuttings for winter wreaths
X	17	goatsbeard	*Aruncus dioicus*	3–8	mid season white flowers; U.S. native woodland plant
Y	4	compact inkberry	*Ilex glabra* 'Compacta'	4–9	evergreen
Z	22	'Ruby Star' coneflower	*Echinacea purpurea* 'Ruby Star'	3–8	magenta flowers summer–fall; good cut flower
aa	3	rhubarb	*Rheum*	3–8	needs cold winters; edible stalks in spring
bb	1	'Sundance dwarf apple tree	*Malus* 'Co-op 29'	5–8	very disease resistant yellow variety
bb	1	'Liberty' dwarf apple tree	*Malus* 'Liberty'	5–8	very disease resistant red variety
cc	9	'Crandall' clove currant	*Ribes odoratum* 'Crandall'	4–8	yellow spring flowers; edible fall fruit
dd	3	Newport viburnum	*Viburnum plicatum* 'Newzam'	5–9	snowball white flowers in spring; burgundy fall color
ee	2	'Glenform' serviceberry	*Amelanchier canadensis* 'Glenform'	4–9	spring flowers; edible fruits in summer
ff	9	'Beauté Vendômoise' hydrangea	*Hydrangea macrophylla* 'Beauté Vendômoise'	6–9	pale blue lacecap flowers
gg	8	'Sixteen Candles' summersweet	*Clethra alnifolia* 'Sixteen Candles'	3–9	white summer flowers; good fall color
hh	22	'Honorine Jobert' Japanese anemone	*Anemone ×hybrida* 'Honorine Jobert'	4–8	white fall flowers for shade
ii	14	fiddlehead ostrich fern	*Matteuccia struthiopteris*	3–7	edible fiddleheads in early spring
jj	18	'Thriller' lady's mantle	*Alchemilla mollis* 'Thriller'	4–7	summer flowers for fresh and dried arrangements
kk	6	'King of Hearts' bleeding heart	*Dicentra* 'King of Hearts'	5–9	long blooming, pink flowers
ll	14	'Jack Frost' Siberian bugloss	*Brunnera macrophylla* 'Jack Frost'	3–7	blue spring flowers
mm	33	wild ginger	*Asarum canadense*	3–7	U.S. native groundcover for shade
nn	17	hostas	*Hosta*	3–9	plant a variety of hostas

emphasis on fall and spring color so that they could enjoy the garden. The young couple likes to cook and have friends over so they also wanted a kitchen garden to grow some of their own food and greens. They needed shrubs and trees to help screen the view directly into the neighbor's yard. The clients will install the design themselves as finances dictate beginning with the trees and kitchen garden.

The design illustrates concepts and addresses some common problems that may be helpful for you in designing your own landscape to be fruitful and colorful. One major issue of this site is the lack of sun. Huge oak trees and old pine trees straddle the property line of this lot in an old suburban neighborhood. So what do you do when you want an edible garden with little direct light?

We studied the site for sun patterns, making notes hourly of the sunny spots. Two small areas on the property receive ample sun to grow vegetables, herbs, and flowers. We located the kitchen garden in one, just at the end of the driveway. This space has room and sun for two dwarf apple trees: 'Co-op 29' and 'Liberty'. Both are new varieties that are extremely disease resistant. The family won't be spraying their apples. The second sunny site is at the edge of the patio where there is room for fall-blooming cut flowers, such as stonecrop, Prairie black-eyed Susan, and 'Tiny Dancer' sneezeweed; these are drought tolerant and easy-to-grow care-free plants with a long bloom time.

Shade-tolerant plants with edible fruit like elderberry, black chokeberry, clove currant, and serviceberry fill in the back yard and help to create the form of the garden. Edible groundcovers like wintergreen, ostrich fern, and wild ginger help prevent erosion and cover the ground with lush green.

Spicebush and 'Alice' oakleaf hydrangea (*Hydrangea quercifolia*) were selected to create the garden space and to help screen the views from the neighbors. Both shrubs will grow large over time, are native, and will provide cut flowers for the table—fragrant blooms in the spring from the spicebush and white hydrangeas in the summer and fall.

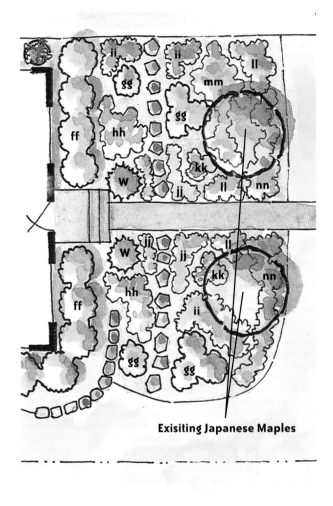

Exisiting Japanese Maples

Detail of front yard plantings.

FORMAL POTAGER: FALL

This is the fall planting plan for the formal potager introduced in spring (page 56) and seen in summer (page 126). As some of the summer vegetables languish, it's time to plant the cool-season varieties again. In this zone 8 garden the fall greens and vegetables remain in the garden for the entire winter. The owner harvests mustards, collards, and greens even in the cold days of midwinter (January). Pansies, which come in a multitude of hues, add color to the fall and winter potager. The bare spots on the fall planting plan are where the garlic has been planted. It will remain in the garden to be harvested the following summer.

Bed 1
'Tadorna' leek
'Champion' collards

Bed 2
22 'Deep Purple' pansy
'German Extra-Hardy' garlic

Bed 3
22 'Deep Purple' pansy
'German Extra-Hardy' garlic

Bed 4
4 'Cheddar' cauliflower
'Tadorna' leek

Bed 5
early mizuna
mâche

Bed 6
'Golden Sunrise' Swiss chard
4 'Nero di Toscano' kale
4 'Rossa di Verona a Palla'
    radicchio

Bed 7
4 'Redbor' kale
4 'Castelfranco' radicchio
'Bianca Riccia' endive

Bed 8
'Joi Choi' bok choy
'Atomic Red' carrot

Bed 9
4 'Ruby Perfection' cabbage
'Red Russian' kale

Bed 10
4 'Redbor' kale
12 'Magenta Sunset' Swiss
    chard
4 'Grumolo Rossa di Verona'
    radicchio

Bed 11
'Osaka Purple' mustard
12 'Bright Lights' Swiss chard
'Bianca Riccia' endive

Bed 12
4 'Ruby Perfection' cabbage
'Chioggia' beet

Bed 13
'Bordeaux' smooth-leaf
    spinach
4 'Oliver' Brussels sprouts

Bed 14
22 'Deep Purple' pansy
'Russian Red' garlic

Bed 15
22 'Deep Purple' pansy
'Russian Red' garlic

Bed 16
'Tyee' Savoy-leaf spinach
4 'Oliver' Brussels sprouts

FALL PLANTING PLAN OF A FORMAL POTAGER

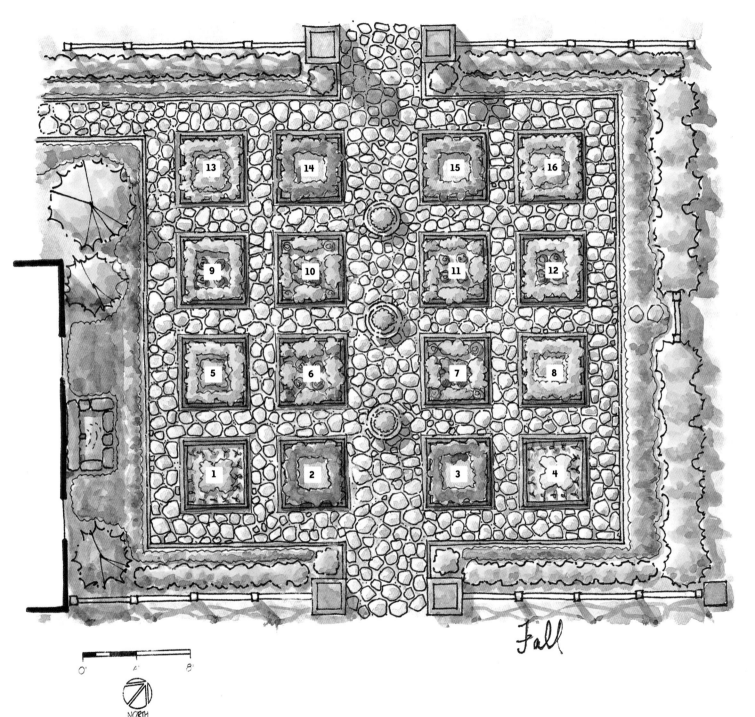

Fall

NORTH

BULB DESIGN

Fall is the time to plant spring-blooming bulbs that extend the season of color and cut flowers in your garden. So many bulb catalogs are good sources of information on the height, color, and bloom times (early, mid or late). In general, daffodils in much of the northern United States are perennial and many naturalize well to come back each spring with faithful color. Tulips are not reliably perennial and I view them as annuals.

In warmer regions, only certain varieties of daffodils tolerate the lack of cold winter and summer heat so check to make sure daffodils will come back

LABEL	NO. OF PLANTS	COMMON NAME	SCIENTIFIC NAME	ZONE	NOTES
A	2000	English bluebells	*Hyacinthoides non-scripta*	4–9	bloom lasts for weeks in late spring; fragrant; heirloom
B	740	'Avalanche' daffodil	*Narcissus* (Division 8 Tazetta) 'Avalanche'	6–9	early–mid spring; heirloom, good for Southern gardens; fragrant; heirloom
C	600	'Hillstar' daffodil	*Narcissus* (Division 7 Jonquilla) 'Hillstar'	4–9	mid spring; good for Southern gardens
D	500	'Geranium' daffodil	*Narcissus* (Division 8 Tazetta) 'Geranium'	5–9	mid to late spring; good for Southern gardens; heirloom

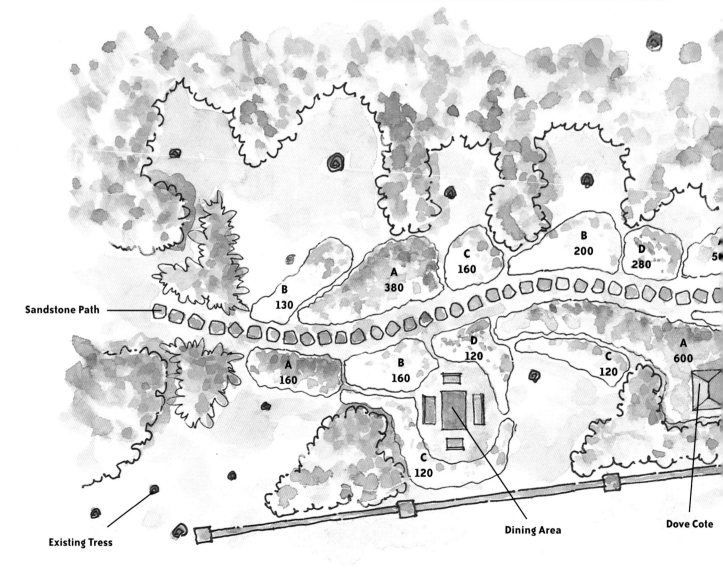

Sandstone Path

Existing Tress

Dining Area

Dove Cote

in your area before ordering. Bulbs can be planted as an under layer of color in an existing garden. The planting plan shown here is for an existing shade garden in the American south. It's really a secret woodland garden filled with profuse spring-blooming azaleas and dogwood.

The first to bloom in early spring are the heirloom 'Avalanche' daffodils with pale white petals and a yellow center. This variety dates back to 1700. In mid-season the 'Hillstar' daffodils bloom yellow with a white center. In late spring the English bluebells are violet blue and in bloom along with the 'Geranium' daffodils, another heirloom variety with white petals and an orange center. These daffodils are either in the Jonquilla division or the Tazetta division so they endure the heat of the warmer climates. Bulbs are part of the overall plan to have something to pick for the vase throughout every season of the year.

A bulb planting plan for a secret woodland garden in a warmer climate. The bulbs will bloom in sequence from early to late spring, perennialize, and return every year.

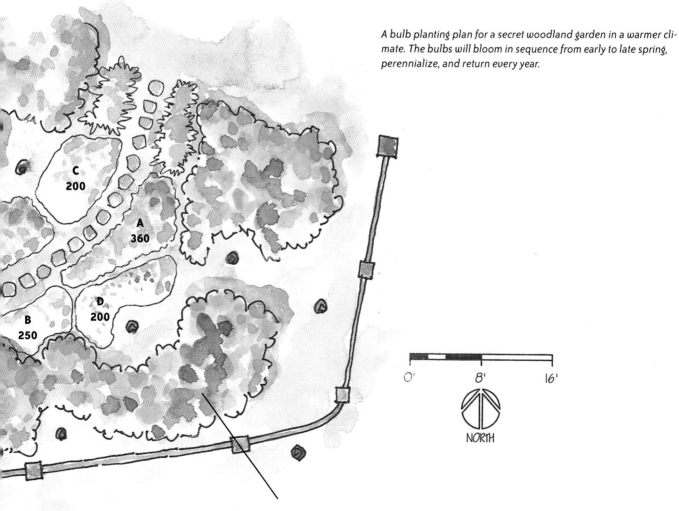

C
200

A
360

D
200

B
250

0'   8'   16'

NORTH

Azaleas and Existing Plantings

EDIBLE FRONT YARD: FALL

In fall the seasonal front-yard garden (first shown on page 60) displays yet another side of its multiseason interest. The dwarf fothergilla turns a vibrant gold and orange. Asters, coneflowers, goldenrod, and sneezeweed burst with the hues of fall—purple, yellow, and orange. Currants are ready to harvest.

Fruit from the quince can be made into jelly. When the leaves fall off the crabapple trees, they reveal the red fruit which can be used to supply pectin in jellies. Annual cool-season greens, mustards, and vegetables take the place in the annual bed in the center.

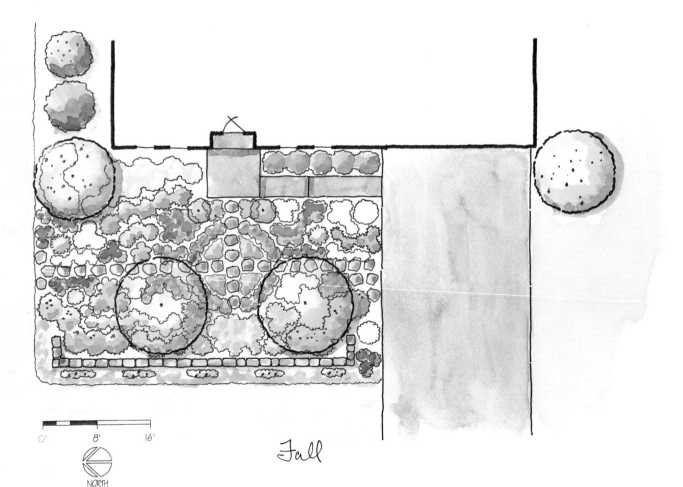

0'   8'   16'

NORTH

Fall

The edible seasonal front yard garden in fall. The shrubs, flowers, and trees with interest or bloom at this time of year are highlighted in color.

Fall Chores

 Continue to check for disease and damage from insects.

 Plant bareroot or container-grown currants and gooseberries if you live in cooler regions or in areas where spring planting is difficult because of soggy, cold soils. Currants and gooseberries bloom early in the spring.

 Plant cool-season greens and vegetables.

☑ Plant garlic and shallots.

☑ Plant daffodil and tulip bulbs.

☑ Clean up the garden. Remove dead foliage from around plants and perennials and put it in the compost. Seed heads can be left on coneflowers, black-eyed Susans, and sedums to attract birds or for winter interest outdoors; they can also be used for winter arrangements and wreaths. Grasses can also be left for winter interest and to provide cover for wild life.

☑ Clean and store tools for the season.

FALL MENUS

One
Fall-Garden Spring Rolls with
 Three Dipping Sauces
Swiss Chard Lo Mein
Fennel Pickles
Pawpaw-Apple Cake
Bouquet of crabapples, viburnum
 berries, asters, and Japanese
 anemones

Two
Pork Tenderloin with Apple and
 Onion Gravy
Crispy Roasted Potatoes with
 Rosemary and Herbs
Quick Spanakopita
Braised Fresh Kale with Bacon and
 Onions
Squash Soup
Mrs. Foster's Crusty Baked Apples
Bouquet of black-eyed
 Susans, coneflowers, sweet
 coneflowers, and sneezeweed

Three
Tofu or Sirloin Kabobs with
 Béarnaise Sauce
Broccoli Florets
Brown Rice
Pear Baklava
Bouquet of 'Chocolate' Joe
 pye weed, goldenrod, and
 sneezeweed

Winter

Winter is a time of rest for many gardens, but that doesn't mean the landscape is without beauty or usefulness. If the garden is near the house, it can be enjoyed visually even in winter. That's where careful design comes in. When planning a multiseasonal garden, integrate evergreen plants or shrubs with interesting twigs or colorful berries in the garden to give structure and color to the garden when perennials have died back and deciduous flowering shrubs have lost their leaves.

Take another look at the winter garden as a fruitful productive garden. You may not be harvesting edibles daily, but with a little planning you can be snipping bright evergreens and colorful berries for your own wreaths and arrangements. With protection in northern gardens you may be able to grow fresh greens and root vegetables well into the winter months. In mild climates, root vegetables and greens will grow all winter in cold frames or under cloches. In southern gardens it goes without saying that you can grow a variety of spinach, parsley, Swiss chard, kale, mustard, leeks, carrots, and onions without protection, outside in the garden.

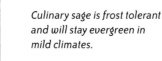

Culinary sage is frost tolerant and will stay evergreen in mild climates.

The gloom of the world
is but a shadow.
Behind it, yet within our reach, is joy.
~TASHA TUDOR~

Extend the Season

Magnolia leaves, evergreens, and bows decorate a storefront window in Granville, Ohio.

CLOCHES

A cloche (French for bell) is a miniature glass greenhouse shaped like a bell, wide at the bottom and narrowly rounded on top. These glass jars protect seedlings and fragile plants from wind and cold weather. Their original use dates to the 1600s in France. Jean-Baptiste de La Quintinie, a lawyer turned kitchen garden designer, in his book *Instruction pour les Jardins Fruitiers et Potagers* (1690), reveals how he was able to send to the table of Louis XIV asparagus and sorrel in December, radishes, lettuces, and mushrooms in January, cauliflowers in March, strawberries early in April, peas in May, and melons in June. Cloches, cold frames, intensive-gardening methods, and of course, a myriad of workers at your disposal all were part of the strategy for cool-season gardening for royalty at Versailles. Think of it: fresh radishes and lettuce from the garden in January. It's the asparagus in December I find surprising.

Try growing cool-season greens like spinach in cold frames through the winter, or at least extend the growing season.

(left) Cloches add just the right amount of protection for cool-season crops in the winter. They also add a decorative element to the winter garden. This photo was taken in late winter when the thermometer read 10 degrees below zero (Fahrenheit).

Market gardeners in France and England used cloches in the mid-nineteenth century to cover individual heads of lettuce and cabbage. Row after row of glass jars were lined up to protect acres of greens. This was a labor-intensive method of farming as each cloche needed to be propped open in the heat of the day and then let down at night. Old photographs have always impressed me, not just for the back-breaking commitment, but for the sheer elegance of it. Glass in the garden looks cool.

COLD FRAMES

Cold frames are boxes with glass lids that protect seedlings. They can be constructed from old windows bought at garage sales or salvaged from buildings. Use the size of the window to gauge the size of the box and build a bottomless frame to fit. Add a hinge to the back of the window frame for easy access.

Sink it in the ground a few inches or prop it on a foundation of bricks loosely laid on the ground. Add compost and good soil to a depth of 12 to 15 inches (30–38 cm), but make sure the box extends high enough for plants to grow; 18 inches (45 cm) should be adequate. Prop open the glass when a sunny day warms up and close it at night for protection. Bump the frame up against a building for even more protection and make sure the site faces south. Lay the long dimension east and west so most of the window has the southerly exposure. Build the frame at an angle to capture the rays of the low winter sun.

Cold frames can also be permanent structures built onto the side of a greenhouse. They can be constructed out of brick, stone, or concrete block. Even with a cold frame, you may need to add extra insulation during the coldest winter days in northern gardens. An old blanket will work.

Winter Greens

A variety of greens can survive outside where winters are mild. Kale, mustard, spinach, Swiss chard, arugula, and broccoli raab are worth a try in zone 6 or warmer. Cloches and cold frames will help extend your growing season and may make it possible to grow greens in zone 4 or 5, at least for part of the winter.

MÂCHE (*Valerianella*)
Annual
Seed to table: 45 to 50 days

For me the most successful cold-hardy green that reliably survives in my climate is mâche, also called corn salad or lamb's lettuce. I sow it in the fall when days are still warm to give the seeds a few weeks of growing weather, then cover the seedlings with glass cloches when the temperatures stay consistently low. The tasty greens survive the entire winter under glass. There is something very satisfying about putting on my winter coat, hat, and gloves, traipsing through the snow, pushing ice and snow away from the wooden gate so I can open it, lifting the frosted jar, and harvesting bright green seedlings in defiance of winter. The color green in the form of tiny salad greens goes with anything in the winter: on hot bean soup or in a party dip or salad.

SPINACH (*Spinacia oleracea*)
Annual
Seed to table: 35 to 40 days

Continue to harvest fresh spinach leaves from plants grown in cold frames or under cloches. Varieties with heavily crinkled leaves are best for winter. See more on spinach in the Spring and Fall chapters (pages 41 and 159, respectively).

Spinach dip redux made with fresh baby greens from the cold frame served with toasted bread. The sage was picked from the garden.

Spinach Dip Redux

Remember the spinach dip made with a soup mix? You won't miss the dehydrated version at all. Fresh greens and vegetables taste better than freeze-dried; the onions, fresh parsley, and fresh greens add all of the flavor you need. Add chopped fresh artichoke hearts when they are in season.

Makes about 3 cups dip

8 ounces cream cheese, at room temperature

1 cup sour cream

½ cup plain yogurt

2 cups fresh spinach, chopped

2 cups mixed winter greens, such as kale, mâche, or
    Swiss chard, chopped

6–8 green onions, chopped

2–3 small leeks, chopped

1 carrot, grated

½ cup fresh flat-leaf parsley, finely chopped

½ cup sliced almonds, toasted

4 ounces parmesan cheese, coarsely grated

⅛ teaspoon hot pepper flakes

Preheat oven to 350°F. Beat the cream cheese in a mixer and add the sour cream and yogurt in small amounts, mixing well after each addition. Add the remaining ingredients and combine using stir speed until well mixed. Pour into an oven-proof dish and heat for 25–30 minutes or until bubbly. Serve hot, or chill and serve cold without heating. Serve with pita bread or wheat crackers.

This photograph was taken a week after the one of the snow covered cloches on page 179. During a brief respite in the weather the snow melted. Mâche (corn salad) magically survived the subzero temperatures under glass. I pulled out a few precious green seedlings, root and all, to sprinkle on a winter soup.

Like other root crops, turnips can be left in the ground until it freezes in the winter.

Winter Root Vegetables

Root vegetables can be left outside in the garden where winters are mild. Sow seed of carrots, parsnips, rutabaga, and turnips in summer when the weather is still warm so the seeds germinate and have time to grow. Give extra protection to the root crops by covering with a layer of leaves, leaf compost, grass clippings, or straw. Harvest the root crops before the ground is frozen.

PARSLEY ROOT (*Petroselinum*)
Biennial grown as an annual
Seed to table: 75 to 85 days

Parsley root is grown for the root instead of the leafy tops like the herb. It looks like a parsnip but thinner. It also resembles a white carrot. Parsley root can be grown like carrots in rich, loose soil. The seeds can be sown directly in the garden in mid to late summer so they will be ready to harvest after the first few frosts. 'Fakir' is a variety that is readily available to the home gardener. Like all of the root vegetables, parsley root can be sliced and added to soups or roasted with a little olive oil.

Parsnips are a wonderful winter vegetable. The frost-tolerant roots can be left in the ground in the winter in mild climates and harvested as needed. In cooler climates try mulching well to protect the ground from freezing.

PARSNIP (*Pastinaca sativa*)
Biennial grown as an annual
Seed to table: 100 to 120 days

Parsnips look like fat white carrots. In fact, they are in the same family as the carrot. Somewhere along the line orange was singled out as a preferred color and over the years the two diverged.

Harvest parsnips after a few frosts or anytime through the winter but before new growth begins in the early spring. Just before the spring growth begins the root begins turning starch to sugar. This makes for a very sweet flavor. Parsnips are unfamiliar to many but in Great Britain the roots are part of traditional Christmas dinners.

Cut off the green tops and mature parsnips will keep in the refrigerator for four to five months and still be good. Use in soups and stews or boil and mash. This root vegetable is really sweet and tasty when roasted.

RUTABAGA (*Brassica napus*)
Biennial grown as an annual
Seed to table: 90 to 110 days

A rutabaga is like a turnip but with yellow flesh. It's actually a cross between a cabbage and a turnip. Harvest when the round vegetable is 4 to 5 inches (10–12.5 cm) in diameter and has been exposed to some frosts. It can stay in the winter garden until the ground is frozen. Peel and boil rutabaga until it's tender, then mash and serve like mashed potatoes with butter, salt, and pepper. Rutabaga keeps for a few months in the refrigerator. 'American Purple Top' is an heirloom variety from before 1920.

TURNIP (*Brassica rapa*)
Biennial grown as an annual
Seed to table: 35 to 58 days

Turnips are grown for the greens or the roots or both. The round root usually has white flesh and can be eaten raw, boiled and mashed, or roasted. Turnips can be left in the ground until it is completely frozen in the winter. Like other root crops, turnips become sweeter with a few frosts. 'Red Round' is an Asian variety with small red globe-shaped roots and stems.

Roasting winter roots like parsnips, turnips, and rutabaga brings out the natural sweetness of the vegetables.

Roasted White Winter Vegetables

Try all these winter vegetables roasted to see which ones you like. Roasted turnips, parsnips, and rutabagas each have a distinct flavor.

Serves 4
1 small turnip
3–4 parsnips
1 small rutabaga
Extra virgin olive oil
Coarse salt

Preheat oven to 400°F. Peel and slice vegetables to make about 3 cups. Place in a roasting pan. Drizzle with good olive oil and coarse salt. Roast for 25–30 minutes until vegetables are tender. Serve immediately.

From the Pantry

DRIED BEANS

You can dry beans in the late fall by simply leaving them in the garden on the trellis until the sun dries them. When the outer shell turns brown, collect them and separate the hard beans. Discard any that are damaged.

Beans that are not dry when cold wet weather sets in at the end of the season can be hung in a dry place inside. Gather the vines off the trellis and hang them up until the shells are brown and dry. Then sort.

Store the shelled beans in airtight containers in a cupboard. Dried beans last for a long time, maybe forever, so what isn't used this year can be stored for next.

Preparing beans takes a little forethought; put them on to soak the night before you need them. Dried beans triple in size when cooked so they need abundant water.

> **To cook dried beans**, first rinse and sort beans. Use 3–4 cups water or stock for every 1 cup of dry beans. Soak beans in water overnight. Then bring to boil and simmer until tender. Or skip the soaking and bring to a boil, then simmer for 1–2 hours until tender. Add more water if necessary to prevent burning.

Chorizo and black bean soup is perfect when it's cold outside. Here it is served with a topping of corn salad mâche fresh from the outside garden.

Chorizo and Black Bean Soup

Serves 4

2 cups dried black beans
6 cups water
1 pound chorizo sausage
6–8 green onions, sliced
3 garlic cloves, chopped
½ teaspoon cumin
2–3 carrots, chopped
2–3 small potatoes, peeled and chopped
6 cups chicken or vegetable stock
Coarse salt
Fresh cilantro (optional)
Sour cream (optional)

Soak the beans in 6 cups of water overnight, then drain. This will shorten the cooking time for the soup.

Cook the Chorizo sausage in a large, heavy soup pot; break into small pieces as you cook. Drain the sausage. Add the green onion, garlic, and cumin and sauté until aromatic. Add the carrots, potatoes, black beans, and chicken stock. Salt to taste.

Simmer covered for one or two hours until potatoes, beans, and carrots are tender, add more stock to the pot to prevent sticking. Serve with chopped fresh cilantro and a dollop of sour cream.

Dried heirloom rattlesnake beans, grown in the author's garden.

DRIED FRUITS

Dried fruits are readily available in grocery stores or use fruits from your own trees that you dried at the end of summer.

Winter squash has a tough waxy shell that makes it suitable for long term storage. This red and blue Hubbard squash is ready for winter storage.

DRIED TOMATOES (*Lycopersicum*)

Dried tomatoes, like other dried vegetables and fruits, are readily available in grocery stores or you can dry tomatoes harvested from your own garden. See more on tomatoes in the Summer and Fall chapters (pages 84 and 144, respectively).

WINTER SQUASH (*Cucurbita*)

Even without a root cellar, you can store the hard-shelled winter squashes through the winter. Keep them in a cool, dry place, such as a basement. Butternut, acorn, and Hubbard squash store well because they develop a hard skin that protects them. See more on squash in the Summer and Fall chapters (pages 81 and 142, respectively).

Fruit cake with dried fruits and nuts can be made with fruits you gathered from your garden or the farmer's market and dried yourself. It stores well, just periodically drizzle on some brandy.

Fruit Cake with Dried Fruits and Nuts

This fruit cake uses naturally dried fruit without added food coloring, citron, or corn syrup.

Makes 4 (6-inch) Bundt cakes
1½ cups dried cherries
1 cup dried apricots, coarsely chopped
1 cup golden raisins
½ cup brandy, plus more for drizzle
Butter for pans
1 small piece (1 inch) fresh ginger root
1 orange with peel, quartered, seeded, and ends
    removed
1 cup butter, softened
1 cup brown sugar
1 cup all-purpose flour
1 cup hickory nuts, black walnuts, or walnuts, whole or
    coarsely chopped
1 cup pecans, whole or coarsely chopped

In a medium bowl, combine the cherries, apricots, and raisins and soak in brandy overnight until all the liquid is absorbed into the fruit.

The next day, preheat oven to 325°F. Butter bottom and sides of four small Bundt pans. Cover bottom of pan with parchment paper and butter again. Set aside.

Process ginger and orange in food processor until finely chopped. Cream butter and brown sugar until well blended and light. Blend in flour until well-mixed. Add in dried fruits, ginger, orange, and nuts and stir just to blend. Pour mixture into prepared baking pans. Bake for 1 hour or until done in center.

When the cakes are cool, drizzle a few tablespoons brandy over each cake. Wrap and store. Add additional brandy over cake every few days.

Linguine with Oven-Roasted Garlic and (Sun-)Dried Tomatoes

Serves 4 to 6
1 cup vegetable or chicken stock
1 cup dried tomatoes, rehydrated
6 garlic cloves, sliced
⅓ cup extra-virgin olive oil
1 tablespoon butter
¼ cup pine nuts
½ cup walnuts, coarsely chopped
¼ cup Kalamata or mixed olives, pitted
Juice of ½ lemon
Salt and freshly ground pepper
1 pound linguine, uncooked
4 ounces goat cheese, crumbled

To rehydrate dried tomatoes for use the same day, bring the stock to a boil in a sauce pan. Turn off the heat, add the chopped dried tomatoes, and cover for an hour until tender and the liquid is absorbed. Or, to rehydrate dried tomatoes for use the next day, chop them into pieces and mix with the stock. Store in the refrigerator overnight.

Preheat oven to 350°F. Pour the rehydrated tomatoes into a heavy Dutch oven. Add the garlic, olive oil, butter, pine nuts, walnuts, olives, and lemon juice. Salt and pepper to taste. Cover tightly and roast for 30–35 minutes or until hot and tomatoes are tender and walnuts are toasted.

While the sauce is cooking in the oven, bring a large pot of water to boiling and cook the pasta to the al dente stage. When pasta is ready, drain, rinse, and put on a serving platter. Pour the sauce over it and crumble goat cheese on top. The goat cheese will melt into the hot pasta blending with the roasted flavors to create a creamy, flavorful winter pasta. Serve immediately.

Winter tacos are made with winter squash, sweet potatoes, and dried beans. Homemade red chile can be served on the side.

Winter Tacos with Red Chile

This is a great winter dish which can be made from the vegetables you grew in the summer and are storing in the winter. It makes use of dried beans and winter squashes and is baked in the oven to warm the kitchen.

Serves 6
½ cup dried pinto beans
2 cups water
½ butternut (or other winter) squash
3 small potatoes
1 medium sweet onion
3 sweet potatoes
Olive oil
½ teaspoon coarse sea salt
½ cup (1 bunch) fresh cilantro, finely chopped
1 small jalapeño pepper, chopped
6–8 green onions, chopped
16 soft corn tortillas
Red Chile (recipe follows)
½ cup white cheddar cheese, grated

To prepare the beans: One day before, combine the dried beans and water in a bowl and let soak overnight. The next day, cook the beans and water over low heat until the beans are soft, about one to two hours. Check periodically so beans do not burn. Add more water if necessary.

To prepare the vegetables: Preheat oven to 400°F. Cut unpeeled squash into large chunks (it's easier to roast with the rind on, then peel when soft). Peel and cut the potatoes, sweet onion, and sweet potatoes into bite-size pieces. Drizzle olive oil over the cut vegetables, mix well, and sprinkle with coarse sea salt. Roast for 25–30 minutes. Onions should begin to caramelize and squash will be tender. Cool slightly; cut winter squash into bite-size pieces, discarding rind. Combine cooked beans and cooked vegetables. Add cilantro, jalapeño, and green onions. Stir to combine. Sprinkle with salt and pepper. This filling can be made a day ahead.

To prepare the corn tortillas: Heat oven to 350°. Brush cookie sheet with olive oil. Place corn tortillas on cookie sheet and brush each with additional olive oil. Heat for a few minutes until soft and hot. Turn over and heat for a few more minutes. Do not overcook. Stack and cover warm tortillas with foil until ready to use.

To assemble the tacos: Place a small amount of filling in each tortilla, sprinkle with cheese. Fold and place in casserole dish. Repeat with other tortillas. Bake at 350° until cheese is melted, about 30 minutes. Serve with red chile.

Red Chile

While traveling and living in New Mexico many years ago, I was intrigued by the nuances in the art of cooking with chile peppers. I had no idea the state took such pride in distinguishing the flavors of their sauces based on when the pepper was harvested. Pick the pepper at the green stage, roast it over an open fire, and you have the basis for green chile. Allow the pepper to mature to its full red and ripe color, then dry naturally and you have the basic ingredient for red chile. Dried chile peppers can be stored through the winter.

The recipe following is for red chile cooked in the traditional way, with dried chile peppers picked from your own ristra, if you have the dry climate to manage it. When made with mild dried chiles, this sauce is ideal for enchiladas or served on the side as a dipping sauce with Mexican food. For a spicier sauce, add more dried cayenne chiles or red pepper flakes.

10–12 dried red chiles, mild
1–3 dried cayenne chiles
Salt to taste

Remove and discard stems and seeds from dried chiles by cutting off the stem and slicing dried chile in half. Scrape out the seeds. Place chiles in sauce pan with just enough water to cover. Cook until soft, about 20 minutes.

Pour mixture into food processor and process until smooth. Add more water for a smooth consistency. Add salt to taste.

Preheat oven to 375°F. Add a small amount of olive oil to the bottom of a heavy Dutch oven. Cut the top off of an acorn squash or small butternut squash, reserving the top for another use. Remove the seeds from the squash to create a bowl. Place the squash in the Dutch oven.

In a separate bowl combine ½ cup pearled barley, green onions, garlic, and mushrooms. Add salt and pepper to taste. Stir the ingredients together and fill squash bowls with mixture.

Pour ½ cup of vegetable stock into each squash bowl, filling to the top with liquid. Place almonds on top. Cover the pot with a tight lid and roast for 35 minutes. Squash should be tender and almonds crisp. Serve immediately.

When stuffed squash bowls are baked in a heavy Dutch oven with a lid, the almonds are roasted as the squash and barley cook.

Barley in Squash Bowl

This is the perfect winter meal, easy to make with ingredients you probably have on hand and easy to clean up. It's made in one bowl and that bowl is made of squash. The barley is cooked to perfection along with the squash.

Serves 2
Olive oil
2 small acorn or butternut squash (about 3–4 inches across)
½ cup quick pearled barley, uncooked
2–3 green onions, chopped
1 garlic clove, finely chopped
½ cup mushrooms, chopped
Salt and freshly ground pepper
1 cup vegetable stock
Water as needed
¼ cup sliced almonds

Small squash varieties like this acorn squash can be filled and baked for a single serving. Fill with butter and brown sugar or honey for something sweet or add savory ingredients like barley with garlic, mushrooms, and green onions.

Meyer lemons can be grown outdoors in the winter in very warm climates; elsewhere they must be grown indoors.

Grow Citrus Trees Indoors

It never fails, every winter in January or February I yearn for something lemony and sweet like lemon bars or lemon pie. It's probably not lemons I'm yearning for, but summer. There may actually be a biological reason we crave lemon treats during the short dreary days of winter, as the aroma of fresh lemons relaxes us and improves our mood. Cutting lemons makes us happier. So start slicing and breathe deeply.

Gardeners who live in warm places like California, Texas, or Florida may be able to pick fresh from their own outdoor lemon trees in midwinter, but elsewhere gardeners must bring citrus containers indoors to an orangery or a sunny draft-free room in the house. Citrus trees need eight hours of light during the winter. This can be supplied from a window or supplemented by complete spectrum lighting put on a timer set to turn on at sunrise and off at sunset. Citrus trees also need a consistent supply of water, not a lot of water, but a regular schedule so that the tree doesn't dry out and then get saturated. The soil should be kept just moist.

Following are some of the best citrus varieties for growing indoors in containers. These trees will produce fruit year-round and won't grow too large. Grow them in painted wood boxes with wheels and the fruit trees can be wheeled outside during the summer when temperatures are warm. If you don't grow your own fruit, Meyer lemons can be found in abundance during the winter months at the grocery.

IMPROVED MEYER LEMON (*Citrus ×meyeri* 'Improved Meyer')

Meyer lemon trees were first introduced into the United States by Frank Meyer in 1908. He discovered them growing as ornamental potted plants in China. Evergreen Meyer lemons have a long history of being grown in containers; maybe that's a good omen.

Meyer lemons (*Citrus ×meyeri*) are a cross between sweet oranges (*Citrus sinensis*) and lemons (*Citrus limon*) and are less sour than regular lemons. The sweeter taste is perfect for tarts and pies. The trees will bloom twice a year with the heaviest fruiting in midwinter (January). The plants are hardier than other lemon varieties and the fruit does not require heat to ripen.

'Improved Meyer' lemon is a virus-free clone released by the University of California in the 1970s. It's identical to the Meyer lemon but without the virus. When 'Improved Meyer' lemon is grafted to a dwarf rootstock it makes a great container plant easily maintained at 3 to 5 feet (90–150 cm) or even smaller with pruning. It's probably the only variety sold now, but double-check when you purchase.

Lemony pie is not too sweet and not too sour. It's a welcome treat in the depths of winter when we crave lemons and citrus.

Lemony Pie

This winter treat uses lemons sliced very thin that are baked right into the pie. It also has a top crust which seals in the flavor and produces the right delectable lemon custard consistency. This pie is the right balance of tart and sweet. Use Meyer lemons if you can get them or substitute regular lemons.

Makes 1 (9-inch) pie
1 cup butter
1½ cups all-purpose flour, plus more
1 tablespoon sugar
Dash of salt
6–8 teaspoons cold water
2 tablespoons butter, melted
3 eggs
2½ cups sugar

2 tablespoons butter, melted
Dash of salt
½ cup water
3 Meyer lemons, peeled, seeded, and sliced very thin

Preheat oven to 350°F. To make the pie crust, process 1 cup butter, flour, 1 tablespoon sugar, and salt in a food processor just until butter is cut into small pieces. With processor running, slowly add the cold water a teaspoon at a time. Process until dough just sticks together. Divide dough into two equal portions. Turn out one of the balls of dough onto a floured surface and roll out for the bottom pie crust, about ¼ inch thick. Place into a 9-inch pie pan, covering the bottom and sides. Roll out the remaining dough to make the top crust. Set aside.

Combine the eggs, 2½ cups sugar, melted butter, salt, and water in a bowl and stir well. Add sliced lemons, then pour mixture into an unbaked pie shell. Top with the top crust and crimp the edges as desired. Bake for 35 minutes or until done.

Lemon and Key Lime Curd

Homemade lemon curd is easy to make. The classic sweet tart flavor is wonderful on toast or biscuits and a perfect partner to a cup of tea for an afternoon energy boost. This recipe uses juice from lemons and key limes for a variation to the traditional lemon curd. Regular limes could be used in place of key limes.

Makes 1 cup
3 eggs
1½ cups sugar
Juice of 3–4 lemons (about ½ cup)
Juice of 4 key limes (about ½ cup)
Zest of 3 lemons (about 2 tablespoons)
¾ cup cold butter, cut into pieces

Whisk the eggs, sugar, juices, and zest in a heavy sauce pan over medium-low heat. Keep whisking until the mixture is hot. Add the butter one piece at a time allowing each to melt. Continue cooking and stirring until whisk marks stay in and small bubbles begin to appear. Remove from heat. Cover and store in refrigerator. Serve on toast or as a dessert with dried fruit. Make it again in the summer and serve with fresh blueberries.

LIMES (*Citrus, Limonia*)

Limes are sensitive to frost and must be brought indoors when temperatures approach freezing. Growing them in containers makes it easier to move them.

The bumpy texture of the Thai lime (*Citrus hystrix*) reminds me of miniature hedge apples from the Osage orange tree but a darker green. The small limes impart a unique flavor to Thai cooking; the juice is tart but the rind is often used in curries. Some use the juice of this lime more for cleaning than for cooking. The evergreen leaves are used in many Thai dishes; thinly slice the leaves to impart the authentic flavor. The tree reaches 6 to 8 feet (1.8–2.4 m) if planted in a container but will grow larger in the landscape.

Key lime (*Limonia aurantifolia*), also known as Mexican lime, grows well in containers. It is a spiny, shrubby evergreen. The fruit is juicy with a tropical flavor, the inspiration for the famous key lime pies. Key lime trees will produce fruit year-round.

Winter Herbs

I have been able to pick fresh sage and thyme from the outdoor potager in mild winters in my zone 5 garden, but it's not a sure thing. To ensure fresh pungent herbs even in the harshest winters, you have to grow them indoors. A sunny window will do, but a better way is to set up grow lights. I purchased a 2-foot (60-cm) light and mounted it under my countertop, connected it to a timer, and now have fresh herbs growing next to my stove.

The biggest problem with growing herbs indoors during the winter is the lack of moisture. The plants may need water everyday because of dry indoor heat combined with the intense lights. To help add moisture to the air around the plants, place some decorative stones in a tray, fill the tray with water, then set the potted herbs on top of the stones. The water in the stones will evaporate around the plants supplying moisture to the air. Add water to the stones daily and check the soil around the pots frequently.

Some indispensable herbs for an indoor winter herb garden, at the risk of sounding like a Simon and Garfunkel record, are flat-leaf Italian parsley, sage, rosemary, and thyme.

ROSEMARY (*Rosmarinus*)

Rosemary is a fragrant culinary herb useful for winter cooking. Fresh sprigs are wonderful with roasted poultry or sprinkled on roasted potatoes. The aromatic leaves can be sprinkled on focaccia before baking or blended into the bread dough. Rosemary is harvested and used throughout the summer but is especially valued in the winter when we do more baking and roasting to warm the kitchen.

This evergreen herb is hardy in southern gardens but must be brought indoors in northern climates. Little pots of rosemary on the counter are a refreshing sight in the winter when we crave something green. Rosemary is tricky to grow indoors: it needs

Shiso, oregano, and thyme grow indoors under lights next to the stove in my kitchen in the winter.

Whole Wheat Focaccia with Rosemary and Onion

Fresh rosemary and coarsely grated parmesan cheese are blended with the dough in this whole wheat focaccia. Garlic and olive oil are brushed on top right before baking.

Makes 1 rectangular loaf
½ cup milk
½ cup water
1 cup whole wheat flour
2 cups unbleached flour
2 ½ teaspoons yeast
¾ teaspoon salt
1 teaspoon honey
7 tablespoons extra-virgin olive oil, divided, plus more
2 tablespoons fresh rosemary, finely chopped
½ cup parmesan cheese, coarsely grated
2 sweet onions, chopped
2 garlic cloves, finely chopped
Coarse salt

Preheat oven to 350°F. In a small saucepan, combine the milk and water and heat until very warm to the touch.

Combine the flours, yeast, and salt in a mixing bowl at low speed until blended. Add the milk and water mixture, honey, and 4 tablespoons olive oil and mix well. Blend with a dough hook until dough is pliable and soft but not sticky. Knead with the dough hook for 5–8 minutes, periodically kneading by hand to make sure the dough is well blended. Add the rosemary and cheese and continue mixing and kneading until both are incorporated through the dough.

Remove the dough from the bowl, put a bit of olive oil on the bottom of the bowl, place the dough back in the bowl, and turn the dough upside down to coat the top with oil. Cover the bowl and let the dough rise in a warm place about an hour.

While the dough is rising, cook the onions in a heavy skillet with a little olive oil until the onions are lightly browned and soft, about an hour, stirring periodically.

Place the dough on a lightly oiled cookie sheet and flatten to a rectangle about 9 by 12 inches. Cover and let rise for ½ an hour.

To make the toppings, combine the garlic with 3 tablespoons olive oil. Brush on top of dough. Place the caramelized onions on top and sprinkle with coarse salt. Bake for 25 minutes or until flatbread is done. Serve immediately.

Roasted Cornish game hens with sage and thyme make a pretty presentation at a holiday meal.

Cornish Game Hen with Sage and Thyme

Serves 6
6 Cornish game hens
12 fresh sage leaves
Extra virgin olive oil
Coarse salt and freshly ground pepper
Sprigs of fresh thyme (optional)

Preheat oven to 400°F. Remove giblets from the game hens. Insert a whole sage leaf under the skin of each breast. Place game hens breast side up and cover with a light drizzle of good olive oil. Sprinkle with salt and pepper. Roast for an hour. Garnish with sprigs of thyme and serve.

Toasted Bread Stuffing with Fresh Herbs

This is a variation of the classic stuffing I watched my grandmother and then my mother make every Thanksgiving when I was a child. You don't need to use prepared, cubed stuffing in a bag. Any bread will do. I find this works especially well for French bread that's a few days old and hard. Whole grain breads work well, too. I make some to stuff the bird and some with vegetable stock baked separately for the vegetarians at the table.

Makes 12 cups of stuffing
1 loaf day-old French bread
½ cup butter
6–8 green onions, chopped
3–4 stalks celery, chopped
3–4 fresh sage leaves, finely chopped
Few sprigs fresh thyme, finely chopped
2 cups chicken or vegetable stock
Salt and freshly ground pepper

Preheat oven to 350°F. Break bread into bite-size pieces and leave on trays in open air until dry. Place in a large baking pan. Set aside.

Melt butter in a large saucepan and sauté green onion and celery for a few minutes. Add herbs and stock and heat through. Pour over bread, mixing well. Bread will absorb the liquid and become soft. Add salt and pepper to taste.

Bake for 35 minutes until desired crispness. Heat longer if crunchier stuffing is desired.

water. Do not allow the soil to dry out. This is really counterintuitive because rosemary is native to the Mediterranean region and is drought tolerant outdoors in the garden. Place the pot near a sunny window or under lights. Did I mention water often? See more about rosemary in the Summer chapter (page 111).

SAGE (*Salvia officinalis*)

Culinary or common sage is another evergreen herb that is native to the Mediterranean region. It naturally prefers Mediterranean growing conditions, namely, full sun and sandy, well-drained soils. It does not tolerate heavy, wet, clay soils. The difficulty growing sage in the midwestern and northern United States may be, in fact, the wet, winter soils and not the low temperatures. Nevertheless, I find some varieties of culinary sage not hardy in my zone 5 garden. Try it in well-drained pots indoors for the winter. See more about sage in the Summer chapter (page 111).

Evergreens, berries, and grasses collected from the author's garden for a simple winter container. The greens will stay fresh and green in the cold all winter. Insert cut branches directly in the soil before the soil freezes. Use a container suitable for your climate--terra cotta and pottery must be brought indoors or stored in a garage in cold climates.

Create Winter Color Inside and Out

The day after Thanksgiving marks the time when the holiday frenzy begins in the United States. Shopping, baking, decorating—all of the memories of our own childhoods and now our expectations of the ideal holiday can overwhelm us. One strategy is to tune out the din of the advertisers, avoid the shopping mall, and walk your own property with an eye for twigs, berries, and greens that can be gathered and brought inside to decorate the mantle, table, or indoor containers. These evergreens and berries can also be placed in outdoor containers at the front door for a bright greeting.

To simplify the season, connect with nature. Put your pruners in your back pocket, bundle up, and invite someone to walk outdoors with you. See what you can glean from your own garden.

Winter Berries

BARBERRY (*Berberis*)
Deciduous shrub
Zones 4 to 8

Fendler's barberry (*Berberis fendleri*) is a deciduous shrub native to Colorado and New Mexico. It has multiseason appeal. The hanging clusters of bright red edible berries stay on the shrub all through the winter. The shrub grows in part sun and reaches 6 to 8 feet (18–2.4 m) tall.

BEAUTYBERRY (*Callicarpa*)
Deciduous shrub
Zones 5 to 11 (varies with variety)

American beautyberry (*Callicarpa americana*) is an American Southeast native that produces vibrant lavender-purple berries in the late summer. The berries persist on the bare stems into winter. The intense color of the berries will surprise you. This deciduous shrub grows to a height of 6 to 8 feet (1.8–2.4 m) and prefers part shade, as in woodland conditions, and is often found growing under tall pine trees. It's a coarse shrub but perfect for an informal woodland border. For best fruit production cut the plant back severely every year. I have seen the branches for sale by the bunch at Christmas time at local nurseries. American beautyberry is hardy in zones 7 to 11. There are other varieties that are hardy in cooler climates.

Purple beautyberry (*Callicarpa dichotoma*), also known as Korean beautyberry, is not native to the United States but is similar to American beautyberry with a neater habit. It is hardy in zones 5 to 8 and also sports the bright lavender berries.

Japanese beautyberry (*Callicarpa japonica*) is hardy in zones 5 to 8. 'Leucocarpa' has white fruit.

CHOKEBERRY (*Aronia*)
Deciduous shrub
Zones 3 to 9

Black chokeberry (*Aronia melanocarpa*) is a deciduous native American shrub that produces edible black berries in the fall. The berries are suitable for jams, jellies, or pies. The white flowers in spring and the black berries in autumn make it an attractive plant even if you don't eat the fruit. The shrub prefers part shade and wet conditions. 'Autumn Magic' has excellent fall color. 'Viking' is one of the best varieties for fruit.

Red chokeberry (*Aronia arbutifolia*) is a multiseason shrub for color in the garden. 'Brilliantissima' has abundant red berries in the fall that persist through winter because the birds find the fruit a bit astringent. It also has brilliant red fall foliage.

HAWTHORN (*Crataegus*)
Deciduous shrub or small tree
Zones 3 to 9 (varies with the variety)

Hawthorns are a large group of trees that vary in character but in general are small, often thorny, deciduous trees or large shrubs that produce fruit. The fruits range from black to red, vary in size, and create food for birds and wild life. Sometimes the fruit is edible to humans. Mayhaw trees (*Crataegus aestivalis*) are native to the American Southeast and hardy in zones 7 to 9. They produce red fruit for locally prized amber-orange Mayhaw jelly.

Some hawthorn varieties have been developed for ornamental use in the landscape. These have multiseason appeal in the small garden—white blooms in the spring, attractive bark, good form, and bright red berries that persist into the winter. Not berries for eating, but clusters of fruit that can be cut to decorate outdoor wreaths or brought indoors for arrangements.

Beautyberry produces showy purple berries that can be used for arrangements in the winter. This photograph was taken in the fall before the leaves dropped. The berries are not edible to humans, but the birds love them.

(left) *Bright red berries persist on 'Winter King' hawthorn* (Crataegus viridis) *through the winter. Clip a few for decorations or leave them for the birds.*

'Winter King' hawthorn (*Crataegus viridis* 'Winter King') is one of my favorite varieties because of the wide vase form of the tree, the gray slightly peeling bark, and the large abundant fruit in the winter. I have been admiring my neighbor's tree for years. In the bleakest part of the winter, when the crabapples are long gone, this tree has vibrant red berries that contrast with the dark branches. This is a very useful tree for the middle part of the United States; it brings vivid color when we need it most. Since it will never grow large it's great for small yards. The tree is attractive outside in the winter garden and does double duty as a useful plant for indoor arrangements.

Other recommended varieties are cockspur hawthorn (*Crataegus crus-galli*) and Washington hawthorn (*Crataegus phaenopyrum*) These trees also produce abundant berries for late fall and winter color. Hawthorns prefer sites in full sun.

The bright red berries of 'Bright Horizon' winterberry (Ilex verticillata) persist through the winter. This photograph was taken at Dawes Arboretum in Newark, Ohio in early winter (late December).

WINTERBERRY (*Ilex verticillata*)
Deciduous shrub
Zones 4 to 9

Common winterberry produces bright red fruit that persists through the winter. The shrub prefers full sun and moist, acidic conditions. Like the evergreen hollies, winterberry needs a male pollinator to produce fruit on the female plants. Vibrant red winterberry branches can be cut for arrangements. I've seen individual berry-laden branches for sale at plant nurseries during the winter holidays. Grow your own instead and enjoy the bright fruits whether you cut them or not.

Other berry-producing species in the genus *Ilex* are commonly known as hollies. Cultivars of American holly (*Ilex opaca*) have bright red or yellow berries in addition to evergreen leaves and make excellent cuttings for arrangements or winter wreaths.

'Dunn No. 2' holly (Ilex opaca) produces vivid gold berries as an alternative to red for winter color.

WINTERGREEN (*Gaultheria procumbens*)
Evergreen groundcover
Zones 3 to 8

Wintergreen is a low-growing evergreen groundcover that produces red edible berries. The fragrant leaves can be crushed and used for wintergreen flavoring. The species is native to the eastern half of the United States and Canada and is endangered in Illinois. It takes light to moderate shade and prefers moist acidic soil. Wintergreen is slow to establish but is a good choice for an edible woodland landscape if you have rich, moist acidic soil.

VIBURNUM (*Viburnum*)
Deciduous flowering shrub (sometimes evergreen)
Zones 5 to 8 (depending on the cultivar)

Fruit will remain on some of the viburnums through the winter, if the birds don't eat it. I have had clusters of deep blue berries remain on my *Viburnum nudum* 'Bulk' (Brandywine) through the winter. See more on viburnum in the Spring and Fall chapters (pages 52 and 165, respectively).

Blossoms, Twigs, and Seed Heads

DRIED FLOWERS AND GRASSES

Look for the beauty in dried flowers. Brown is a color, not vivid, not bright, but dried flowers have their own subtle beauty. It is mainly what we see in the winter, but shades can vary from tan to reddish or dark brown. It is the reality of the winter season for perennials. Leave the flower heads on plants in the fall to dry naturally by the sun and wind. Many have interesting shapes that add subtle textures to the landscape when nothing is growing. Dried grasses and flowers also create mounds of interesting textures when snow drifts over them.

The flat flower heads of *Sedum* 'Autumn Joy' naturally dry to a rich dark brown in the late fall. Leave the flowers on the plant for texture or cut some to add with pinecones and evergreens for wreaths and arrangements. Hydrangea blossoms are wonderful dried. No need to elaborately fuss with the flowers, just leave them on the shrub outside. The sun and air will dry them to a pale patina. Gather in early winter before strong winds blow the dried blossoms away. Seed heads of coneflowers (*Echinacea*) and black-eyed Susans (*Rudbeckia*) will feed goldfinches and other birds during the winter.

Ornamental grasses look luminous in the fall when they turn various shades of gold and amber. They are useful in the winter garden for that reason, especially if sited where they are viewed from the house with strong backlighting so they glow. Have you considered growing them for the tall light tan dried plumes?

The strong architectural interest of grasses in the garden is useful indoors in the vase. We created our own decorations for my daughter's wedding and reception. We dried *Miscanthus sinensis* 'Gracillimus' in early spring (before the green spring growth), removed the feathery plumes, placed bunches in simple vases, added a large white ribbon and set them on the dining tables. The arrangements were minimalist, elegant, and added architectural pizzazz to a ballroom with enormously high ceilings. The tall grass arrangements were the perfect scale for such a massive room.

DOGWOOD (*Cornus*)
Deciduous ornamental shrub
Zones 2 to 7 (depending on plant)

Red osier dogwood (*Cornus servicea*) is similar in form to willow. The word *osier* derives from Old French and means willow-like. 'Cardinal' has bright red stems. 'Silver and Gold' has variegated leaves

'The Blues' little bluestem grass (Schizachyrium scoparium) and Limelight hydrangeas (Hydrangea paniculata 'Zwijnenburg') were cut in late fall to make this winter arrangement. The reddish hue of the native grass looks beautiful whether it's left outside or brought indoors.

and yellow stems. 'Flaviramea' also has bright yellow stems. These shrubs will grow 7 to 10 feet (2.1–3 m) tall and 10 to 15 feet (3–4.5 m) wide so need plenty of room. They can be kept smaller by coppicing (cutting down to the ground) in late fall. Cut all stems to 2 to 3 inches (5–7.5 cm) above the base. This ensures a smaller plant and vivid straight stems as the new growth has the most intense color.

Red osier dogwood is an excellent plant for the rain garden; it tolerates a variety of soils from saturated to dry. It prefers full sun but will tolerate shade. The species is native to much of the northern and western United States.

Blood twig dogwood (*Cornus sanguinea* 'Midwinter Fire') is hardy in zones 5 to 7 and has golden orange stems at the base that transition to orange-red at the tips. It also should be cut back each year.

HELLEBORES (*Helleborus ×hybridus*)
Evergreen perennial
Zones 4 to 9

Plant hellebores in the shade garden for winter color. The flowers bloom in late winter and early spring (from February through April). Hellebores prefer part to full shade in well-drained, humus-rich alkaline soil. The hybrids come in a range of colors from creamy white to yellow and reddish purple to dark black purple. The foliage remains evergreen. The flowers can be used for cut flowers when not much else is in bloom. Plant with hostas, ferns, and ramps in the woodland garden.

QUINCE (*Chaenomeles speciosa*)
Deciduous shrub
Zones 4 to 8

Common flowering quince is a large sprawling shrub that produces fragrant colorful blooms in late winter. The shrub is twiggy and coarse in the landscape but unparalleled for providing colorful blooms when nothing else is blooming. The branches can be cut

Red osier dogwood (Cornus servicea 'Flaviramea') has bright yellow stems in winter. If you have the room, plant in mass in the garden for the most impact. Cut all of the stems to the ground in early spring because the new growth is the most vibrant.

while still in the bud stage and brought indoors to flower even earlier. The simple, sculptural branches and blossoms are long lasting in the vase.

Flowering quince produces small edible fruits in the fall that can be used in jellies and preserves but these should not be confused with the fruiting quince tree (*Cydonia oblonga*), which produces large golden pear-apple-like fruits that are also used to make jellies. Flowering quince prefers full sun but will take part sun.

WILLOW (*Salix*)
Deciduous shrub or tree
Zones 2 to 8 (depending on the variety)

Willows have vivid stems in the winter that range from copper red to bright yellow. Coral bark willow (*Salix alba* 'Britzensis') has intense orange-red coloring. 'Flame' willow (*Salix* 'Flame') will grow to a

This arrangement of flowering quince (Chaenomeles speciosa) was picked in midwinter in a client's garden in the southeastern United States. The goal is to pick something for the vase or to munch on throughout the year.

The bright orange-red stems of coral bark willow (Salix alba 'Britzensis') can be cut for arrangements or left in the winter garden. Cut back stems in early spring because the new growth is the most vivid and it will keep the willow at garden size.

height of 15 to 30 feet (4.5–9 m) if left unpruned but can be kept smaller.

Willows are a natural plant for wet sites but tolerate drought once established. They are fast-growing shrubs and some will grow into large trees if left unpruned, so understand the yearly maintenance requirements for this plant on your site. Willows prefer full sun and moist soil.

Cut the stems down to the ground every year in late winter to keep them at a manageable landscape size and to produce the most intense coloring which only appears on new growth. The stems that are cut yearly can be used for baskets, twig furniture, wattle fencing, and flower arrangements.

Willows can also be pollarded yearly to keep them manageable. Cut the branches off to a stub that is 3 to 5 feet (90–150 cm) high. The effect is a single stem tree with a mass of branches at the node. Each year cut all of the branches back to the node.

Pussy willow (*Salix discolor*) is a large shrub with fuzzy catkins in late winter. These are perfect for winter arrangements and for children. There are male plants and female plants of pussy willows. Choose the male variety for the best display. Pussy willows produce pollen early to provide food for beneficial insects in the garden early in the season.

Curly willow (*Salix matsudana* 'Tortuosa' produces twisted, contorted stems. This is what florists and decorators use in arrangements, but you can grow your own.

Fragrant yellow blossoms cover the branches of one of the hybrid witch hazels, Hamamelis ×intermedia 'Westerstede', in early spring. Vernal witch hazel (H. vernalis) blooms a little earlier.

WITCH HAZEL (*Hamamelis*)
Deciduous shrub or small tree
Zones 4 to 8 (depending on variety)

Witch hazels can vary in form from an upright vase shape to a spreading horizontal tree depending on the cultivar. They can be grown in full sun or in part shade. The large shrub or small tree is one of the first shrubs to bloom in cold weather. Cut a few blooms to bring indoors.

Common witch hazel (*Hamamelis virginiana*) is a native multistemmed shrub or tree with winter bloom. It blooms in late fall or early winter with yellow flowers appearing as early as October to as late as December in my area.

Vernal witch hazel (*Hamamelis vernalis*) is also a native shrub and one of the first to bloom for the year. Yellow to orange red blooms emerge in mid to late winter (January or February). Use it for naturalizing in the woodland.

The hybrid witch hazels (*Hamamelis ×intermedia*) bloom in late winter to early spring (February or early March). The fragrant blooms range in color from pale yellow to russet red. 'Arnold Promise' has bright yellow flowers. 'Diane' has russet-red flowers. 'Pallida' has clear yellow flowers.

Evergreens have a variety of textures: (left to right) pine (Pinus), boxwood (Buxus), and yew (Taxus).

Evergreens

Evergreens add structure and color to the winter garden. They can be tightly pruned for a formal hedge or planted randomly in a naturalistic garden. Each variety has its own design characteristics from wispy and transparent to dense and opaque. Evergreens make good screens to block out views or separate boundary lines. They can be tall and solid like a wall or diminutive marking a low edge.

BOXWOOD (*Buxus*)
Shrubs and small trees
Zones 4 to 9 (depending on plant)

Boxwood is great for edging the potager to delineate the boundary of the kitchen garden. Every rectilinear raised bed at Villandry has a petite boxwood hedge outline. The hedge is maintained less than a foot (30 cm) high so that exuberant leafy and colorful vegetables project above the neat edge. *Buxus sempervi*rens 'Suffruticosa' is the true English boxwood and will grow less than three feet. *Buxus* 'Green Gem' will grow 2 feet (60 cm) tall and wide and is hardy in zones 5 to 8. *Buxus microphylla* 'Compacta' is the smallest variety, growing only a foot (30 cm) tall. Of course, the large varieties can be pruned to keep them at a desired size, it just means more clipping. Save those clipping chores for the winter holidays and you can use the greens for decorating.

HOLLIES (*Ilex*)
Shrubs and trees
Zones 5 to 9

Hollies are one of the most useful plants for colorful interest in the winter landscape. The conical evergreens among them sport bright red, yellow or orange berries. Evergreen, pointy (and sometimes sharp) leaves vary from dark green to pale green or variegated forms with shades of green and cream. Hollies prefer moist, acidic soil that is high in

A row of boxwood beneath a cover of snow is part of the structure of the formal potager in winter or summer.

(left) A neat row of boxwood in pots creates a movable hedge on the patio. The evergreens will grow outside in containers in winter or summer.

Evergreens cut fresh from the garden, a little here and there, are put into a vase to make a simple arrangement of green during the bleak days of winter.

organic matter in sun or part shade. To ensure fruit production in some varieties you will need a male pollinator.

Hollies make great screens or can be planted as specimens. *Ilex opaca*, the native, American holly is hardy to zone 5. There are over a thousand named cultivars. If you live in zones 6 to 9, your choice in hollies expands. *Ilex ×attenuate* is a group of hybrids crossed between *Ilex cassine* and *Ilex opaca*. There are many varieties. Cut the berries and a few leaves for indoor winter arrangements.

PINES, YEWS, AND JUNIPERS
Shrubs, trees, and ground covers
Zones 2 to 10 (depending on plant)

White pines create a wispy effect in the landscape. The soft sprays of long needles look light and airy, but planted close together the trees are effective at blocking views. Fir trees and spruce trees have a strong pyramidal form with short needles on symmetrical branches. These trees create a dense screen.

Yews and junipers are ubiquitous and if you live on an older property with overgrown evergreens save your pruning chores for the holidays to use the branches for wreaths and decorations. One year, I used mugo pine boughs for the fireplace mantel. I was planning to cut down the overgrown shrubs that had taken over the garden, so I aggressively cut whole branches to bring inside. Harvesting whole plants or taking tiny clippings of evergreens from your landscape means free materials for decorating.

Be careful when clipping branches from evergreen trees or shrubs. I am not advocating hacking at your evergreens, whatever you cut won't grow back. Only take overgrown branches that need pruning anyway. A selective pruning here and there won't harm the tree.

There are some evergreen shrubs that need pruning every year to keep them in bounds in the garden. These would be a renewable source of evergreens for winter decorations. Yew, boxwood, juniper, mugo pine, bird's nest spruce and holly might be some of the evergreen shrubs that are used as foundation plantings around your home. They need pruned every year so save the pruning chores for winter and then make a wreath or bring the greens indoors for table arrangements.

Small evergreen trees can be placed in containers for the winter and then planted in the landscape in the spring. Here a small tree is planted with clipped evergreens and magnolia leaves. Design by Village Flower Basket and Gardens, Granville, Ohio.

Living Christmas trees that are either grown in containers or dug, then balled and burlapped can be planted outdoors after the holidays are over. This makes sense, although the cost of the living tree will be more than a cut tree. It is a way to enhance your property by creating screening and shade. It's a nice way of turning full circle to return something to the land. Some preparation is necessary so that you can transplant the tree in a timely manner. Dig the holes for the trees before the ground freezes. Follow directions from your local nursery on how long to keep a living tree in the house.

PLANT A WINTER CONTAINER

There are a couple of ways to create winter containers. The first is to use living plants. Small evergreens like boxwood or dwarf conifers work well. The second way is to use evergreen boughs, berries, willow stems, dogwood branches, whatever you can glean from the garden and insert them in the soil of the container. Or create a combination of living plants and cut stems.

When choosing a live plant for an outdoor container choose a variety that is hardy a zone beyond yours– if you live in zone 5 select something that is hardy to zone 4. Roots in an outdoor winter container are less protected than plants in the ground.

Create the container early in the winter before everything is frozen. Just insert the stems and cuttings directly in the soil deep enough to secure the plant from the wind.

MAKE A WREATH

Handmade wreaths are easy to make. Collect wisps of evergreens, pinecones, twigs and dried flowers. The only tools required are a wire frame and some florist's wire.

Use the wire to tie boughs of evergreens to the metal frame, working in a circular motion around the wreath, adding more to balance the whole effect. Continue to secure dried flowers, winterberry, grass plumes– whatever you can find until the wreath is as full as you like. Add some ribbon and hang it for a rustic natural artistic creation.

Design for Winter

WINTER WALK

The reality in the midwestern United States is that much of the time flowers are not blooming and trees are without leaves. There is a long period of time from late autumn to late winter (November to February) during which trees and deciduous shrubs are barren sticks. The design presented here celebrates the season by selecting plants that have vivid berries, twigs, or even flowers in the winter. The site is in part sun and connects to the existing kitchen gar-

den. I have left that on the plan to show the transition between the two areas.

'Copper Beauty' witch hazel is planted in mass for the most impact. This hybrid blooms in late winter or early spring. The fragrant copper red flowers cover the branches just before it begins to leaf out. Berry Heavy winterberry holly is planted in a group of seven female plants; these are deciduous and the bright berries will remain on the branches through the winter. 'Southern Gentleman' is the male pollinator for these winterberries.

'Winter King' hawthorn is carefully sited so that as it matures to its full form it will be quite spectacular in the winter with its red berries on horizontal architectural branches. The yellow to orange-red

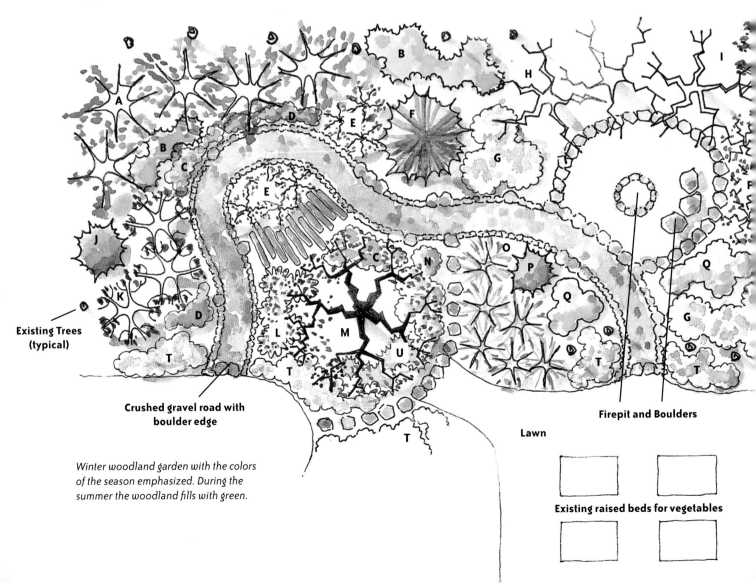

Existing Trees (typical)

Crushed gravel road with boulder edge

Firepit and Boulders

Lawn

Winter woodland garden with the colors of the season emphasized. During the summer the woodland fills with green.

Existing raised beds for vegetables

twigs of 'Midwinter Fire' bloodtwig dogwood are most effective in a grouping of plants. In the summer they will help create a pleasant walk with their green leaves, but in the winter they will be vivid against white snow.

'Viking' chokeberry produces black edible fruits in the fall that remain through the winter if they are not harvested. Wintergreen provides edible berries and evergreen fragrant leaves for a groundcover. 'Early Amethyst' purple beautyberry has bright purple berries that remain on the shrub. Blue Princess holly is planted as a specimen in this design; it will slowly grow into a large evergreen shrub with red berries every winter.

LABEL	NO. OF PLANTS	COMMON NAME	SCIENTIFIC NAME	ZONE	NOTES
A	5	'Copper Beauty' witch hazel	*Hamamelis ×intermedia* 'Jelena'	5–9	copper red flowers in winter, very fragrant
B	10	compact inkberry	*Ilex glabra* 'Compacta'	4–9	evergreen
C	19	Double Queen hybrid Lenten rose	*Helleborus ×hybridus* Double Queen Strain	4–8	mix of yellow, white, and pink flowers in winter
D	23	wintergreen groundcover	*Gaultheria procumbens*	3–7	evergreen, fragrant groundcover; red berries in winter
E	7	red chokeberry	*Aronia arbutifolia* 'Brilliantissima'	4–9	bright red fruits persist on branches through winter
F	1	'Fat Albert' Colorado blue spruce	*Picea pungens* 'Fat Albert'	2–8	stays small
G	8	snowflake hydrangea	*Hydrangea quercifolia* 'Brido'	5–9	white blooms all summer can be dried
H	3	'Autumn Brilliance' apple serviceberry	*Amelanchier ×grandiflora* 'Autumn Brilliance'	4–9	brilliant fall color, edible berries in summer
I	5	'Viking' black chokeberry	*Aronia melanocarpa* 'Viking'	3–7	edible black fruit in fall may persist through winter
J	1	Blue Prince holly	*Ilex ×meserveae* Blue Prince	5–9	male pollinator for 'Blue Princess' holly
K	3	American black elderberry	*Sambucus nigra* subsp. *canadensis*	3–11	flowers for cordial; berries for jelly
L	5	'Early Amethyst' purple beautyberry	*Callicarpa dichotoma* 'Early Amethyst'	5–8	bright purple berries attract birds, use for arrangements
M	1	'Winter King' hawthorn	*Crataegus viridis* 'Winter King'	4–7	attractive tree with red berries that persist through winter
N	5	'Henry's Garnet' Virginia sweetspire	*Itea virginica* 'Henry's Garnet'	5–9	spring flowers, garnet red color in fall
O	6	"Midwinter Fire' bloodtwig dogwood	*Cornus sanguinea* 'Midwinter Fire'	5–7	bright yellow stems tipped with copper orange in winter
P	1	Blue Princess holly	*Ilex ×meserveae* Blue Princess	5–9	red berries on evergreen holly foliage in winter
Q	8	'Mount Airy 'fothergilla	*Fothergilla gardenii* 'Mount Airy'	5–8	spring flowers, great fall color
R	7	Berry Heavy winterberry holly	*Ilex verticillata* 'Spravy' (Berry Heavy)	3–9	profuse red berries through winter
S	1	'Southern Gentleman' winterberry holly	*Ilex verticillata* 'Southern Gentleman'	3–9	male pollinator for 'Spravy' winterberry holly
T	—	perennials for part sun, varies	—	—	—
U	7	red wind Japanese forest grass	*Hakonechloa macra* 'Beni Kaze'	5–9	tips turn red in the fall

8' 16'

NORTH

209

EDIBLE FRONT YARD: WINTER

There are still interesting plants to look at during the winter in the seasonal front-yard garden (first shown on page 60). The female winterberry shrub has red berries. In the early winter the crabapples still have red fruits but the birds will eat them before the end of winter. The grasses have turned amber and are a highlight of the winter garden. They provide structure and golden contrast to winter snow.

The coral bark willow pollarded to a small tree has vivid orange-copper stems. These stems will be cut off at the node in the early spring to stimulate new growth and keep the plant small. The seeds have been left on the coneflowers to attract birds. Even the structures of the plants give some winter interest. The vivid yellow leaves of dwarf fothergilla will remain on the plants for part of the winter.

The plan leaves room for annuals in the center of the design. This space can be filled with pansies, mustards, kale, or parsnips. Decorative cloches will extend the season.

0'   8'   16'

NORTH

Winter

The edible seasonal front yard garden in winter. The shrubs, flowers, and trees with interest or bloom at this time of year are highlighted on color.

Winter Chores

☑ Design a spring, summer, and fall kitchen garden.

☑ Design perennial and shrub borders.

☑ Order seeds and bareroot plants.

☑ Water, fertilize, and care for indoor citrus plants.

☑ Prune and shape fruit trees.

☑ Harvest greens from under cloches and cold frames as they are ready.

☑ Gather evergreen boughs, dried flowers, colorful twigs, and bright berries from your garden to bring indoors.

WINTER MENUS

One
Cornish Game Hen with Sage and
  Thyme
Toasted Bread Stuffing with Fresh
  Herbs
Barley in Squash Bowl
Lemony Pie
Bouquet of evergreen boughs and
  winterberry

Two
Winter Tacos with Red Chile
Roasted White Winter Vegetables
Lemon and Key Lime Curd with
  Dried Fruits
Bouquet of dried hydrangeas and
  grasses

Three
Chorizo and Black Bean Soup
Linguine with Oven-Roasted Garlic
  and Sun-Dried Tomatoes
Whole Wheat Focaccia with
  Rosemary and Onion
Fruit Cake with Dried Fruits and
  Nuts
Bouquet of fresh quince blossoms

Seed and Fruit Sources

Baker Creek Heirloom Seeds
2278 Baker Creek Road
Mansfield, Missouri 65704
417-924-8917
www.rareseeds.com

Botanical Interests
660 Compton Street
Broomfield, Colorado 80020
800-486-2647
www.botanicalinterests.com

The Cook's Garden
P.O. Box C5030
Warminster, Pennsylvania 18974
800-457-9703
www.cooksgarden.com

Gurney's Seed & Nursery Company
P.O. Box 4178
Greendale, Indiana 47025
513-354-1491
www.gurneys.com

Hartmann's Plant Co.
310 60th Street
Grand Junction, Michigan 49056
269-253-4281
www.hartmannsplantcompany.com

Indiana Berry & Plant Company
5218 West 500 South
Huntingburg, Indiana 47542
800-295-2226
www.indianaberry.com

John Scheepers Kitchen Garden
    Seeds
23 Tulip Drive
P.O. Box 638
Bantam, Connecticut 06750
www.kitchengardenseeds.com

Johnny's Selected Seeds
955 Benton Avenue
Winslow, Maine 04901
877-564-6697
www.johnnyseeds.com

Miller Nurseries
5060 West Lake Road,
Canandaigua, New York 14424
800-836-9630
www.millernurseries.com

Mulberry Creek Herb Farm
3312 Bogart Road
Huron, Ohio 44839
419-433-6126
www.mulberrycreek.com

North Creek Nurseries
388 North Creek Road
Landenberg, Pennsylvania 19350
877-326-7584
www.northcreeknurseries.com

Nourse Farms
41 River Road
South Deerfield, Massachusetts
    01373
413-665-2658
www.noursefarms.com

Park Seed Company
1 Parkton Avenue
Greenwood, South Carolina 29647
800-213-0076
www.parkseed.com

Peterson Pawpaws
P.O. Box 1011
Harpers Ferry, West Virginia 25425
www.petersonpawpaws.com

Prairie Nursery
P.O. Box 306
Westfield, Wisconsin 53964
800-476-9453
www.prairienursery.com

Renee's Garden Seeds
6060A Graham Hill Road
Felton, California 95018
888-880-7228
www.reneesgarden.com

Seed Savers Exchange
3094 North Winn Road
Decorah, Iowa 52101
563-382-5990
www.seedsavers.org

Seeds of Change
3209 Richards Lane
Santa Fe, New Mexico 87507
888-762-7333
www.seedsofchange.com

Stark Bro's Nursery
P.O. Box 1800
Louisiana, Missouri 63353
800-325-4180
www.starkbros.com

Territorial Seed Company
P.O. Box 158
Cottage Grove, Oregon 97424
800-626-0866
www.territorialseed.com

Index

About the Author

JENNIFER R. BARTLEY is a landscape architect and author of *Designing the New Kitchen Garden*. She owns the design firm American Potager, and creates garden spaces for clients devoted to using fresh, seasonal, and local food. These enclosed gardens are both productive and elegant year-round, and allow gardeners to embrace a simpler life more connected to the landscape, the seasons, and the food they eat. Bartley earned her undergraduate and master's degrees in landscape architecture from Ohio State University and now lives in Granville, Ohio, where she enjoys photography, cooking for friends and family, growing heirloom vegetables from seed, and visiting gardens in faraway places. Her website is www.americanpotager.com.